OXFORD READINGS IN PHILOSOPHY

THE CONCEPT OF EVIDENCE

THE CONCEPT OF EVIDENCE

EDITED BY

PETER ACHINSTEIN

OXFORD UNIVERSITY PRESS
1983

Oxford University Press, Walton Street, Oxford OX2 6DP

London Glasgow New York Toronto
Delhi Bombay Calcutta Madras Karachi
Kuala Lumpur Singapore Hong Kong Tokyo
Nairobi Dar es Salaam Cape Town
Melbourne Auckland

and associated companies in
Beirut Berlin Ibadan Mexico City Nicosia

Oxford is a trade mark of Oxford University Press

Published in the United States
by Oxford University Press, New York

British Library Cataloguing in Publication Data
The concept of evidence. – (Oxford readings in philosophy)
  1. Science – Philosophy
  I. Achinstein, Peter
  501   Q175
  ISBN 0-19-875062-5

Library of Congress Cataloging in Publication Data
Main entry under title:

The Concept of evidence.

  (Oxford readings in philosophy)
  Bibliography: p.
  Includes index.
  Contents: Studies in the logic of confirmation / by Carl A.
Hempel – The stucture of a scientific system / by R. B. Braithwaite –
The logic of discovery / by Norwood Russell Hanson – [etc.]
  1. Evidence–Addresses, essays, lectures. 2. Logic – Addresses,
essays, lectures. I. Achinstein, Peter. II. Series.
BC173.C66 1983   121'.65   83-8266
ISBN 0-19-875062-5 (pbk.)

Set in IBM Press Roman by ROD-ART, Abingdon, England
Printed in the United States of America

For my father, Asher Achinstein

CONTENTS

INTRODUCTION

EVIDENCE is a concept central to the empirical sciences. Whether to believe, or even take seriously, a scientific hypothesis or theory depends on the quantity and character of the evidence in its favour. The choice between conflicting theories, for example, between Newtonian and Einsteinian physics, or between the Darwinian theory of gradual evolution and the contemporary theory that evolution occurs in more sudden bursts, cannot be made without examining the evidence for each. If no evidence could in principle be discovered that would favour a theory over its competitors, or if what counts as evidence is completely unclear, the theory may be deemed unscientific or pseudo-scientific. One reason scientists reject astrology is that many of its claims are so vague that it is unclear what would count as evidence that they are true or false.

A study of evidence will help illuminate the nature of scientific method. It is widely assumed that the scientist at some point must test a hypothesis or set of hypotheses by deriving consequences from it and determining whether these are true by experiment and observation. A theory of evidence will indicate what relationship has to exist between the observation reports and the hypotheses for the former to constitute evidence for the latter. Such a theory will clarify what sort of information the scientist should seek when he performs experiments and makes observations. Does any true consequence of a set of hypotheses constitute confirming evidence? If not, which ones do?

Rudolf Carnap, who has written extensively about evidence, distinguishes three concepts: classificatory, comparative, and quantitative. In the first case we are concerned with whether or not a body of information is evidence for (or 'confirms' or 'supports') a given hypothesis. For example, is the fact that the Moon's surface appears blotchy through the telescope evidence that there are craters on the Moon (as Galileo claimed in 1610)? Does it confirm or support that hypothesis? In the second case we ask whether a body of information confirms or supports a certain hypothesis more than some body of information (the same or another) supports a second hypothesis. For example, we ask whether the fact that the Moon's surface appears blotchy through the telescope supports the hypothesis that the Moon contains craters more than it supports the hypothesis that the telescope distorts the light coming from the Moon (as Galileo's critics insisted). In the third case we assess the *degree* to which a body of information confirms or supports a hypothesis. For example, we ask to what extent Galileo's hypothesis about the lunar surface is supported by his telescopic observations. Those who study this third concept generally assume that some precise number can be given to measure the degree of evidential support.

Since the 1940s philosophers of science have focused primarily on the classificatory and quantitative concepts. Discussion of the latter is usually very technical and invokes the mathematical theory of probability. Discussion of the classificatory concept is less technical, and more 'philosophical'. It has engendered the widest controversy. Some would claim (though even this is controversial, as we shall see) that it is the most basic and important of the three concepts for the empirical sciences. In any case, the classificatory concept is the subject of the present volume.

What should a theory of the classificatory concept of evidence or confirmation accomplish? Its aim is to provide conditions that determine when a body of information is evidence that some hypothesis or theory is true. These conditions should be both 'theoretically' and 'practically' informative. They should help us better understand the concept of evidence used in the sciences by relating that concept to others that are well (or at least better) understood. For example, as we shall see, some philosophers want to define evidence in terms of probability, which, they argue, is well understood. Others want to define it completely by reference to fundamental concepts of deductive logic. The conditions defining evidence should also be informative from a practical viewpoint. Using them it should be possible to determine in actual cases whether a body of information is evidence for a hypothesis. A definition in terms of probabilities would be less than ideal if the probabilities invoked are impossible or very difficult to determine.

The selections in this volume represent a broad spectrum of theories of evidence, and include material critical of rival viewpoints. They provide the reader with an opportunity to study seminal discussions in the field and the ensuing controversy. Perhaps the most influential article is the one by Hempel (selection I in this volume) which appeared in 1945. It outlines the need for a study of confirmation; it formulates various intuitive 'conditions of adequacy' that a definition of confirmation might be thought to satisfy, and generates the notorious 'paradox of the ravens' based on some of these conditions; and it proposes a 'satisfaction' definition of confirmation using concepts definable within deductive logic. The basic idea is that a hypothesis is confirmed by an observation report if the hypothesis is satisfied by the class of individuals mentioned in that report. Consider a simple example. Let h be the hypothesis that all ravens are black, which we write as:

  h: For any x, if x is a raven then x is black.

Now suppose we perform an 'experiment': we pick out three objects, a, b, and c, and observe whether or not they are ravens and whether or not they are black. Here is the outcome of our 'experiment':

  (1) a is a raven and a is black
      b is not a raven and b is black
      c is not a raven and c is not black.

Does the information in (1) constitute evidence for (does it confirm) hypothesis h? To decide, Hempel introduces the concept of the *development of a hypothesis for a class of individuals*—what the hypothesis would assert if only those individuals existed. The development of hypothesis h above for the class consisting of the three individuals a, b, and c is the conjunction:

  (2) If a is a raven then a is black, and
      if b is a raven then b is black, and
      if c is a raven then c is black.

Now, Hempel suggests, an observation report O *directly confirms* a hypothesis H if O deductively entails the development of H for the class of individuals mentioned in O. And an observation report O *confirms* a hypothesis H if H is deductively entailed by a class of sentences each of which is directly confirmed by O. These two claims constitute Hempel's definition of confirmation. In the example above, the observation report is given in (1). The development of the hypothesis h for the class of individuals mentioned in this observation report is given in (2). Construing the logical connectives 'and' and 'if-then' truth-functionally, (1) deductively entails (2). Therefore, by Hempel's definition, (1) directly confirms (and also confirms) hypothesis h. Intuitively, the hypothesis that all ravens are black is confirmed by an observation report indicating that each of the individuals observed is something other than a non-black raven.

  One limitation of this account is that it restricts evidence for a hypothesis to that which can be formulated using terms primarily in the hypothesis itself. This may seem reasonable when the hypotheses are 'observational' in nature (as Hempel is taking them to be in his theory)—when they are expressible using terms applying to what can be directly observed or measured. But what happens when scientists seek evidence for 'theoretical' hypotheses—for example, that protons are composed of three quarks? Such hypotheses are not expressible using terms applying to what can be directly observed. The evidence physicists discover for the hypothesis that protons are composed of three quarks is not of the form 'a is a proton and a is composed of 3 quarks, and b is not a proton and b is not composed of 3 quarks'. Because of the importance of such theoretical cases in science we might turn to a different approach, the hypothetico-deductive (h-d) picture of science formulated by R. B. Braithwaite in the second selection.

According to this, a scientific theory is a deductive system containing high-level hypotheses as 'axioms' and lower-level propositions ('theorems') which follow deductively. Among the latter will be 'observational' propositions which are directly testable. If some of these are false then the set of axioms is false and must be revised or discarded. However, if the observational conclusions are true then this is evidence for the high-level axioms, which may include 'theoretical' propositions that are not directly testable. More precisely, suppose that a theory T consists of a set of axioms which deductively entail an observational conclusion O and which is such that if any of these axioms is deleted the entailment is cancelled. Then, if O is observed to be true, this constitutes evidence for the set of axioms, as well as (indirect) evidence for each axiom in the set. On the h-d view the theoretical proposition that protons are composed of three quarks is one hypothesis within the larger quark theory. From this theory together with auxiliary hypotheses from physics one deduces certain observational consequences, which, if true, provide evidence for the theory and hence for the proposition that protons are composed of three quarks. Unlike example (1) above, illustrating Hempel's satisfaction theory, the evidence for this proposition need not consist in observation reports of the form 'a is (or is not) a proton and a is (not) composed of three quarks'.

The h-d idea is powerful because there are no restrictions on the types of axioms considered. It is also simple because, as in Hempel's theory, it is formulated using simple concepts definable in deductive logic. Yet several of its features are criticized by authors in this volume. With Glymour (selection VII) one might question the idea that a true observational consequence of a theory constitutes evidence for *each* higher-level hypothesis in the theory. That is, one might suppose that a piece of information can be evidence for one part of a theory without necessarily being evidence for another. Again, there is no requirement in the h-d view that the high-level hypotheses in a theory have any independent probability or plausibility (an idea criticized in selections III, VI, and VIII). On the h-d view the scientist may invent any hypotheses that strike his fancy, so long as these are testable by deriving observational conclusions. Yet, as Hanson emphasizes in selection III, scientists will not derive consequences from just any hypotheses but only from ones to which they assign some initial plausibility. And, he insists, there is an important type of reasoning to the plausibility of a hypothesis which h-d theorists unfortunately ignore. What kind of reasoning is this?

Borrowing a term (as well as some ideas) from Charles Peirce, Hanson calls it retroductive reasoning. The basic notion is that the scientist begins with some surprising phenomenon P and then reasons that a hypothesis h is probable, or plausible, or at least worth considering, on the grounds that if true it would (correctly) *explain* that phenomenon. One simple way in which Hanson formulates retroduction is as follows:

> Some surprising phenomenon P is observed
> P would be explicable as a matter of course if H were true
> Hence there is reason to think that H is true.[1]

Although Hanson does not explicitly do so, one might readily use these ideas to characterize a concept of evidence. One might say that e is evidence for the hypothesis h provided that h if true would correctly explain e. In terms of Hanson's own example, Tycho Brahe's data regarding the observed positions of the planet Mars at various times of the year constitute evidence for the hypothesis that Mars travels in an elliptical orbit around the sun because the latter hypothesis, if true, would correctly explain Brahe's data; it would correctly explain why Mars is seen where it is in the sky at different times of the year. On this view evidence is to be defined by reference to *explanation*, a concept not usually considered definable entirely in terms of concepts in deductive logic. As with the h-d view this proposal allows evidence for 'theoretical' as well as 'observational' hypotheses. Unlike the h-d view, it does not require evidence for one hypothesis in a theory to be evidence for the set of them or for any other in the set. If the truth of h_1 would correctly explain e, it does not necessarily follow that h_1 and h_2 (or h_2 by itself), if true, would also correctly explain e.

[1] This formulation is taken from Hanson's *Patterns of Discovery* (Cambridge University Press, 1958), p. 86.

Some may object that unless explanation is itself defined by reference to simpler concepts a definition of evidence that appeals to it is not sufficiently informative. Others may defend such an approach by admitting that although it does not provide a complete solution it suggests a promising direction. One should recognize (it might be said) that the claim that e is evidence that h requires some explanatory connection between e and h, and abandon attempts to define evidence entirely in terms of implication and related concepts from deductive logic. Someone who is sympathetic to this approach should then consider whether the definition of evidence in the previous paragraph suffices or whether complications are necessary. (See selection VIII, sections 3–4, for a discussion of this.)

A major difficulty facing any theory of evidence is the powerful 'grue' paradox introduced by Nelson Goodman. The problem is particularly apparent in the case of a theory such as Hempel's. Suppose that each emerald observed so far has been green. Then, on Hempel's theory, this information confirms the hypothesis that all emeralds are green. Now consider the predicate 'grue' which is defined so as to apply to all things examined before t just in case they are green, and to other things just in case they are blue. Let t be some time in the future, say the year 2000. Then since all the emeralds examined so far have been green they have also been grue. Therefore, without some restrictions on Hempel's theory, we can say that the hypothesis that all emeralds are grue is confirmed by our information that all examined emeralds are grue. But this hypothesis entails that emeralds not examined before 2000 are blue, not green, which conflicts with the hypothesis that all emeralds (including the ones not examined before 2000) are green. Yet both hypotheses seem equally confirmed by the observed emeralds, each of which is green as well as grue. More generally, for any universal hypothesis of the form 'All A's are B's' confirmed by all of its examined instances (e.g., by all of the A's observed to be B's) we can construct a conflicting hypothesis of the form 'All A's are C's' which has just as many confirming instances. The problem, which Hempel's theory does not address, is how to distinguish hypotheses such as 'All emeralds are green' whose instances are confirming from a hypothesis such as 'All emeralds are grue' whose instances are not. In selection IV Goodman presents a theory designed to solve this problem.

The theory is based on the idea that a predicate such as 'green' is much better *entrenched* than one such as 'grue'. 'Green' (or other terms true of the same class of things) has been used much more frequently than 'grue' (or other coextensive predicates) in hypotheses of the form 'All A's are B's' that have actually come to be adopted. Goodman is concerned with when a hypothesis is 'projectible', i.e., when it can be said to be confirmed by its instances, and his theory consists of a set of conditions that provide an answer. Suppose that two conflicting hypotheses of the form 'All A's are B's' and 'All A's are C's' are such that all their examined instances are true. But suppose that the term 'B' is better entrenched than the term 'C'. Then, on Goodman's theory, the hypothesis 'All A's are C's' is not projectible. It does not receive confirmation from its instances. Accordingly, the hypothesis 'All emeralds are grue'—although all of its examined instances are true—does not receive confirming support from those instances. The reason is that it is 'overridden' by the conflicting hypothesis 'All emeralds are green' which has equal numbers of examined instances but uses the better entrenched term 'green' and conflicts with no hypothesis with still better entrenched terms. Under these circumstances examined instances of green emeralds will confirm the hypothesis that all emeralds are green.

So far the theories described treat the classificatory notion of evidence as basic. A contrasting viewpoint is that of Carnap in selection V, according to which a classificatory concept of evidence can be defined only in terms of a quantitative one: the degree to which evidence e confirms hypothesis h. The latter is explicated by Carnap in terms of numerical probability. Carnap writes quantitative confirmation statements as follows:

$$c(h, e) = r,$$

which means that the degree to which e confirms h is the number r. Carnap's c-functions obey the standard axioms of the probability calculus, so that r is some number between 0 and 1. Now, Carnap suggests, an important classificatory concept of confirmation can be understood in terms of the quantitative one. When we say that e is confirming evidence for h we may mean that the degree of confirmation of h (the probability of h) is increased by e. Suppose that the degree of confirmation of h on the basis of general background information b that we possess is some number r_1. Suppose that we obtain some new information e which together with b makes h's degree of confirmation some larger number r_2. Then, Carnap proposes, e confirms h (in the classificatory sense). In short, e confirms h, given b, if and only if:

$$c(h, e\&b) > c(h, b).$$

This is sometimes called the 'positive relevance' sense of evidence.

Carnap uses it to criticize Hempel's satisfaction definition as well as several of the conditions of adequacy on which it is based.

In selection VI Wesley Salmon agrees with Carnap that in general when we speak about confirming evidence (using the qualitative, classificatory concept) we are doing so in the sense of positive relevance. In other words, he accepts the definition according to which e is evidence that h if and only if e raises h's probability. But he argues that knowing that e is evidence that h tells us very little. The qualitative concept is 'too crude . . . and it doesn't carry enough information to be useful'. He bases this conclusion upon the fact that a set of startling, counter-intuitive consequences follow from the use of this concept. Employing examples first introduced by Carnap, Salmon shows how, in the positive relevance sense, each of two evidence statements may confirm a hypothesis while their conjunction disconfirms it; how a piece of evidence may confirm each of two hypotheses while disconfirming their conjunction; and how a piece of evidence may confirm each of two hypotheses while disconfirming their disjunction. (These are just some of the disquieting consequences.) Salmon concludes that the classificatory concept is not very serviceable and that to understand the logic of evidential support the quantitative concept of degree of confirmation will need to be employed.

Clark Glymour would not agree. In selection VII, developing his novel 'bootstrap' approach, he defends the idea that a reasonable classificatory concept of evidence can be defined, indeed that this can be done without invoking probabilities or any notion of degree of confirmation. Glymour's claim is that something confirms a hypothesis only in relation to a theory consisting of a set of hypotheses. So e may confirm h relative to theory T_1 without necessarily confirming h relative to theory T_2. His basic idea, the 'bootstrap' condition, is that e confirms hypothesis h with respect to theory T if and only if from e it is possible, using the theory T itself, to derive an instance of h (where the derivation is such as not to guarantee an instance of h no matter what e had been chosen). To use Glymour's example, suppose theory T consists of the following equations:

1. $A_1 = E_1$
2. $B_1 = G_1 + G_2 + E_2$
3. $A_2 = E_1 + E_2$
4. $B_2 = G_1 + G_2$
5. $A_3 = G_1 + E_1$
6. $B_3 = G_2 + E_2$

The A's and B's are directly measurable quantities, the E's and G's are 'theoretical' quantities whose values can be determined only indirectly through the theory by determining the values of the A's and B's. How do we proceed to obtain evidence for hypothesis 1, for example? We determine a value for A_1 directly by experiment, since A_1 is directly measurable. We obtain a value for the 'theoretical' quantity E_1 by obtaining values for the 'observables' B_1, B_3, and A_3, and then by using certain hypotheses from the theory, namely, 2, 5, and 6, mathematically computing a value for E_1. If the value for A_1 which is determined by experiment is the same as the computed value for E_1 then the observed values of A_1, B_1, B_3, and A_3 constitute confirming evidence for hypothesis 1 in the theory.

Accordingly, like hypothetico-deductivists, and unlike Hempel, Glymour stresses the role of theories in confirmation. However, unlike h-d supporters, he shows how evidence can confirm one part of a theory without confirming all parts. (In the example the observed values of A_1, B_1, B_3, and A_3 confirm hypothesis 1 but not hypothesis 3.) Glymour agrees with Hempel that we test hypotheses by testing their instances. But, unlike Hempel, he shows how to do so for 'theoretical' as well as 'observational' hypotheses. In the appendix of selection VIII some difficulties in Glymour's theory are suggested.

The final selection, a paper of my own, develops a theory of evidence that combines concepts of probability and explanation. The Carnapian examples used by Salmon should, I think, lead us to draw a different conclusion from Salmon's. They show not that the classificatory concept of evidence is useless but that this concept is not adequately defined as positive relevance. In my paper I present even simpler examples to demonstrate why 'e is evidence that h' cannot be defined either as 'e increases the probability of h' (positive relevance) or as 'the probability of h, given e, is high'. Other examples suggest why we cannot adopt a simple retroductivist-inspired definition in terms of explanation. Yet if we combine some of these ideas the result is more successful. My proposal is to require that the probability of h, given e, be high, and that the probability be high that there is an explanatory connection between h and e, given that h and e are both true. This avoids counter-intuitive consequences of the probability and explanation definitions I discuss. Since it rejects positive relevance as necessary or sufficient for evidence it also avoids the embarrassing examples invoked by Salmon.[2]

² For help in the preparation of this volume I am grateful to George Wilson, David Zaret, Vera Herst, and Nancy McCarthy.

I
STUDIES IN THE LOGIC
OF CONFIRMATION

CARL G. HEMPEL

1. OBJECTIVE OF THE STUDY[1]

THE DEFINING characteristic of an empirical statement is its capability of being tested by a confrontation with experiential findings, i.e. with the results of suitable experiments or focused observations. This feature distinguishes statements which have empirical content both from the statements of the formal sciences, logic and mathematics, which require no experiential test for their validation, and from the formulations of transempirical metaphysics, which admit of none.

The testability here referred to has to be understood in the comprehensive sense of "testability in principle" or "theoretical testability"; many empirical statements, for practical reasons, cannot actually be tested now. To call a statement of this kind testable in principle means that it is possible to state just what experiential findings, if they were actually obtained, would constitute favourable evidence for it, and what findings or "data", as we shall say for brevity, would constitute unfavourable evidence; in other words, a statement is called testable in principle if it is possible to describe the kind of data which would confirm or disconfirm it.

From *Aspects of Scientific Explanation* by Carl G. Hempel (Free Press, 1965), pp. 3–25, 30–9 where it is reprinted with revisions from *Mind*, 54 (1945), pp. 1–26, 97–121. By permission of the author and Basil Blackwell Publisher.

[1] The present analysis of confirmation was to a large extent suggested and stimulated by a co-operative study of certain more general problems which were raised by Dr Paul Oppenheim, and which I have been investigating with him for several years. These problems concern the form and the function of scientific laws and the comparative methodology of the different branches of empirical science.

In my study of the logical aspects of confirmation, I have benefited greatly by discussions with Professor R. Carnap, Professor A. Tarski, and particularly Dr Nelson Goodman, to whom I am indebted for several valuable suggestions which will be indicated subsequently.

A detailed exposition of the more technical aspects of the analysis of confirmation presented in this essay is included in my article 'A Purely Syntactical Definition of Confirmation', *Journal of Symbolic Logic*, 8 (1943).

The concepts of confirmation and of disconfirmation as here under-stood are clearly more comprehensive than those of conclusive verification and falsification. Thus, e.g., no finite amount of experi-ential evidence can conclusively verify a hypothesis expressing a general law such as the law of gravitation, which covers an infinity of potential instances, many of which belong either to the as yet inaccessible future or to the irretrievable past; but a finite set of relevant data may well be "in accord with" the hypothesis and thus constitute confirming evidence for it. Similarly, an existential hypothesis, asserting, say, the existence of an as yet unknown chemical element with certain specified characteristics, cannot be conclusively proved false by a finite amount of evidence which fails to "bear out" the hypothesis; but such unfavourable data may, under certain conditions, be considered as weakening the hypothesis in question, or as constituting disconfirming evidence for it.[2]

While, in the practice of scientific research, judgments as to the confirming or disconfirming character of experiential data obtained in the test of a hypothesis are often made without hesitation and with a wide consensus of opinion, it can hardly be said that these judgments are based on an explicit theory providing general criteria of con-firmation and of disconfirmation. In this respect, the situation is comparable to the manner in which deductive inferences are carried out in the practice of scientific research: this, too, is often done without reference to an explicitly stated system of rules of logical inference. But while criteria of valid deduction can be and have been supplied by formal logic, no satisfactory theory providing general criteria of confirmation and disconfirmation appears to be available so far.

In the present essay, an attempt will be made to provide the elements of a theory of this kind. After a brief survey of the signifi-cance and the present status of the problem, I propose to present a detailed critical analysis of some common conceptions of confirmation and disconfirmation and then to construct explicit definitions for these concepts and to formulate some basic principles of what might be called the logic of confirmation.

2. SIGNIFICANCE AND PRESENT STATUS OF THE PROBLEM

The establishment of a general theory of confirmation may well be regarded as one of the most urgent desiderata of the present method-

[2] This point as well as the possibility of conclusive verification and conclusive falsification will be discussed in some detail in section 10 of the present paper [omitted].

ology of empirical science. Indeed, it seems that a precise analysis of the concept of confirmation is a necessary condition for an adequate solution of various fundamental problems concerning the logical structure of scientific procedure. Let us briefly survey the most outstanding of these problems.

(*a*) In the discussion of scientific method, the concept of relevant evidence plays an important part. And while certain inductivist accounts of scientific procedure seem to assume that relevant evidence, or relevant data, can be collected in the context of an inquiry prior to the formulation of any hypothesis, it should be clear upon brief reflection that relevance is a relative concept; experiential data can be said to be relevant or irrelevant only with respect to a given hypothesis; and it is the hypothesis which determines what kind of data or evidence are relevant for it. Indeed, an empirical finding is relevant for a hypothesis if and only if it constitutes either favourable or unfavourable evidence for it; in other words, if it either confirms or disconfirms the hypothesis. Thus, a precise definition of relevance presupposes an analysis of confirmation and disconfirmation.

(*b*) A closely related concept is that of instance of a hypothesis. The so-called method of inductive inference is usually presented as proceeding from specific cases to a general hypothesis of which each of the special cases is an "instance" in the sense that it conforms to the general hypothesis in question, and thus constitutes confirming evidence for it.

Thus, any discussion of induction which refers to the establishment of general hypotheses on the strength of particular instances is fraught with all those logical difficulties—soon to be expounded—which beset the concept of confirmation. A precise analysis of this concept is, therefore, a necessary condition for a clear statement of the issues involved in the problem complex of induction and of the ideas suggested for their solution—no matter what their theoretical merits or demerits may be.

(*c*) Another issue customarily connected with the study of scientific method is the quest for "rules of induction". Generally speaking, such rules would enable us to infer, from a given set of data, that hypothesis or generalization which accounts best for all the particular data in the given set. But this construal of the problem involves a misconception: while the process of invention by which scientific discoveries are made is as a rule *psychologically guided and stimulated* by antecedent knowledge of specific facts, its results are *not logically determined* by them; the way in which scientific hypotheses or theories are discovered cannot be mirrored in a set of general rules of inductive inference.[3] One of the crucial considerations which leads to this conclusion is the following: take a scientific theory such as the atomic theory of matter. The evidence on which it rests may be described in terms referring to directly observable phenomena, namely to certain macroscopic aspects of the various experimental and observational data which are relevant to the theory. On the other hand, the theory itself contains a large number of highly abstract, non-observational terms such as 'atom', 'electron', 'nucleus', 'dissociation', 'valence', and others, none of which figures in the description of the observational data. An adequate rule of induction would therefore have to provide, for this and for every other conceivable case, mechanically applicable criteria determining unambiguously, and without any reliance on the inventiveness or additional scientific knowledge of its user, all those new abstract concepts which need to be created for the formulation of the theory that will account for the given evidence. Clearly, this requirement cannot be satisfied by any set of rules, however ingeniously devised; there can be no general rules of induction in the above sense; the demand for them rests on a confusion of logical and psychological issues. What determines the soundness of a hypothesis is not the way it is arrived at (it may even have been suggested by a dream or a halluci-nation), but the way it stands up when tested, i.e. when confronted with relevant observational data. Accordingly, the quest for rules of induction in the original sense of canons of scientific discovery has to be replaced, in the logic of science, by the quest for general objective criteria determining (A) whether, and—if possible—even (B) to what degree, a hypothesis H may be said to be corroborated by a given body of evidence E. This approach differs essentially from the inductivist conception of the problem in that it presupposes not only E, but also H as given, and then seeks to determine a certain logical relationship between them. The two parts of this latter problem can be related in somewhat more precise terms as follows:

(A) To give precise definitions of the two non-quantitative relational concepts of confirmation and of disconfirmation; i.e. to define the meaning of the phrases 'E confirms H' and 'E disconfirms H'. (When

[3] See the lucid presentation of this point in Karl Popper's *Logik der Forschung* (Wien, 1935), esp. sections 1, 2, 3, and 25, 26, 27; cf. also Albert Einstein's remarks in his lecture *On the Method of Theoretical Physics* (Oxford, 1933), 11, 12. Also of interest in this context is the critical discussion of induction by H. Feigl in "The Logical Character of the Principle of Induction", *Philosophy of Science*, 1 (1934).

E neither confirms nor disconfirms H, we shall say that E is neutral, or irrelevant, with respect to H.)

(B) (1) To lay down criteria defining a metrical concept "degree of confirmation of H with respect to E", whose values are real numbers; or, failing this,

(2) To lay down criteria defining two relational concepts, "more highly confirmed than" and "equally well confirmed as", which make possible a non-metrical comparison of hypotheses (each with a body of evidence assigned to it) with respect to the extent of their confirmation.

Interestingly, problem B has received much more attention in methodological research than problem A; in particular, the various theories of the so-called probability of hypotheses may be regarded as concerning this problem complex; we have adopted[4] the more neutral term 'degree of confirmation' instead of 'probability' because the latter is used in science in a definite technical sense involving reference to the relative frequency of the occurrence of a given event in a sequence, and it is at least an open question whether the degree of confirmation of a hypothesis can generally be defined as a probability in this statistical sense.

The theories dealing with the probability of hypotheses fall into two main groups: the "logical" theories construe probability as a logical relation between sentences (or propositions; it is not always clear which is meant);[5] the "statistical" theories interpret the probability of a hypothesis in substance as the limit of the relative frequency of its confirming instances among all relevant cases.[6] Now it is a remarkable fact that none of the theories of the first type which have been developed so far provides an explicit general definition of the probability (or degree of confirmation) of a hypothesis H with respect to a body of evidence E; they all limit themselves essentially to the construction of an uninterpreted postulational system of logical

[4] Following R. Carnap's use in "Testability and Meaning", *Philosophy of Science*, 3 (1936) and 4 (1937); esp. section 3 (in vol. 3).

[5] This group includes the work of such writers as Janina Hosiasson-Lindenbaum [cf. for instance, her article "Induction et analogie: Comparison de leur fondement", *Mind*, 50 (1941)], H. Jeffreys, J. M. Keynes, B. O. Koopman, J. Nicod, St. Mazurkiewicz, and F. Waismann. For a brief discussion of this conception of probability, see Ernest Nagel, *Principles of the Theory of Probability* (International Encyclopedia of Unified Science, vol. 1, no. 6, Chicago, 1939), esp. sections 6 and 8.

[6] The chief proponent of this view is Hans Reichenbach; cf. especially "Ueber-Induktion und Wahrscheinlichkeit", *Erkenntnis*, 5 (1935), and *Experience and Prediction* (Chicago, 1938), Chap. V.

probability.[7] For this reason, these theories fail to provide a complete solution of problem B. The statistical approach, on the other hand, would, if successful, provide an explicit numerical definition of the degree of confirmation of a hypothesis; this definition would be formulated in terms of the numbers of confirming and disconfirming instances for H which constitute the body of evidence E. Thus, a necessary condition for an adequate interpretation of degrees of confirmation as statistical probabilities is the establishment of precise criteria of confirmation and disconfirmation; in other words, the solution of problem A.

However, despite their great ingenuity and suggestiveness, the attempts which have been made so far to formulate a precise statistical definition of the degree of confirmation of a hypothesis seem open to certain objections,[8] and several authors[9] have expressed doubts as to the possibility of defining the degree of confirmation of a hypothesis as a metrical magnitude, though some of them consider it as possible, under certain conditions, to solve at least the less exacting problem B (2), i.e. to establish standards of non-metrical comparison between hypotheses with respect to the extent of their confirmation. An adequate comparison of this kind might have to take into account a variety of different factors;[10] but again the numbers of the confirming and of the disconfirming instances which the given evidence includes will be among the most important of those factors.

Thus, of the two problems, A and B, the former appears to be the more basic one, first, because it does not presuppose the possibility of

[7] (Added in 1964). Since this article was written, R. Carnap has developed a theory of inductive logic which, for formalized languages of certain types, makes it possible explicitly to define—without use of the qualitative notion of confirming instance—a quantitative concept of degree of confirmation which has the formal characteristics of a probability; Carnap refers to it as inductive, or logical, probability. For details, see especially R. Carnap, "On Inductive Logic", *Philosophy of Science*, 12 (1945); *Logical Foundations of Probability* (Chicago, 1950; 2nd ed", 1962); *The Continuum of Inductive Methods* (Chicago, 1952); "The Aim of Inductive Logic" in E. Nagel, P. Suppes, and A. Tarski (eds.), *Logic, Methodology, and Philosophy of Science, Proceedings of the 1960 International Congress* (Stanford, 1962).

[8] Cf. Karl Popper, *Logik der Forschung* (Wien, 1935), section 80; Nagel, loc. cit., section 8, and "Probability and the Theory of Knowledge", *Philosophy of Science*, 6 (1939); C. G. Hempel, "Le problème de la vérité", *Theoria* (Göteborg), 3 (1937), section 5, and "On the Logical Form of Probability Statements", *Erkenntnis,* 7 (1937–8), esp. section 5. Cf. also Morton White, "Probability and Confirmation", *Journal of Philosophy*, 36 (1939).

[9] See, for example, J. M. Keynes, *A Treatise on Probability* (London, 1929), esp. ch. III; Ernest Nagel, *Principles of the Theory of Probability*, esp. p. 70; cf. also the somewhat less definitely sceptical statement by Carnap, loc. cit. section 3, p. 427.

[10] See especially the survey of such factors given by Ernest Nagel in *Principles of the Theory of Probability* , pp. 66–73.

defining numerical degrees of confirmation or of comparing different hypotheses as to the extent of their confirmation; and second because our considerations indicate that any attempt to solve problem B—unless it is to remain in the stage of an axiomatized system without interpretation—is likely to require a precise definition of the concepts of confirming and disconfirming instance of a hypothesis before it can proceed to define numerical degrees of confirmation, or to lay down non-metrical standards of comparison.

(d) It is now clear that an analysis of confirmation is of fundamental importance also for the study of a central problem of epistemology, namely, the elaboration of standards of rational belief or of criteria of warranted assertibility. In the methodology of empirical science this problem is usually phrased as concerning the rules governing the test and the subsequent acceptance or rejection of empirical hypotheses on the basis of experimental or observational findings, while in its epistemological version the issue is often formulated as concerning the validation of beliefs by reference to perceptions, sense data, or the like. But no matter how the final empirical evidence is construed and in what terms it is accordingly expressed, the theoretical problem remains the same: to characterize, in precise and general terms, the conditions under which a body of evidence can be said to confirm, or to disconfirm, a hypothesis of empirical character; and that is again our problem A.

(e) The same problem arises when one attempts to give a precise statement of the empiricist and operationalist criteria for the empirical meaningfulness of a sentence; these criteria, as is well known, are formulated by reference to the theoretical testability of the sentence by means of experiential evidence,[11] and the concept of theoretical testability, as was pointed out earlier, is closely related to the concepts of confirmation and disconfirmation.[12]

Considering the great importance of the concept of confirmation, it is surprising that no systematic theory of the non-quantitative relation of confirmation seems to have been developed so far. Perhaps this fact reflects the tacit assumption that the concepts of confirmation and of disconfirmation have a sufficiently clear meaning to make explicit

[11] Cf., for example, A. J. Ayer, *Language, Truth and Logic* (London and New York, 1936), ch. I; R. Carnap, "Testability and Meaning", sections 1, 2, 3; H. Feigl, "Logical Empiricism" (in *Twentieth Century Philosophy*, ed. by Dagobert D. Runes, New York, 1943); P. W. Bridgman, *The Logic of Modern Physics* (New York, 1928).

[12] It should be noted, however, that in his essay "Testability and Meaning", R. Carnap has constructed definitions of testability and confirmability which avoid reference to the concept of confirming and of disconfirming evidence; in fact, no proposal for the definition of these latter concepts is made in that study.

definitions unnecessary or at least comparatively trivial. And indeed, as will be shown below, there are certain features which are rather generally associated with the intuitive notion of confirming evidence, and which, at first, seem well suited to serve as defining characteristics of confirmation. Closer examination will reveal the definitions thus obtainable to be seriously deficient and will make it clear that an adequate definition of confirmation involves considerable difficulties.

Now the very existence of such difficulties suggests the question whether the problem we are considering does not rest on a false assumption: perhaps there are no objective criteria of confirmation; perhaps the decision as to whether a given hypothesis is acceptable in the light of a given body of evidence is no more subject to rational, objective rules than is the process of inventing a scientific hypothesis or theory; perhaps, in the last analysis, it is a "sense of evidence," or a feeling of plausibility in view of the relevant data, which ultimately decides whether a hypothesis is scientifically acceptable.[13] This view is comparable to the opinion that the validity of a mathematical proof or of a logical argument has to be judged ultimately by reference to a feeling of soundness or convincingness; and both theses have to be rejected on analogous grounds: they involve a confusion of logical and psychological considerations. Clearly, the occurrence or non-occurrence of a feeling of conviction upon the presentation of grounds for an assertion is a subjective matter which varies from person to person, and with the same person in the course of time; it is often deceptive and can certainly serve neither as a necessary nor as a sufficient condition for the soundness of the given assertion.[14] A rational reconstruction of the standards of scientific validation cannot, therefore, involve reference to a sense of evidence; it has to be based on objective criteria. In fact, it seems reasonable to require that the criteria of empirical confirmation, besides being objective in character, should contain no reference to the specific subject-matter of the hypothesis or of the evidence in question; it ought to be possible, one feels, to set up purely formal criteria of confirmation in a manner similar to that in which deductive logic provides purely formal criteria for the validity of deductive inference.

With this goal in mind, we now turn to a study of the non-quantitative concept of confirmation. We shall begin by examining some current conceptions of confirmation and exhibiting their logical

---

[13] A view of this kind has been expressed, for example, by M. Mandelbaum in "Causal Analyses in History", *Journal of the History of Ideas*, 3 (1942); cf. esp. pp. 46–7.

[14] See Popper's statement, loc. cit. section 8.

and methodological inadequacies; in the course of this analysis, we shall
develop a set of conditions for the adequacy of any proposed definition
of confirmation; and finally, we shall construct a definition of
confirmation which satisfies those general standards of adequacy.

3. NICOD'S CRITERION OF CONFIRMATION
AND ITS SHORTCOMINGS

We consider first a conception of confirmation which underlies many
recent studies of induction and of scientific method. A very explicit
statement of this conception has been given by Jean Nicod in the
following passage: "Consider the formula or the law: *A entails B*.
How can a particular proposition, or more briefly, a fact, affect its
probability? If this fact consists of the presence of B in a case of A,
it is favorable to the law '*A entails B*'; on the contrary, if it consists
of the absence of B in a case of A, it is unfavorable to this law. It is
conceivable that we have here the only two direct modes in which a
fact can influence the probability of a law. ... Thus, the entire
influence of particular truths or facts on the probability of universal
propositions or laws would operate by means of these two elementary
relations which we shall call *confirmation* and *invalidation*."[15] Note
that the applicability of this criterion is restricted to hypotheses of the
form '*A entails B*'. Any hypothesis *H* of this kind may be expressed in
the notation of symbolic logic[16] by means of a universal conditional
sentence, such as, in the simplest case,

$$(x)[P(x) \supset Q(x)]$$

i.e. 'For any object *x*: if *x* is a *P*, then *x* is a *Q*,' or also 'Occurrence of
the quality *P* entails occurrence of the quality *Q*.' According to the
above criterion this hypothesis is confirmed by an object *a* if *a* is *P*
and *Q*; and the hypothesis is disconfirmed by *a* if *a* is *P*, but not *Q*.[17]
In other words, an object confirms a universal conditional hypothesis if
and only if it satisfies both the antecedent (here: '*P(x)*') and the consequent (here: '*Q(x)*') of the conditional; it disconfirms the hypothesis if

[15] Jean Nicod, *Foundations of Geometry and Induction* (transl. by P. P.
Wiener), London, 1930, 219; cf. also R. M. Eaton's discussion of "Confirmation
and Infirmation", which is based on Nicod's views; it is included in ch. III of his
General Logic (New York, 1931).
[16] In this essay, only the most elementary devices of this notation are used;
the symbolism is essentially that of *Principia Mathematica*, except that
parentheses are used instead of dots, and that existential quantification is
symbolized by '(E)' instead of by the inverted 'E.'
[17] (Added in 1964). More precisely we would have to say, in Nicod's parlance,
that the hypothesis is confirmed by the *proposition* that *a* is both *P* and *Q*, and is
disconfirmed by the *proposition* that *a* is *P* but not *Q*.

and only if it satisfies the antecedent, but not the consequent of the conditional; and (we add this to Nicod's statement) it is neutral, or irrelevant, with respect to the hypothesis if it does not satisfy the antecedent.

This criterion can readily be extended so as to be applicable also to universal conditionals containing more than one quantifier, such as 'Twins always resemble each other', or, in symbolic notation, '$(x)(y)$(Twins$(x, y) \supset$ Rsbl(x, y)))'. In these cases, a confirming instance consists of an ordered couple, or triple, etc., of objects satisfying the antecedent and the consequent of the conditional. (In the case of the last illustration, any two persons who are twins and resemble each other would confirm the hypothesis; twins who do not resemble each other would disconfirm it; and any two persons not twins—no matter whether they resemble each other or not—would constitute irrelevant evidence.)

We shall refer to this criterion as Nicod's criterion.[18] It states explicitly what is perhaps the most common tacit interpretation of the concept of confirmation. While seemingly quite adequate, it suffers from serious shortcomings, as will now be shown.

(*a*) First, the applicability of this criterion is restricted to hypotheses of universal conditional form; it provides no standards of confirmation for existential hypotheses (such as 'There exists organic life on other stars', or 'Poliomyelitis is caused by some virus') or for hypotheses whose explicit formulation calls for the use of both universal and existential quantifiers (such as 'Every human being dies some finite number of years after his birth', or the psychological hypothesis, 'You can fool all of the people some of the time and some of the people all of the time, but you cannot fool all of the people all of the time', which may be symbolized by '$(x)(Et)$Fl(x, t) · $(Ex)(t)$Fl(x, t) · $\sim (x)(t)$Fl(x, t)', (where 'Fl(x, t)' stands for 'You can fool person x at time t'). We note, therefore, the desideratum of establishing a criterion of confirmation which is applicable to hypotheses of *any* form.[19]

---

[18] This term is chosen for convenience, and in view of the above explicit formulation given by Nicod; it is not, of course, intended to imply that this conception of confirmation originated with Nicod.

[19] For a rigorous formulation of the problem, it is necessary first to lay down assumptions as to the means of expression and the logical structure of the language in which the hypotheses are supposed to be formulated; the desideratum then calls for a definition of confirmation applicable to any hypothesis which can be expressed in the given language. Generally speaking, the problem becomes increasingly difficult with increasing richness and complexity of the assumed language of science.

(b) We now turn to a second shortcoming of Nicod's criterion. Consider the two sentences

$$S_1: \text{'}(x)[\text{Raven}(x) \supset \text{Black}(x)]\text{'};$$
$$S_2: \text{'}(x)[\sim\text{Black}(x) \supset \sim \text{Raven}(x)]\text{'}$$

(i.e. 'All ravens are black' and 'Whatever is not black is not a raven'), and let *a, b, c, d* be four objects such that *a* is a raven and black, *b* a raven but not black, *c* not a raven but black, and *d* neither a raven nor black. Then according to Nicod's criterion, *a* would confirm S_1, but be neutral with respect to S_2; *b* would disconfirm both S_1 and S_2; *c* would be neutral with respect to both S_1 and S_2, and *d* would confirm S_2, but be neutral with respect to S_1.

But S_1 and S_2 are logically equivalent; they have the same content, they are different formulations of the same hypothesis. And yet, by Nicod's criterion, either of the objects *a* and *d* would be confirming for one of the two sentences, but neutral with respect to the other. This means that Nicod's criterion makes confirmation depend not only on the content of the hypothesis, but also on its formulation.[20]

One remarkable consequence of this situation is that every hypothesis to which the criterion is applicable—i.e. every universal conditional—can be stated in a form for which there cannot possibly exist any confirming instances. Thus, e.g. the sentence

$$(x)[(\text{Raven}(x) \cdot \sim \text{Black}(x)) \supset (\text{Raven}(x) \cdot \sim \text{Raven}(x))]$$

is readily recognized as equivalent to both S_1 and S_2 above; yet no object whatever can confirm this sentence, i.e. satisfy both its antecedent and its consequent; for the consequent is contradictory. An analogous transformation is, of course, applicable to any other sentence of universal conditional form.

4. THE EQUIVALENCE CONDITION

The results just obtained call attention to the following condition which an adequately defined concept of confirmation should satisfy, and in the light of which Nicod's criterion has to be rejected as inadequate:

Equivalence condition: Whatever confirms (disconfirms) one of two equivalent sentences, also confirms (disconfirms) the other.

Fulfilment of this condition makes the confirmation of a hypothesis independent of the way in which it is formulated; and no doubt it will be conceded that this is a necessary condition for the adequacy of any

---

[20] This difficulty was pointed out, in substance, in my article "Le problème de la vérité", *Theoria* (Göteborg), 3 (1937), esp. p. 222.

proposed criterion of confirmation. Otherwise, the question as to whether certain data confirm a given hypothesis would have to be answered by saying: "That depends on which of the different equivalent formulations of the hypothesis is considered"—which appears absurd. Furthermore—and this is a more important point than an appeal to a feeling of absurdity—an adequate definition of confirmation will have to do justice to the way in which empirical hypotheses function in theoretical scientific contexts such as explanations and predictions; but when hypotheses are used for purposes of explanation or prediction,[21] they serve as premisses in a deductive argument whose conclusion is a description of the event to be explained or predicted. The deduction is governed by the principles of formal logic, and according to the latter, a deduction which is valid will remain so if some or all of the premisses are replaced by different but equivalent statements; and indeed, a scientist will feel free, in any theoretical reasoning involving certain hypotheses, to use the latter in whichever of their equivalent formulations are most convenient for the development of his conclusions. But if we adopted a concept of confirmation which did not satisfy the equivalence condition, then it would be possible, and indeed necessary, to argue in certain cases that it was sound scientific procedure to base a prediction on a given hypothesis if formulated in a sentence S_1, because a good deal of confirming evidence had been found for S_1; but that it was altogether inadmissible to base the prediction (say, for convenience of deduction) on an equivalent formulation S_2, because no confirming evidence for S_2 was available. Thus, the equivalence condition has to be regarded as a necessary condition for the adequacy of any definition of confirmation.

5. THE PARADOXES OF CONFIRMATION

Perhaps we seem to have been labouring the obvious in stressing the necessity of satisfying the equivalence condition. This impression is likely to vanish upon consideration of certain consequences which derive from a combination of the equivalence condition with a most

---

[21]   For a more detailed account of the logical structure of scientific explanation and prediction, cf. C. G. Hempel, "The Function of General Laws in History", *Journal of Philosophy*, 39 (1942), esp. sections 2, 3, 4. The characterization, given in that paper as well as in the above text, of explanations and predictions as arguments of a deductive logical structure, embodies an over-simplification: as will be shown in section 7 of the present essay [omitted], explanations and predictions often involve "quasi-inductive" steps besides deductive ones. This point, however, does not affect the validity of the above argument.

natural and plausible assumption concerning a sufficient condition of confirmation.

The essence of the criticism we have levelled so far against Nicod's criterion is that it certainly cannot serve as a necessary condition of confirmation; thus, in the illustration given in the beginning of section 3, object a confirms S_1 and should therefore also be considered as confirming S_2, while according to Nicod's criterion it is not. Satisfaction of the latter is therefore not a necessary condition for confirming evidence.

On the other hand, Nicod's criterion might still be considered as stating a particularly obvious and important sufficient condition of confirmation. And indeed, if we restrict ourselves to universal conditional hypotheses in one variable[22]—such as S_1 and S_2 in the above illustration—then it seems perfectly reasonable to qualify an object as confirming such a hypothesis if it satisfies both its antecedent and its consequent. The plausibility of this view will be further corroborated in the course of our subsequent analyses.

Thus, we shall agree that if a is both a raven and black, then a certainly confirms S_1: '(x) (Raven$(x) \supset$ Black(x))', and if d is neither black nor a raven, d certainly confirms S_2: '(x) [$\sim$ Black$(x) \supset \sim$ Raven(x)]'.

Let us now combine this simple stipulation with the equivalence condition. Since S_1 and S_2 are equivalent, d is confirming also for S_1; and thus, we have to recognize as confirming for S_1 any object which

---

[22] This restriction is essential: in its general form which applies to universal conditionals in any number of variables, Nicod's criterion cannot even be construed as expressing a sufficient condition of confirmation. This is shown by the following rather surprising example: Consider the hypothesis:

$$S_1 : (x)(y)[\sim(R(x,y) \cdot R(y,x)) \supset (R(x,y) \cdot \sim R(y,x))].$$

Let a, b be two objects such that $R(a,b)$ and $\sim R(b,a)$. Then clearly, the couple (a,b) satisfies both the antecedent and the consequent of the universal conditional S_1; hence, if Nicod's criterion in its general form is accepted as stating a sufficient condition of confirmation, (a, b) constitutes confirming evidence for S_1. But S_1 can be shown to be equivalent to

$$S_2 : (x)(y)R(x,y)$$

Now, by hypothesis, we have $\sim R(b, a)$; and this flatly contradicts S_2 and thus S_1. Thus, the couple (a, b), although satisfying both the antecedent and the consequent of the universal conditional S_1, actually constitutes disconfirming evidence of the strongest kind (conclusively disconfirming evidence, as we shall say later) for that sentence. This illustration reveals a striking and—as far as I am aware—hitherto unnoticed weakness of that conception of confirmation which underlies Nicod's criterion. In order to realize the bearing of our illustration upon Nicod's original formulation, let A and B be $\sim (R(x, y) \cdot R(y, x))$ and $R(x, y) \cdot \sim R(y, x)$, respectively. Then S_1 asserts that A entails B, and the couple (a, b) is a case of the presence of B in the presence of A; this should, according to Nicod, be favourable to S_1.

is neither black nor a raven. Consequently, any red pencil, any green leaf, any yellow cow, etc., becomes confirming evidence for the hypothesis that all ravens are black. This surprising consequence of two very adequate assumptions (the equivalence condition and the above sufficient condition of confirmation) can be further expanded: The sentence S_1 can readily be shown to be equivalent to S_3: '(x) [(Raven(x) v $\sim$ Raven(x)) $\supset$ ($\sim$ Raven(x) v Black(x))]', i.e. 'Anything which is or is not a raven is either no raven or black'. According to the above sufficient condition, S_3 is certainly confirmed by any object, say e, such that (1) e is or is not a raven and, in addition (2) e is not a raven or is also black. Since (1) is analytic, these conditions reduce to (2). By virtue of the equivalence condition, we have therefore to consider as confirming for S_1 any object which is either no raven or also black (in other words: any object which is no raven at all, or a black raven).

Of the four objects characterized in section 3, a, c and d would therefore constitute confirming evidence for S_1, while b would be disconforming for S_1. This implies that any non-raven represents confirming evidence for the hypothesis that all ravens are black.[23]

We shall refer to these implications of the equivalence condition and of the above sufficient condition of confirmation as the *paradoxes of confirmation*.

How are these paradoxes to be dealt with? Renouncing the equivalence condition would not represent an acceptable solution, as it is shown by the considerations presented in section 4. Nor does it seem possible to dispense with the stipulation that an object satisfying two conditions, C_1 and C_2, should be considered as confirming a general hypothesis to the effect that any object which satisfies C_1 also satisfies C_2.

But the deduction of the above paradoxical results rests on one other assumption which is usually taken for granted, namely, that the meaning of general empirical hypotheses, such as that all ravens are black, or that all sodium salts burn yellow, can be adequately expressed by means of sentences of universal conditional form, such as '(x) [Raven(x) $\supset$ Black(x)]' and '(x) (Sod. Salt(x) $\supset$ Burn yellow (x))',

[23] (Added in 1964). The following further "paradoxical" consequence of our two conditions might be noted: any hypothesis of universal conditional form can be equivalently rewritten as another hypothesis of the same form which, even if true, can have no confirming instances in Nicod's sense at all, since the proposition that a given object satisfies the antecedent and the consequent of the second hypothesis is self-contradictory. For example, '(x) [$P(x)$ $\supset$ $Q(x)$]' is equivalent to the sentence '(x) [($P(x)$ $\cdot$ $\sim$ $Q(x)$) $\supset$ ($P(x)$ $\cdot$ $\sim$ $P(x)$)]', whose consequent is true of nothing.

etc. Perhaps this customary mode of presentation has to be modified; and perhaps such a modification would automatically remove the paradoxes of confirmation? If this is not so, there seems to be only one alternative left, namely to show that the impression of the paradoxical character of those consequences is due to misunderstanding and can be dispelled, so that no theoretical difficulty remains. We shall now consider these two possibilities in turn: subsections 5.11 and 5.12 are devoted to a discussion of two different proposals for a modified representation of general hypotheses; in subsection 5.2, we shall discuss the second alternative, i.e. the possibility of tracing the impression of paradoxicality back to a misunderstanding.

5.11. It has often been pointed out that while Aristotelian logic, in agreement with prevalent everyday usage, confers existential import upon sentences of the form 'All P's are Q's', a universal conditional sentence, in the sense of modern logic, has no existential import; thus, the sentence

$$'(x) \ [\text{Mermaid}(x) \supset \text{Green}(x)]'$$

does not imply the existence of mermaids; it merely asserts that any object either is not a mermaid at all, or a green mermaid; and it is true simply because of the fact that there are no mermaids. General laws and hypotheses in science, however—so it might be argued—are meant to have existential import; and one might attempt to express the latter by supplementing the customary universal conditional by an existential clause. Thus, the hypothesis that all ravens are black would be expressed by means of the sentence S_1: '$[(x) \ (\text{Raven}(x) \supset \text{Black}(x)] \ \cdot \ (Ex)\text{Raven}(x)$'; and the hypothesis that no non-black things are ravens by S_2: '$(x)[\sim\text{Black}(x) \supset \sim \text{Raven}(x)] \ \cdot \ (Ex) \sim \text{Black}(x)$'. Clearly, these sentences are not equivalent, and of the four objects a, b, c, d characterized in section 3, part (b), only a might reasonably be said to confirm S_1, and only d to confirm S_2. Yet this method of avoiding the paradoxes of confirmation is open to serious objections.

(a) First of all, the representation of every general hypothesis by a conjunction of a universal conditional and an existential sentence would invalidate many logical inferences which are generally accepted as permissible in a theoretical argument. Thus, for example, the assertions that all sodium salts burn yellow, and that whatever does not burn yellow is no sodium salt are logically equivalent according to customary understanding and usage, and their representation by universal conditionals preserves this equivalence; but if existential clauses are added, the two assertions are no longer equivalent, as is illustrated above by the analogous case of S_1 and S_2.

(*b*) Second, the customary formulation of general hypotheses in empirical science clearly does not contain an existential clause, nor does it, as a rule, even indirectly determine such a clause unambiguously. Thus, consider the hypothesis that if a person after receiving an injection of a certain test substance has a positive skin reaction, he has diphtheria. Should we construe the existential clause here as referring to persons, to persons receiving the injection, or to persons who, upon receiving the injection, show a positive skin reaction? A more or less arbitrary decision has to be made; each of the possible decisions gives a different interpretation to the hypothesis, and none of them seems to be really implied by the latter.

(*c*) Finally, many universal hypotheses cannot be said to imply an existential clause at all. Thus, it may happen that from a certain astrophysical theory a universal hypothesis is deduced concerning the character of the phenomena which would take place under certain specified extreme conditions. A hypothesis of this kind need not (and, as a rule, does not) imply that such extreme conditions ever were or will be realized; it has no existential import. Or consider a biological hypothesis to the effect that whenever man and ape are crossed, the offspring will have such and such characteristics. This is a general hypothesis; it might be contemplated as a mere conjecture, or as a consequence of a broader genetic theory, other implications of which may already have been tested with positive results; but unquestionably the hypothesis does not imply an existential clause asserting that the contemplated kind of cross-breeding referred to will, at some time, actually take place.

5.12. Perhaps the impression of the paradoxical character of the cases discussed in the beginning of section 5 may be said to grow out of the feeling that the hypothesis that all ravens are black is about ravens, and not about non-black things, nor about all things. The use of an existential clause was one attempt at exhibiting this presumed peculiarity of the hypothesis. The attempt has failed, and if we wish to express the point in question, we shall have to look for a stronger device. The idea suggests itself of representing a general hypothesis by the customary universal conditional, supplemented by the indication of the specific "field of application" of the hypothesis; thus, we might represent the hypothesis that all ravens are black by the sentence '(x) [Raven$(x) \supset$ Black(x)]' or any one of its equivalents, plus the indication 'Class of ravens', characterizing the field of application; and we might then require that every confirming instance should belong to the field of application. This procedure would exclude the objects c and d from those constituting confirming evidence and would thus avoid those undesirable consequences of the existential-clause device which were pointed out in 5.11 (*c*). But apart from this advantage, the second method is open to objections similar to those which apply to the first: (*a*) The way in which general hypotheses are used in science never involves the statement of a field of application; and the choice of the latter in a symbolic formulation of a given hypothesis thus introduces again a considerable measure of arbitrariness. In particular, for a scientific hypothesis to the effect that all *P*'s are *Q*'s, the field of application cannot simply be said to be the class of all *P*'s; for a hypothesis such as that all sodium salts burn yellow finds important application in tests with negative results; e.g., it may be applied to a substance of which it is not known whether it contains sodium salts, nor whether it burns yellow; and if the flame does not turn yellow, the hypothesis serves to establish the absence of sodium salts. The same is true of all other hypotheses used for tests of this type. (*b*) Again, the consistent use of a field of application in the formulation of general hypotheses would involve considerable logical complications, and yet would have no counterpart in the theoretical procedure of science, where hypotheses are subjected to various kinds of logical transformation and inference without any consideration that might be regarded as referring to changes in the fields of application. This method of meeting the paradoxes would therefore amount to dodging the problem by means of an *ad hoc* device which cannot be justified by reference to actual scientific procedure.

5.2 We have examined two alternatives to the customary method of representing general hypotheses by means of universal conditionals; neither of them proved an adequate means of precluding the paradoxes of confirmation. We shall now try to show that what is wrong does not lie in the customary way of construing and representing general hypotheses, but rather in our reliance on a misleading intuition in the matter: the impression of a paradoxical situation is not objectively founded; it is a psychological illusion.

(*a*) One source of misunderstanding is the view, referred to before, that a hypothesis of the simple form 'Every *P* is a *Q*', such as 'All sodium salts burn yellow', asserts something about a certain limited class of objects only, namely, the class of all *P*'s. This idea involves a confusion of logical and practical considerations: our interest in the hypothesis may be focused upon its applicability to that particular class of objects, but the hypothesis nevertheless asserts something about, and indeed imposes restrictions upon, *all* objects (within the logical type of the variable occurring in the hypothesis, which in the case of our last illustration might be the class of all physical objects). Indeed, a hypothesis of the form 'Every P is a Q' forbids the occurrence of any objects having the property P but lacking the property Q; i.e. it restricts all objects whatsoever to the class of those which either lack the property P or also have the property Q. Now, every object either belongs to this class or falls outside it, and thus, every object—and not only the P's—either conforms to the hypothesis or violates it; there is no object which is not implicitly referred to by a hypothesis of this type. In particular, every object which either is no sodium salt or burns yellow conforms to, and thus bears out, the hypothesis that all sodium salts burn yellow; every other object violates that hypothesis.

The weakness of the idea under consideration is evidenced also by the observation that the class of objects about which a hypothesis is supposed to assert something is in no way clearly determined, and that it changes with the context, as was shown in 5.12 (a).

(b) A second important source of the appearance of paradoxicality in certain cases of confirmation is exhibited by the following consideration.

Suppose that in support of the assertion 'All sodium salts burn yellow' somebody were to adduce an experiment in which a piece of pure ice was held into a colourless flame and did not turn the flame yellow. This result would confirm the assertion, 'Whatever does not burn yellow is no sodium salt' and consequently, by virtue of the equivalence condition, it would confirm the original formulation. Why does this impress us as paradoxical? The reason becomes clear when we compare the previous situation with the case where an object whose chemical constitution is as yet unknown to us is held into a flame and fails to turn it yellow, and where subsequent analysis reveals it to contain no sodium salt. This outcome, we should no doubt agree, is what was to be expected on the basis of the hypothesis that all sodium salts burn yellow—no matter in which of its various equivalent formulations it may be expressed; thus, the data here obtained constitute confirming evidence for the hypothesis. Now the only difference between the two situations here considered is that in the first case we are told beforehand the test substance is ice, and we happen to "know anyhow" that ice contains no sodium salt; this has the consequence that the outcome of the flame-colour test becomes entirely irrelevant for the confirmation of the hypothesis and thus can yield no new evidence for us. Indeed, if the flame should not turn yellow, the hypothesis requires that the substance contain no sodium salt—and we know beforehand that ice does not; and if the flame should turn yellow, the hypothesis would impose no further restrictions on the substance: hence, either of the possible outcomes of the experiment would be in accord with the hypothesis.

The analysis of this example illustrates a general point: in the seemingly paradoxical cases of confirmation, we are often not actually judging the relation of the given evidence E alone to the hypothesis H (we fail to observe the methodological fiction, characteristic of every case of confirmation, that we have no relevant evidence for H other than that included in E); instead, we tacitly introduce a comparison of H with a body of evidence which consists of E in conjunction with additional information that we happen to have at our disposal; in our illustration, this information includes the knowledge (1) that the substance used in the experiment is ice, and (2) that ice contains no sodium salt. If we assume this additional information as given, then, of course, the outcome of the experiment can add no strength to the hypothesis under consideration. But if we are careful to avoid this tacit reference to additional knowledge (which entirely changes the character of the problem), and if we formulate the question as to the confirming character of the evidence in a manner adequate to the concept of confirmation as used in this paper, we have to ask: Given some object a (it happens to be a piece of ice, but this fact is not included in the evidence), and given the fact that a does not turn the flame yellow and is no sodium salt: does a then constitute confirming evidence for the hypothesis? And now—no matter whether a is ice or some other substance—it is clear that the answer has to be in the affirmative; and the paradoxes vanish.

So far, in section (b), we have considered mainly that type of paradoxical case which is illustrated by the assertion that any non-black non-raven constitutes confirming evidence for the hypothesis, 'All ravens are black'. However, the general idea just outlined applies as well to the even more extreme cases exemplified by the assertion that any non-raven as well as any black object confirms the hypothesis in question. Let us illustrate this by reference to the latter case. If the given evidence E—i.e. in the sense of the required methodological fiction, all data relevant for the hypothesis—consists only of one object which, in addition, is black, then E may reasonably be said to support even the hypothesis that all objects are black, and *a fortiori* E supports the weaker assertion that all ravens are black. In this case, again, our factual knowledge that not all objects are black tends to create an impression of paradoxicality which is not justified on logical grounds. Other paradoxical cases of confirmation may be dealt with analogously. Thus it turns out that the paradoxes of confirmation, as formulated above, are due to a misguided intuition in the matter rather than to a logical flaw in the two stipulations from which they were derived.[24,25]

6. CONFIRMATION CONSTRUED AS A RELATION BETWEEN SENTENCES

Our analysis of Nicod's criterion has so far led to two main results: the rejection of that criterion in view of several deficiencies, and the emergence of the equivalence condition as a necessary condition of adequacy for any proposed definition of confirmation. Another aspect of Nicod's criterion requires consideration now. In our formulation of the criterion, confirmation was construed as a dyadic relation between an object or an ordered set of objects, representing the evidence, and a sentence, representing the hypothesis. This means that confirmation

[24] The basic idea of section (b) in the above analysis is due to Dr Nelson Goodman, to whom I wish to reiterate my thanks for the help he rendered me, through many discussions, in clarifying my ideas on this point.

[25] The considerations presented in section (b) above are also influenced by, though not identical in content with, the very illuminating discussion of the paradoxes by the Polish methodologist and logician Janina Hosiasson-Lindenbaum; cf. her article 'On Confirmation', *Journal of Symbolic Logic*, 5 (1940), especially section 4. Dr Hosiasson's attention had been called to the paradoxes by my article 'Le problème de la vérité' (cf. note 20) and by discussions with me. To my knowledge, hers has so far been the only publication which presents an explicit attempt to solve the problem. Her solution is based on a theory of degrees of confirmation, which is developed in the form of an uninterpreted axiomatic system, and most of her arguments presuppose that theoretical framework. I have profited, however, by some of Miss Hosiasson's more general observations which proved relevant for the analysis of the paradoxes of the non-graduated or qualitative concept of confirmation which forms the object of the present study.

One point in those of Miss Hosiasson's comments which rest on her theory of degrees of confirmation is of particular interest, and I should like to discuss it briefly. Stated in reference to the raven hypothesis, it consists in the suggestion that the finding of one non-black object which is no raven, while constituting confirming evidence for the hypothesis, would increase the degree of confirmation of the hypothesis by a smaller amount than the finding of one raven which is black. This is said to be so because the class of all ravens is much less numerous than that of all non-black objects, so that—to put the idea in suggestive though somewhat misleading terms—the finding of one black raven confirms a larger portion of the total content of the hypothesis than the finding of one non-black non-raven. In fact, from the basic assumptions of her theory, Miss Hosiasson is able to derive a theorem according to which the above statement about the relative increase in degree of confirmation will hold provided that actually the number of all ravens is small compared with the number of all non-black objects. But is this last numerical assumption actually warranted in the present case and analogously in all other "paradoxical" cases? The answer depends in part upon the logical structure of the language of science. If a "coordinate language" is used, in which, say, finite space-time regions figure as individuals, then the raven hypothesis assumes some such form as 'Every space-time region which contains a raven contains something black'; and even if the total number of ravens ever to exist is finite, the class of space-time regions containing a raven has the power of the continuum, and so does the class of space-time regions containing something was conceived of as a semantical relation[26] obtaining between certain extra-linguistic objects[27] on one hand and certain sentences on the other. It is possible, however, to construe confirmation in an alternative fashion as a relation between two sentences, one describing the given evidence, the other expressing the hypothesis. Thus, instead of saying that an object a which is both a raven and black (or the fact of a being both a raven and black) confirms the hypothesis that all ravens are black, we may say that the evidence sentence, 'a is a raven and a is black', confirms the hypothesis-sentence (briefly, the hypothesis), 'All ravens are black'. We shall adopt this conception of confirmation as a relation between sentences here for the following reasons: first, the evidence adduced in support or criticism of a scientific hypothesis is always expressed in sentences, which frequently have the character of observation reports; and second, it will prove very fruitful to pursue the parallel, alluded to in section 2 above, between the concepts of confirmation and of logical consequence. And just as in the theory of the consequence relation, i.e. in deductive logic, the premises of which a given conclusion is a consequence are construed as sentences rather than as "facts", so we propose to construe the data which confirm a given hypothesis as given in the form of sentences.

The preceding reference to observation reports suggests a certain restriction which might be imposed on evidence sentences. Indeed, the evidence adduced in support of a scientific hypothesis or theory consists, in the last analysis, in data accessible to what is loosely called direct observation, and such data are expressible in the form of "observation reports". In view of this consideration, we shall restrict the evidence sentences which form the domain of the relation of confirmation to sentences of the character of observation reports. In

non-black; thus, for a co-ordinate language of the type under consideration, the above numerical assumption is not warranted. Now the use of a co-ordinate language may appear quite artificial in this particular illustration; but it will seem very appropriate in many other contexts, such as, e.g., that of physical field theories. On the other hand, Miss Hosiasson's numerical assumption may well be justified on the basis of a "thing language", in which physical objects of finite size function as individuals. Of course, even on this basis, it remains an empirical question, for every hypothesis of the form 'All P's are Q's', whether actually the class of non-Q's is much more numerous than the class of P's; and in many cases this question will be very difficult to decide.

[26] For a detailed account of this concept, see C. W. Morris, *Foundations of the Theory of Signs* (Internat. Encyclopedia of Unified Science, vol. I, No. 2, Chicago, 1938) and R. Carnap *Introduction to Semantics* (Cambridge, Mass., 1962), esp. sections 4 and 37.

[27] Instead of making the first term of the relation an object or a sequence of objects we might construe it as a state of affairs (or perhaps as a fact, or a proposition, as Nicod puts it), such as that state of affairs which consists in a being a black raven, etc.

order to give a precise meaning to the concept of observation report, we shall assume that we are given a well-determined "language of science", in terms of which all sentences under consideration, hypotheses as well as evidence sentences, are formulated. We shall further assume that this language contains, among other terms, a clearly delimited "observational vocabulary" which consists of terms designating more or less directly observable attributes of things or events, such as, say, 'black', 'taller than', 'burning with a yellow light', etc., but no theoretical constructs such as 'aliphatic compound', 'circularly polarized light', 'heavy hydrogen', etc.

We shall now understand by a *hypothesis* any sentence which can be expressed in the assumed language of science, no matter whether it is a generalized sentence, containing quantifiers, or a particular sentence referring only to a finite number of particular objects. An *observation report* will be construed as a finite class (or a conjunction of a finite number) of observation sentences; and an observation sentence as a sentence which either asserts or denies that a given object has a certain observable property (e.g. 'a is a raven', 'd is not black'), or that a given sequence of objects stand in a certain observable relation (e.g. 'a is between b and c').

Now the concept of observability itself obviously is relative to the techniques of observation used. What is unobservable to the unaided senses may well be observable by means of suitable devices such as telescopes, microscopes, polariscopes, lie-detectors, Gallup polls, etc. If by direct observation we mean such observational procedures as do not make use of auxiliary devices, then such property terms as 'black', 'hard', 'liquid', 'cool', and such relation terms as 'above', 'between', 'spatially coincident', etc., might be said to refer to directly observable attributes; if observability is construed in a broader sense, so as to allow for the use of certain specified instruments or other devices, the concept of observable attribute becomes more comprehensive. If, in our study of confirmation, we wanted to analyse the manner in which the hypotheses and theories of empirical science are ultimately supported by "evidence of the senses", then we should have to require that observation reports refer exclusively to directly observable attributes. This view was taken, for simplicity and concreteness, in the preceding parts of this section. Actually, however, the general logical characteristics of that relation which obtains between a hypothesis and a group of empirical statements which support it, can be studied in isolation from this restriction to direct observability. All we will assume here is that in the context of the scientific test of a given hypothesis or theory, certain specified techniques of observation have been agreed upon; these determine an observational vocabulary, namely, a set of terms designating properties and relations observable by means of the accepted techniques. For our purposes it is entirely sufficient that these terms, constituting the observational vocabulary, be given. An observation sentence is then defined simply as a sentence affirming or denying that a given object, or sequence of objects, possesses one of those observable attributes.[28]

Let it be noted that we do not require an observation sentence to be true, nor to be accepted on the basis of actual observations; rather, an observation sentence expresses something that is decidable by means of the accepted techniques of observation. In other words, an observation sentence describes a possible outcome of the accepted observational techniques; it asserts something that might conceivably be established by means of those techniques. Possibly, the term "observation-type sentence" would be more suggestive; but for convenience we give preference to the shorter term. An analogous comment applies, of course, to our definition of an observation report as a class or a conjunction of observation sentences. The need for this broad conception of observation sentences and observation reports is readily recognized: confirmation as here conceived is a logical relationship between sentences, just as logical consequence is. Now whether a sentence S_2 is a consequence of a sentence S_1 does not depend on whether or not S_1 is true (or known to be true); and analogously, the criteria of whether a given statement, expressed in terms of the

---

[28] The concept of observation sentence has, in the context of our study, a status and a logical function closely akin to that of the concepts of protocol statement or basis sentence, etc., as used in many recent studies of empricism. However, the conception of observation sentence which is being proposed in the present study is more liberal in that it renders the discussion of the logical problems of testing and confirmation independent of various highly controversial epistemological issues; thus, e.g., we do not stipulate that observation reports must be about psychic events, or about sense perceptions (i.e. that they have to be expressed in terms of a vocabulary of phenomenology, or of introspective psychology). According to the conception of observation sentence adopted in the present study, the "objects" referred to in an observation sentence may be construed in any one of the senses just referred to, or in various other ways; for example, they might be space-time regions, or again physical objects such as stones, trees, etc. (most of the illustrations given throughout this article represent observation sentences belonging to this kind of "thing language"); all that we require is that the few very general conditions stated above be satisfied.

These conditions impose on observation sentences and on observation reports certain restrictions with respect to their form; in particular, neither kind of sentence may contain any quantifiers. This stipulation recommends itself for the purposes of the logical analysis here to be undertaken; but we do not wish to claim that this formal restriction is indispensable. On the contrary, it is quite possible and perhaps desirable also to allow for observation sentences containing quantifiers: our simplifying assumption is introduced mainly in order to avoid considerable logical complications in the definition of confirmation.

observational vocabulary, confirms a certain hypothesis cannot depend on whether the statements in the report are true, or based on actual experience, or the like. Our definition of confirmation must enable us to indicate what kind of evidence *would* confirm a given hypothesis *if* it were available; and clearly the sentence characterizing such evidence can be required only to express something that *might* be observed, but not necessarily something that has actually been established by observation.

It may be helpful to carry the analogy between confirmation and consequence one step further. The truth or falsity of S_1 is irrelevant for the question of whether S_2 is a consequence of S_1 (whether S_2 can be validly inferred from S_1); but in a logical inference which justifies a sentence S_2 by showing that it is a logical consequence of a conjunction of premisses, S_1, we can be certain of the truth of S_2 only if we know S_1 to be true. Analogously, the question of whether an observation report stands in the relation of confirmation to a given hypothesis does not depend on whether the report states actual or fictitious observational findings; but for a decision as to the soundness or acceptability of a hypothesis which is confirmed by a certain report, it is of course necessary to know whether the report is based on actual experience or not. Just as a conclusion of a logical inference, shown to be true, must be (a1) validly inferred from (a2) a set of true premisses, so a hypothesis, to be scientifically acceptable, must be (b1) formally confirmed by (b2) reliable reports on observational findings.

The central problem of this essay is to establish general criteria for the formal relation of confirmation as referred to in (b1); the analysis of the concept of a reliable observation report, which belongs largely to the field of pragmatics,[29] falls outside the scope of the present study. One point, however, deserves mention here. A statement in the form of an observation report (for example, about the position of the pointer of a certain thermograph at 3 a.m.) may be accepted or rejected in science either on the basis of direct observation, or because it is indirectly confirmed or disconfirmed by other accepted observation sentences (in the example, these might be sentences describing the curve traced by the pointer during the night); and because of this possibility of indirect confirmation, our study has a bearing also on the question of the acceptance of hypotheses which have themselves the form of observation reports.

The conception of confirmation as a relation between sentences analogous to that of logical consequence suggests yet another require-

[29] An account of the concept of pragmatics may be found in the publications listed in note 26.

ment for the attempted definition of confirmation: While logical consequence has to be conceived of as a basically semantical relation between sentences, it has been possible, for certain languages, to establish criteria of logical consequence in purely syntactical terms. Analogously, confirmation may be conceived of as a semantical relation between an observation report and a hypothesis; but the parallel with the consequence relation suggests that it should be possible, for certain languages, to establish purely syntactical criteria of confirmation. The subsequent considerations will indeed eventuate in a definition of confirmation based on the concept of logical consequence and other purely syntactical concepts.

The interpretation of confirmation as a logical relation between sentences involves no essential change in the central problem of the present study. In particular, all the points made in the preceding sections can readily be rephrased in accordance with this interpretation. Thus, for example, the assertion that an object a which is a swan and white confirms the hypothesis '(x) [Swan$(x) \supset$ White(x)]' can be expressed by saying that the observation report 'Swan$(a)\cdot$ White(a)' confirms that hypothesis. Similarly, the equivalence condition can be reformulated as follows: if an observation report confirms a certain sentence, then it also confirms every sentence which is logically equivalent with the latter. Nicod's criterion as well as our grounds for rejecting it can be reformulated along the same lines. We presented Nicod's concept of confirmation as referring to a relation between non-linguistic objects on one hand and sentences on the other because this approach seemed to approximate most closely to Nicod's own formulations,[30] and because it enabled us to avoid certain technicalities which are actually unnecessary in that context.

[Section 7 omitted]

8. CONDITIONS OF ADEQUACY FOR ANY DEFINITION OF CONFIRMATION

. . .

First of all, it will be agreed that any sentence which is logically entailed by a given observation report has to be considered as

[30] (Added in 1964.) Actually this is not correct; cf. note 17 above. But, as is readily seen, the objections raised in this article against Nicod's criterion remain in force also when that criterion is understood as taking general hypotheses to be confirmed or disconfirmed by propositions rather than by objects.

confirmed by that report: entailment is a special case of confirmation. Thus, e.g., we want to say that the observation report 'a is black' confirms the sentence (hypothesis) 'a is black or grey'; and the observation sentence '$R_2(a, b)$' should certainly be confirming evidence for the sentence '$(Ez)R_2(a, z)$'. We are therefore led to the stipulation that any adequate definition of confirmation must insure the fulfilment of the

(8.1) *Entailment Condition.* Any sentence which is entailed by an observation report is confirmed by it.[31]

This condition is suggested by the preceding consideration, but of course not proved by it. To make it a standard of adequacy for the definition of confirmation means to lay down the stipulation that a proposed definition of confirmation will be rejected as logically inadequate if it is not constructed in such a way that (8.1) is unconditionally satisfied. An analogous remark applies to the subsequently proposed further standards of adequacy.

Second, an observation report which confirms certain hypotheses would invariably be qualified as confirming any consequence of those hypotheses. Indeed: any such consequence is but an assertion of all or part of the combined content of the original hypotheses and has therefore to be regarded as confirmed by any evidence which confirms all of the latter. This suggests the following condition of adequacy:

(8.2) *Consequence Condition.* If an observation report confirms every one of a class K of sentences, then it also confirms any sentence which is a logical consequence of K.

If (8.2) is satisfied, then the same is true of the following two more special conditions:

(8.21) *Special Consequence Condition.* If an observation report confirms a hypothesis H, then it also confirms every consequence of H.

(8.22) *Equivalence Condition.* If an observation report confirms a hypothesis H, then it also confirms every hypothesis which is logically equivalent with H.

(8.22) follows from (8.21) in view of the fact that equivalent hypotheses are mutual consequences of each other. Thus, the satis-

[31] As a consequence of this stipulation, a contradictory observation report, such as [Black(a), $\sim$ Black(a)] confirms every sentence, because it has every sentence as a consequence. Of course, it is possible to exclude contradictory observation reports altogether by a slight restriction of the definition of 'observation report'. There is, however, no important reason to do so.

faction of the consequence condition entails that of our earlier
equivalence condition, and the latter loses its status of an independent
requirement.

In view of the apparent obviousness of these conditions, it is
interesting to note that the definition of confirmation in terms of
successful prediction, while satisfying the equivalence condition, would
violate the consequence condition. Clearly, if the observational findings
B_2 can be predicted on the basis of the findings B_1 by means of the
hypothesis H, the same prediction is obtainable by means of any
equivalent hypothesis, but not generally by means of a weaker one.

On the other hand, any prediction obtainable by means of H can
obviously also be established by means of any hypothesis which is
stronger than H, i.e. which logically entails H. Thus while the
consequence condition stipulates in effect that whatever confirms a
given hypothesis also confirms any weaker hypothesis, the relation of
confirmation defined in terms of successful prediction would satisfy
the condition that whatever confirms a given hypotheses also confirms
every stronger one.

But is this "converse consequence condition", as it might be called,
not reasonable enough, indeed should it not be included among our
standards of adequacy for the definition of confirmation? The second
of these two suggestions can be readily disposed of: The adoption of
the new condition, in addition to (8.1) and (8.2), would have the
consequence that any observation report B would confirm any
hypothesis H whatsoever. Thus, e.g., if B is the report 'a is a raven' and
H is Hooke's law, then, according to (8.1), B confirms the sentence 'a is
a raven'; hence B would, according to the converse consequence
condition, confirm the stronger sentence 'a is a raven, and Hooke's
law holds'; and finally, by virtue of (8.2), B would confirm H, which is
a consequence of the last sentence. Obviously, the same type of
argument can be applied in all other cases.

But is it not true, after all, that very often observational data which
confirm a hypothesis H are considered also as confirming a stronger
hypothesis? Is it not true, for example, that those experimental findings
which confirm Galileo's law, or Kepler's laws, are considered also as
confirming Newton's law of gravitation?[32] This is indeed the case, but
it does not justify the acceptance of the converse consequence
condition as a general rule of the logic of confirmation; for in the cases
just mentioned, the weaker hypothesis is connected with the stronger

[32] Strictly speaking, Galileo's law and Kepler's laws can be deduced from the
law of gravitation only if certain additional hypotheses—including the laws of
motion—are presupposed; but this does not affect the point under discussion.

one by a logical bond of a particular kind: it is essentially a substitution instance of the stronger one; thus, e.g., while the law of gravitation refers to the force obtaining between any two bodies, Galileo's law is a specialization referring to the case where one of the bodies is the earth, the other an object near its surface. In the preceding case, however, where Hooke's law was shown to be confirmed by the observation report that a is a raven, this situation does not prevail; and here, the rule that whatever confirms a given hypothesis also confirms any stronger one becomes an entirely absurd principle. Thus, the converse consequence condition does not provide a sound general condition of adequacy.[33]

A third condition remains to be stated:[34]

(8.3) *Consistency Condition.* Every logically consistent observation report is logically compatible with the class of all the hypotheses which it confirms.

The two most important implications of this requirement are the following:

(8.31) Unless an observation report is self-contradictory,[35] it does not confirm any hypothesis with which it is not logically compatible.

(8.32) Unless an observation report is self-contradictory, it does not confirm any hypotheses which contradict each other.

The first of these corollaries will readily be accepted; the second, however,—and consequently (8.3) itself—will perhaps be felt to embody a too severe restriction. It might be pointed out, for example, that a

---

[33] William Barrett, in a paper entitled 'Discussion on Dewey's Logic' (*Philosophical Review*, 50, 1941, 305 ff., esp. p. 312) raises some questions closely related to what we have called above the consequence condition and the converse consequence condition. In fact, he invokes the latter (without stating it explicitly) in an argument which is designed to show that "not every observation which confirms a sentence need also confirm all its consequences," in other words, that the special consequence condition (8.21) need not always be satisfied. He supports his point by reference to "the simplest case: the sentence 'C' is an abbreviation of 'A·B', and the observation O confirms 'A', *and so* 'C', but is irrelevant to 'B', which is a consequence of 'C'." (Italics mine.)

For reasons contained in the above discussion of the consequence condition and the converse consequence condition, the application of the latter in the case under consideration seems to me unjustifiable, so that the illustration does not prove the author's point; and indeed, there seems to be every reason to preserve the unrestricted validity of the consequence condition. As a matter of fact, Barrett himself argues that 'the degree of confirmation for the consequence of a sentence cannot be less than that of the sentence itself'; this is indeed quite sound; but it is hard to see how the recognition of this principle can be reconciled with a renunciation of the special consequence condition, which may be considered simply as its correlate for the non-graduated relation of confirmation.

[34] For a fourth condition, see note 39.

[35] A contradictory observation report confirms every hypothesis (cf. note 31) and is, of course, incompatible with every one of the hypotheses it confirms.

finite set of measurements concerning the changes of one physical magnitude, x, associated with those of another, y, may conform to, and thus be said to confirm, several different hypotheses as to the particular mathematical function in terms of which the relationship of x and y can be expressed; but such hypotheses are incompatible because to at least one value of x, they will assign different values of y.

No doubt it is possible to liberalize the formal standards of adequacy in line with these considerations. This would amount to dropping (8.3) and (8.32) and retaining only (8.31). One of the effects of this measure would be that when a logically consistent observation report B confirms each of two hypotheses, it does not necessarily confirm their conjunction; for the hypotheses might be mutually incompatible, hence their conjunction self-contradictory; consequently, by (8.31), B could not confirm it. This consequence is intuitively rather awkward, and one might therefore feel inclined to suggest that while (8.3) should be dropped and (8.31) retained, (8.32) should be replaced by the requirement (8.33): if an observation sentence confirms each of two hypotheses, then it also confirms their conjunction. But it can readily be shown that by virtue of (8.2) this set of conditions entails the fulfilment of (8.32).

If, therefore, the condition (8.3) appears to be too rigorous, the most obvious alternative would seem to lie in replacing (8.3) and its corollaries by the much weaker condition (8.31) alone. [Added in 1970: But as G. L. Massey has pointed out to me, satisfaction of (8.1), (8.2), and (8.31) logically implies satisfaction of (8.3); hence, that alternative fails.] One of the advantages of a definition which satisfies (8.3) is that it sets a limit, so to speak, to the strength of the hypotheses which can be confirmed by given evidence.[36]

The remainder of the present study, therefore, will be concerned exclusively with the problem of establishing a definition of confirmation which satisfies the more severe formal conditions represented by (8.1), (8.2), and (8.3) together.

The fulfilment of these requirements, which may be regarded as general laws of the logic of confirmation, is of course only a necessary, not a sufficient, condition for the adequacy of any proposed definition of confirmation. Thus, e.g., if 'B confirms H' were defined as meaning 'B logically entails H', then the above three conditions would clearly be satisfied; but the definition would not be adequate because

---

[36] This was pointed out to me by Dr Nelson Goodman. The definition later to be outlined in this essay, which satisfies conditions (8.1), (8.2), and (8.3), lends itself, however, to certain generalizations which satisfy only the more liberal conditions of adequacy just considered.

confirmation has to be a more comprehensive relation than entailment (the latter might be referred to as the special case of *conclusive* confirmation). Thus, a definition of confirmation, to be acceptable, also has to be materially adequate: it has to provide a reasonably close approximation to that conception of confirmation which is implicit in scientific procedure and methodological discussion. That conception is vague and to some extent quite unclear, as I have tried to show in earlier parts of this paper; therefore, it would be too much to expect full agreement as to whether a proposed definition of confirmation is materially adequate. On the other hand, there will be rather general agreement on certain points; thus, e.g., the identification of confirmation with entailment, or the Nicod criterion of confirmation as analysed above, or any definition of confirmation by reference to a "sense of evidence", will probably now be admitted not to be adequate approximations to that concept of confirmation which is relevant for the logic of science.

On the other hand, the soundness of the logical analysis (which, in a clear sense, always involves a logical reconstruction) of a theoretical concept cannot be gauged simply by our feelings of satisfaction at a certain proposed analysis; and if there are, say, two alternative proposals for defining a term on the basis of a logical analysis, and if both appear to come fairly close to the intended meaning, then the choice has to be made largely by reference to such features as the logical properties of the two reconstructions, and the comprehensiveness and simplicity of the theories to which they lead.

9. THE SATISFACTION CRITERION OF CONFIRMATION

As has been mentioned before, a precise definition of confirmation requires reference to some definite "language of science", in which all observation reports and all hypotheses under consideration are assumed to be formulated, and whose logical structure is supposed to be precisely determined. The more complex this language, and the richer its logical means of expression, the more difficult it will be, as a rule, to establish an adequate definition of confirmation for it. However, the problem has been solved at least for certain cases: with respect to languages of a comparatively simple logical structure, it has been possible to construct an explicit definition of confirmation which satisfies all of the above logical requirements, and which appears to be intuitively rather adequate. An exposition of the technical details of this definition has been published elsewhere;[37] in the present study,

[37] In my article referred to in note 1. The logical structure of the languages to which the definition in question is applicable is that of the lower functional

which is concerned with the general logical and methodological aspects of the problem of confirmation rather than with technical details, it will be attempted to characterize the definition of confirmation thus obtained as clearly as possible with a minimum of technicalities.

Consider the simple case of the hypothesis H: '$(x)(\text{Raven}(x) \supset \text{Black}(x))$', where 'Raven' and 'Black' are supposed to be terms of our observational vocabulary. Let B be an observation report to the effect that Raven $(a) \cdot \text{Black}(a) \cdot \sim \text{Raven}(c) \cdot \text{Black}(c) \cdot \sim \text{Raven}(d) \cdot \sim \text{Black}(d)$. Then B may be said to confirm H in the following sense: there are three objects mentioned in B, namely a, c, and d; and as far as these are concerned, B informs us that all those which are ravens (i.e. just the object a) are also black.[38] In other words, from the information contained in B we can infer that the hypothesis H does hold true within the finite class of those objects which are mentioned in B.

Let us apply the same consideration to a hypothesis of a logically more complex structure. Let H be the hypothesis 'Everybody likes somebody'; in symbols: '$(x)(Ey)\text{Likes}(x, y)$', i.e. 'For every (person) x, there exists at least one (not necessarily different person) y such that x likes y'. (Here again, 'Likes' is supposed to be a relation term which occurs in our observational vocabulary.) Suppose now that we are given an observation report B in which the names of two persons, say 'e' and 'f', occur. Under what conditions shall we say that B confirms H? The previous illustration suggests the answer: If from B we can infer that H is satisfied within the finite class $\{e,f\}$; i.e., that within $\{e,f\}$

calculus with individual constants, and with predicate constants of any degree. All sentences of the language are assumed to be formed exclusively by means of predicate constants, individual constants, individual variables, universal and existential quantifiers for individual variables, and the connective symbols of denial, conjunction, alternation, and implication. The use of predicate variables or of the identity sign is not permitted.

As to the predicate constants, they are all assumed to belong to the observational vocabulary, i.e. to denote properties or relations observable by means of the accepted techniques. ("Abstract" predicate terms are supposed to be defined by means of those of the observational vocabulary and then actually to be replaced by their definientia, so that they never occur explicitly.)

As a consequence of these stipulations, an observation report can be characterized simply as a conjunction of sentences of the kind illustrated by '$P(a)$', '$\sim P(b)$', '$R(c,d)$', '$\sim R(e,f)$', etc., where 'P', 'R', etc., belong to the observational vocabulary, and 'a', 'b', 'c', 'd', 'e', 'f', etc., are individual names, denoting specific objects. It is also possible to define an observation report more liberally as any sentence containing no quantifiers, which means that besides conjunctions also alternations and implication sentences formed out of the above kind of components are included among the observation reports.

[38] I am indebted to Dr Nelson Goodman for having suggested this idea; it initiated all those considerations which finally led to the definition to be outlined below.

everybody likes somebody. This in turn means that e likes e or f, and f likes e or f. Thus, B would be said to confirm H if B entailed the statement 'e likes e or f, and f likes e or f'. This latter statement will be called the development of H for the finite class $\{e,f\}$.

The concept of *development of a hypothesis, H, for a finite class of individuals, C,* can be defined precisely by recursion; here it will suffice to say that the development of H for C states what H would assert if there existed exclusively those objects which are elements of C. Thus, e.g., the development of the hypothesis $H_1 =$ '$[(x)(P(x) \text{ v } Q(x))]$' (i.e. 'Every object has the property P or the property Q') for the class $\{a, b\}$ is '$[P(a) \text{ v } Q(a)] \cdot [P(b) \text{ v } Q(b)]$' (i.e. '$a$ has the property P or the property Q, and b has the property P or the property Q'); the development of the existential hypothesis H_2 that at least one object has the property P, i.e. '$(Ex)P(x)$', for $\{a, b\}$ is '$P(a) \text{ v } P(b)$'; the development of a hypothesis which contains no quantifiers, such as H_3 : '$P(c) \text{ v } K(c)$' is defined as that hypothesis itself, no matter what the reference class of individuals is.

A more detailed formal analysis based on considerations of this type leads to the introduction of a general relation of confirmation in two steps; the first consists in defining a special relation of direct confirmation along the lines just indicated; the second step then defines the general relation of confirmation by reference to direct confirmation.

Omitting minor details, we may summarize the two definitions as follows:

(9.1Df). An observation report B directly confirms a hypothesis H if B entails the development of H for the class of those objects which are mentioned in B.

(9.2 Df.) An observation report B confirms a hypothesis H if H is entailed by a class of sentences each of which is directly confirmed by B.

The criterion expressed in these definitions might be called the *satisfaction criterion of confirmation* because its basic idea consists in construing a hypothesis as confirmed by a given observation report if the hypothesis is satisfied in the finite class of those individuals which are mentioned in the report.

Let us now apply the two definitions to our last examples: the observation report B_1: '$P(a) \cdot Q(b)$' directly confirms (and therefore also confirms) the hypothesis H_1, because it entails the development of H_1 for the class $\{a, b\}$, which was given above. The hypothesis H_3 is not directly confirmed by B, because its development, i.e. H_3 itself, obviously is not entailed by B_1. However, H_3 is entailed by H_1, which is directly confirmed by B_1; hence, by virtue of (9.2), B_1 confirms H_3. Similarly, it can readily be seen that B_1 directly confirms H_2.

Finally, to refer to the first illustration in this section: the observation report 'Raven(a) · Black(a) · ~ Raven(c) · Black(c) · ~ Raven(d) · ~ Black(d)' confirms (even directly) the hypothesis '(x)[Raven(x) ⊃ Black(x)]', for it entails the development of the latter for the class {a, c, d}, which can be written as follows: '[Raven(a) ⊃ Black(a)] · [Raven(c) ⊃ Black(c)] · [Raven(d) ⊃ Black(d)]'.

It is now easy to define disconfirmation and neutrality:

(9.3 Df.) An observation report B disconfirms a hypothesis H if it confirms the denial of H.

(9.4 Df.) An observation report B is neutral with respect to a hypothesis H if B neither confirms nor disconfirms H.

By virtue of the criteria laid down in (9.2), (9.3), (9.4), every consistent observation report B divides all possible hypotheses into three mutually exclusive classes; those confirmed by B, those disconfirmed by B, and those with respect to which B is neutral.

The definition of confirmation here proposed can be shown to satisfy all the formal conditions of adequacy embodied in (8.1), (8.2), and (8.3) and their consequences. For the condition (8.2) this is easy to see; for the other conditions the proof is more complicated.[39]

[39] For these proofs, see the article referred to in note 1. I should like to take this opportunity to point out and to remedy a certain defect of the definition of confirmation which was developed in that article, and which has been outlined above: this defect was brought to my attention by a discussion with Dr Olaf Helmer.

It will be agreed that an acceptable definition of confirmation should satisfy the following further condition which might well have been included among the logical standards of adequacy set up in section 8 above: (8.4) If B_1 and B_2 are logically equivalent observation reports and B_1 confirms (disconfirms, is neutral with respect to) a hypothesis H, then B_2 too, confirms (disconfirms, is neutral with respect to) H. This condition is indeed satisfied if observation reports are construed, as they have been in this article, as classes or conjunctions of observation sentences. As was indicated at the end of note 37, however, this restriction of observation reports to a conjunctive form is not essential; in fact, it has been adopted here only for greater convenience of exposition, and all the preceding results, including especially the definitions and theorems of the present section, remain applicable without change if observation reports are defined as sentences containing no quantifiers. (In this case, if 'P' and 'Q' belong to the observational vocabulary, such sentences as '$P(a)$ v $Q(a)$', '$P(a)$ v ~ $Q(b)$', etc., would qualify as observation reports.) This broader conception of observation reports was therefore adopted in the article referred to in note 1; but it has turned out that in this case, the definition of confirmation summarized above does not generally satisfy the requirement (8.4). Thus, e.g., the observation reports, B_1 = '$P(a)$' and B_2 = '$P(a)$ · [$Q(b)$ v ~ $Q(b)$]' are logically equivalent, but while B_1 confirms (and even directly confirms) the hypothesis H_1 = '(x)$P(x)$', the second report does not do so, essentially because it does not entail '$P(a)$ · $P(b)$', which is the development of H_1 for the class of those objects mentioned in B_2. This deficiency can be remedied as follows: The fact that B_2 fails to confirm H_1 is

Furthermore, the application of the above definition of confirmation is not restricted to hypotheses of universal conditional form (as Nicod's criterion is, for example), nor to universal hypotheses in general; it applies, in fact, to any hypothesis which can be expressed by means of property and relation terms of the observational vocabulary of the given language, individual names, the customary connective symbols for 'not', 'and', 'or', 'if-then', and any number of universal and existential quantifiers.

Finally, as is suggested by the preceding illustrations as well as by the general considerations which underlie the establishment of the above definition, it seems that we have obtained a definition of confirmation which is also materially adequate in the sense of being a reasonable approximation to the intended meaning of confirmation.

obviously due to the circumstance that B_2 contains the individual constant 'b', without asserting anything about b: The object b is mentioned only in an analytic component of B_2. The atomic constituent '$Q(b)$' will therefore be said to occur (twice) *inessentially* in B_2. Generally, an atomic constitutent A of a molecular sentence S will be said to occur inessentially in S if by virtue of the rules of the sentential calculus S is equivalent to a molecular sentence in which A does not occur at all. Now an object will be said to be mentioned inessentially in an observation report if it is mentioned only in such components of that report as occur inessentially in it. The sentential calculus provides mechanical procedures for deciding whether a given observation report mentions any object inessentially, and for establishing equivalent formulations of the same report in which no object is mentioned inessentially. Finally, let us say that an object is mentioned essentially in an observation report if it is mentioned, but not only mentioned inessentially, in that report. Now we replace 9.1 by the following definition:

(9.1a) An observation report B directly confirms a hypothesis H if B entails the development of H for the class of those objects which are mentioned essentially in B.

The concept of confirmation as defined by (9.1a) and (9.2) now satisfies (8.4) in addition to (8.1), (8.2), (8.3) even if observation reports are construed in the broader fashion characterized earlier in this footnote.

II

THE STRUCTURE OF A
SCIENTIFIC SYSTEM

R. B. BRAITHWAITE

A scientific system consists of a set of hypotheses which form a
deductive system; that is, which is arranged in such a way that from
some of the hypotheses as premisses all the other hypotheses logically
follow. The propositions in a deductive system may be considered as
being arranged in an order of levels, the hypotheses at the highest level
being those which occur only as premisses in the system, those at the
lowest level being those which occur only as conclusions in the system,
and those at intermediate levels being those which occur as conclusions
of deductions from higher-level hypotheses and which serve as
premisses for deductions to lower-level hypotheses.

Let us consider as an example a fairly simple deductive system with
hypotheses on three levels. This example has been selected principally
because it illustrates excellently the points that need to be made, and
partly because the construction and the establishment of a similar
system by Galileo marks a turning-point in the history of science.

The system has one highest-level hypothesis:

I. Every body near the Earth freely falling towards the Earth falls
with an acceleration of 32 feet per second per second.

From this hypothesis there follows, by simple principles of the
integral calculus,[1] the hypothesis:

II. Every body starting from rest and freely falling towards the
Earth falls $16t^2$ feet in t seconds, whatever number t may be.

From II there follows in accordance with the logical principle (the
applicative principle) permitting the application of a generalization to
its instances, the infinite set of hypotheses:

III*a*. Every body starting from rest and freely falling for 1 second
towards the Earth falls a distance of 16 feet.

From *Scientific Explanation* by R. B. Braithwaite (Cambridge Univ. Press, 1953),
pp. 12–21. By permission of Cambridge University Press.

[1] Hypothesis I can be expressed by the differential equation $d^2s/dt^2 = 32$,
whose solution, under the conditions that $s = o$ and $ds/dt = o$ when $t = o$, is
$s = 16t^2$.

III*b*. Every body starting from rest and freely falling for 2 seconds towards the Earth falls a distance of 64 feet.

And so on.

In this deductive system the hypotheses at the second and third levels (II, III*a*, III*b*, etc.) follow from the one highest-level hypothesis (I); those at the third level (III*a*, III*b*, etc.) also follow from the one at the second level (II).

The hypotheses in this deductive system are empirical general propositions with diminishing generality. The empirical testing of the deductive system is effected by testing the lowest-level hypotheses in the system. The confirmation or refutation of these is the criterion by which the truth of all the hypotheses in the system is tested. The establishment of a system as a set of true propositions depends upon the establishment of its lowest-level hypotheses.

The lowest-level hypothesis III*a* is tested by applying it to a particular case. A body is allowed to fall freely for 1 second and the distance it falls measured.[2] If it is found that it falls 16 feet, the hypothesis is confirmed; if it is found that it falls more, or less, than 16 feet, the hypothesis is refuted.

It is convenient to treat the logic of this procedure as consisting of two steps. A case is either observed, or experimentally produced, of a body falling for 1 second. The following proposition is then empirically known:

e_1. This body freely falls for 1 second towards the Earth, starting from rest.

The general hypothesis III*a* is then applied to this case by first deducing from III*a* the proposition:

III*a'*. It is only the case that this body, starting from rest, freely falls for 1 second towards the Earth if it falls a distance of 16 feet.

From this application of the general hypothesis, together with the proposition e_1, there is deduced:

f_1 This body falls 16 feet.

The testing of a scientific hypothesis thus consists in deducing from it a proposition of the form ≪e_1 only if f_1≫. Then there follows from the conjunction of e_1 with this proposition the third proposition f_1, whose truth or falsity is observed.

If f_1, the logical consequence of e_1 and III*a'*, is observed to be true, the hypothesis III*a* is ordinarily said to be confirmed. The piece of

[2] The system tested by Galileo was, in fact, more complicated than our example. Galileo was unable to measure times of fall of bodies accurately enough to test III*a*; what he tested empirically was a more elaborate system in which the lowest-level hypotheses were propositions about descents of bodies rolling down grooves in inclined planes.

evidence f_1, conjoined with e_1 (which conjunction will be called an *instance* of the hypothesis), is said to support the hypothesis. But it is clear that this one piece of evidence is insufficient to prove the hypothesis. It would only do so if the hypothesis were a logical consequence of the conjunction of f_1 with e_1. This, of course, is not the case. It is perfectly possible for the hypothesis to hold in this one instance, but to be false in some other instance, and consequently false as a general proposition. And, indeed, this is the case however many times the hypothesis is confirmed. However many conjunctions f_1 with e_1, f_2 with e_2, etc., have been examined and found to confirm the hypothesis, there will still be unexamined cases in which the hypothesis might be false without contradicting any of the observed facts.[3] Thus the empirical evidence of its instances never proves the hypothesis: in suitable cases we must say that it *establishes* the hypothesis, meaning by this that the evidence makes it reasonable to accept the hypothesis; but it never *proves* the hypothesis in the sense that the hypothesis is a logical consequence of the evidence.

The situation is different if f_1 is observed to be false. For the conjunction of not-f_1 with e_1 is logically incompatible with the hypothesis being true; the falsity of the hypothesis is a logical consequence of the conjunction of not-f_1 with e_1. Calling this conjunction a *contrary instance* of the hypothesis, we may say that a hypothesis is proved to be false, or refuted, by one known contrary instance.

This asymmetry of confirmation and refutation is a consequence of the fact that all the hypotheses of a science are general propositions of the form ≪ Every A is B ≫. Propositions of the form ≪ Some A's are B's ≫ (existential propositions),[4] which are the contradictories of general propositions, have the reverse asymmetry; they can be proved by one instance, but no number of contrary instances will suffice to disprove them.

It has been said that there is no greater tragedy than the murder of a beautiful scientific hypothesis by one discordant instance. As will

---

[3] Unless, of course, the hypothesis has only a limited number of instances, and not only have all these instances been examined, but it is known that there are no unexamined instances. Generalizations with only a limited number of instances, which can be proved from a knowledge of these instances by what logicians have called *perfect induction*, present no logical problem; since they are of little interest in science, they will not be considered further. All scientific hypotheses will be taken to be generalizations with an unlimited number of instances.

[4] In the terminology of traditional logic my existential propositions would be called "particular propositions" and my general propositions "universal propositions", the term "general proposition" being used to cover both types.

be seen, it is usually possible to save any particular higher-level hypothesis from this fate by choosing instead to sacrifice some other higher-level hypothesis which is essential to the deduction. But the fact that in principle a scientific hypothesis (or a conjunction of scientific hypotheses, if more than one are required for the deduction of the observable facts) can be conclusively disproved by observation, although it can never be conclusively proved, sharply distinguishes the question of the refutation of a scientific theory from that of its establishment. The former question is a simple matter of deductive logic, if the system of hypotheses is taken as a whole;[5] the latter question involves the justification of inductive inference, a problem which has worried philosophers since the time of Hume.

So far as confirmation is concerned the relation between lowest-level hypotheses and a hypothesis on the next higher level is similar to that between instances of a lowest-level hypothesis and the hypothesis itself. In our examples, the third-level hypotheses IIIa, IIIb, etc., are special cases of the second-level hypothesis II; each of them can be seen to follow from II in accordance with the applicative principle, but II is not a logical consequence of any finite number of hypotheses such as IIIa, IIIb, etc. The formula $s = 16t^2$ can hold for any finite number of values of s and t without being true in general. This is most easily seen by representing the lowest-level hypotheses as points on a graph (Fig. II.1). The second-level hypothesis is represented by a curve passing through these points. Any number of curves beside the parabola $s = 16t^2$ can be drawn to pass through any finite number of points. Thus a refutation of IIIa serves to refute II, but a proof of IIIa does not prove II. Nevertheless, evidence in favour of IIIa is evidence in favour of II; and if the evidence is good enough for us to regard IIIa, IIIb, etc., as established, it may also be good enough for us to regard II also as established.

A similar relationship holds between II and I as holds between IIIa and II. The difference is that, whereas the method of deducing IIIa from II is merely the logical principle involved in implying a general proposition to a special case of it (the applicative principle), and this is implicit in the use of any general proposition, the deduction of II from I is made by using methods of the integral calculus, either explicitly by using known theorems of the calculus, or implicitly by constructing a special geometrical proof, as Galileo, ignorant of the calculus, had to do. But this difference is irrelevant to the general

[5] So simple that Karl Popper takes the possibility of falsification by experience as the criterion for a system of hypotheses being an empirical scientific system (*Logik der Forschung* (Vienna, 1935), § 6).

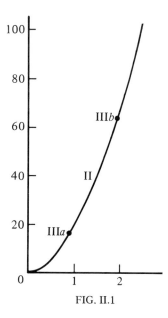

FIG. II.1

nature of the procedure. II is just as much a logical consequence of I as III*a* is of II, although to know the former relationship requires a knowledge of mathematics which must be specially learnt, whereas the latter relationship we learnt when we were taught how to use the word "every".[6]

The general characteristic of a deductive system is that the logical strength of the hypotheses increases the higher their level. Sometimes, although each of the hypotheses at a certain level is weaker than the one hypothesis at the next higher level from which they are all deducible, yet the conjunction of them all is equivalent to that hypothesis. This will happen when there are a limited number of special cases of the higher-level hypothesis, each of which is asserted by one of the lower-level hypotheses. It should be noted that this situation never arises in the relation of a lowest-level hypothesis to its instances, since no hypothesis is a mere enumerative generalization of a finite set of instances.

There are other important points about scientific deductive systems which are illustrated by our example. Since observed instances of III*a*

---

[6] See below, pp. 82ff. [Omitted.]

are evidence for II as well as for IIIa, they are *indirect* evidence[7] for all the logical consequences of II, e.g. IIIb. Thus a hypothesis in a deductive system not at the highest level is empirically supported not only by observation of its instances, or of instances of hypotheses lying below it in the system, but also by observations of instances of other hypotheses in the system. The evidence for a scientific hypothesis is thus frequently much stronger than the *direct* evidence for it of its instances, or of instances of a hypothesis which logically follows from it; it also includes, as indirect evidence, the direct evidence for any higher-level hypothesis from which it logically follows. My reasons for believing that all men are mortal are not confined to knowledge that a great number of men have died; they include also knowledge that a great number of animals have died, which knowledge supports the wider generalization that all animals are mortal. One of the main purposes in organizaing scientifc hypotheses into a deductive system is in order that the direct evidence for each lowest-level hypothesis may become indirect evidence for all the other lowest-level hypotheses; although no amount of empirical evidence suffices to prove any of the hypotheses in the system, yet any piece of empirical evidence for any part of the system helps towards establishing the whole of the system.

But there is one important point about most scientific deductive systems which our simple example does not illustrate. In our example only one higher-level hypothesis is used as a premiss in deductions to lower-level hypotheses. II logically follows from I alone, IIIa, IIIb, etc., from II alone. In most scientific deductive systems, however, each deduction requires more than one premiss. For instance, the example of Galileo's deductive system was incorporated by Newton into a larger deductive system in which I ceased to be the highest-level hypothesis, but was instead presented as deducible from the conjunction of two higher-level hypotheses, one being that called (in the plural) Newton's Laws of Motion and the other being his Law of Universal Gravitation.[8] Consequently most of the deductive systems used in science are not of the simply branching type exemplified by Galileo's system, but are systems in which there are a number of higher-level hypotheses all of which are required to serve as premisses in one or other of the

[7] Observed facts will be said to be *indirect evidence* for a hypothesis p if they are direct evidence for a hypothesis q (or for a set of hypotheses q_1, q_2, etc.) from which p logically follows. A corollary of this definition is that if the observed facts are direct evidence for a set of hypotheses $q_1, q_2, \ldots, q_n$, they are indirect evidence for any one of these hypotheses, since each logically follows from the set.

[8] I am not stating the hypotheses explicitly, because they make use of the terms *force* and *mass* which are theoretical concepts of the sort to be discussed in Chapter III. [Omitted.]

deductions in the system. Of course if we were to extend our meaning
of scientific hypothesis to include conjunctions of generalizations,
we could lump all the premisses together into one conjunctive
hypothesis, and have only one highest-level hypothesis in every system.
Thus any scientific system could be treated as a simply branching
system. But to combine disparate hypotheses into one conjunctive
hypothesis would confuse thought. And it would have the added
disadvantage that we should have to admit as scientific hypotheses
propositions which were not themselves generalizations.

Since the consequences of any set of hypotheses are also
consequences of any set of hypotheses which includes this set, the
highest-level hypotheses could always be increased by adding any
hypothesis to them. But to do this would be to make the observed
facts evidence for a set of hypotheses which included one which played
no part in their deduction from the set, and would thus make them
indirect evidence for the supernumerary hypothesis and for its
consequences. Since the supernumerary hypothesis might be any
generalization whatever, this would have the undesirable result that any
observable fact would be indirect evidence for any generalization
whatever.[9] To avoid this result we stipulate that each of the highest-
level hypotheses in a system must be necessary for the deduction of the
lower-level hypotheses in the system; none must be included which play
no part in the system. Similarly, we must treat as two systems, and not
conflate into one, two systems whose sets of highest-level hypotheses
have no hypothesis in common.

The fact that most scientific deductive systems employ more than
one highest-level hypothesis has an important bearing upon the
empirical testing of these hypotheses. As has been shown, one contrary
instance is sufficient to refute a generalization, and the refutation of
this generalization (a lowest-level hypothesis) will be sufficient to refute
a higher-level hypothesis from which it logically follows. But suppose,
as is frequently the case, that we are considering a deductive system in
which there is no one higher-level hypothesis from which this lowest-
level hypothesis follows, but instead the system is such that this follows
from two or more higher-level hypotheses. Then what will be refuted

[9] C. G. Hempel (*Mind*, n.s., 54 (1945), p. 104 [Selection I in this volume])
raises a point similar to this as an objection to defining the 'confirmation' of a
hypothesis in terms of what can be deduced from the hypothesis in conjunction
with observable propositions. I do not profess to give a precise definition of
'confirmation'; but I believe that the limitation of hypotheses to be themselves
general propositions, and the exclusion of supernumerary hypotheses from a
scientific system, will avoid the difficulties pointed out by Hempel. There is an
elaborate discussion of the whole subject in Rudolf Carnap, *Logical Foundations
of Probability* (Chicago, 1950), §§ 87f [Selection V in this volume.]

by the refutation of the lowest-level hypothesis will be the conjunction of these two or more higher-level hypotheses; what will be a logical consequence of the falsity of the lowest-level hypothesis will be that at least one of the higher-level hypotheses is false.

Thus in the case of almost all scientific hypotheses, except the straightforward generalizations of observable facts which serve as the lowest-level hypotheses in the deductive system, complete refutation is no more possible than is complete proof. What experience can tell us is that there is something wrong somewhere in the system; but we can make our choice as to which part of the system we consider to be at fault. In almost every system it is possible to maintain any one hypothesis in the face of apparently contrary evidence at the expense of modifying the others. Ptolemy was able to save the geocentric hypothesis by supposing that the planets moved in complicated orbits round the earth. But at some time a point is reached at which the modifications in a system required to save a hypothesis become more implausible than the rejection of the hypothesis; and then the hypothesis is rejected.

The scientific deductive system which physics has gradually built up by incorporating the original deductive systems of Galileo and his contemporaries has developed by the rejection of hypotheses when the system which included them led to the prediction of observable results which were found not to be observed. But exactly which hypothesis was to be rejected at each point was a matter for the 'hunch' of the physicist. Generally speaking, a hypothesis was not rejected until an alternative hypothesis was available to take its place. Long before Einstein propounded his theory of gravitation it was known that Newton's theory could not account by itself for the observed motion of Mercury's perihelion. But Newton's theory was not dethroned until Einstein's theory was available to take its place. The process of refuting a scientific hypothesis is thus more complicated than it appears to be at first sight.

There is no hard and fast line at the point at which the common-sense synthesis of experience becomes a scientific ordering in a scientific system. Just as in tracing back common-sense thought either in the individual or in the race there is no point at which there were no generalizations believed, so in the history of a science there is rarely any one historical date at which it is possible to say that the first hypothesis was adumbrated. The history of a science is the history of the development of scientific systems from those containing so few generalizations, and these so flimsily established that one might well hesitate to call them systems at all, into imposing structures with a hierarchy of hypotheses. This development takes place by the establishment of some of the original hypotheses, by the replacement of others by better established hypotheses, and by the construction of higher-level hypotheses under which the lower-level hypotheses can be subsumed. The problems raised by this development are of many different kinds. There are historical problems, both as to what causes the individual scientist to discover a new idea, and as to what causes the general acceptance of scientific ideas. The solution of these historical problems involves the individual psychology of thinking and the sociology of thought. None of these questions are our business here. What we are concerned with are the straight logical problems of the internal structure of scientific systems and of the roles played in such systems by the formal truths of logic and mathematics, and also the problems of inductive logic or epistemology concerned with the grounds for the reasonableness or otherwise of accepting well-established scientific systems.

III
THE LOGIC OF DISCOVERY

NORWOOD RUSSELL HANSON

J. S. MILL[1] was wrong in his account of Kepler's discovery [of the elliptical orbit of Mars ed.] It is impossible to reconcile the labours of the *Astronomia Nova*, and the delicate adjustment between theory, hypothesis, and observation recorded in *De Motibus Stellae Martis*, with Mill's irresponsible statement that Kepler's First Law is just "a compendious expression for the one set of directly observed facts". Mill cannot have understood Kepler.[2] *A System of Logic* is as misleading about scientific research and discovery as any account which proceeded *via* what Bacon called "Inductio per enumerationem simplicem, ubi non reperitur instantia contradictoria."[3] In another way the accounts of H-D [Hypothetico-Deductive] theorists are equally misleading.

An H-D account of Kepler's First Law would treat it as a high-level hypothesis in an H-D system. It would be regarded as a quasi-axiom, from the assumption of which observation-statements can be shown to follow. If these are true—if, e.g., they imply that Uranus' orbit is an ellipse and that its apparent velocity at $90°$ will be greater than at aphelion,—then insofar is the First Law confirmed.[4]

From *Journal of Philosophy*, 55 (1958), pp. 1079–89. By permission of the Managing Editor, The Journal of Philosophy.

[1] *A System of Logic*, Bk. III, chs. 2–3.

[2] As Peirce notes, *Collected Papers*, I, 31. It is equally questionable whether Reichenbach understood Kepler: "Kepler's laws of the elliptic motion of celestial bodies were inductive generalizations of observed facts. . . . [He] observed a series of . . . positions of the planet Mars and found that they may be connected by a mathematical relation . . ." (*Experience and Prediction*, p. 371).

[3] Reichenbach observes: "It is the great merit of John Stuart Mill to have pointed out that all empirical inferences are reducible to the *inductio per enumerationem simplicem* . . ." (op. cit., p. 389).

[4] Thus Braithwaite writes: "A scientific system consists of a set of hypotheses which form a deductive system . . . arranged in such a way that from some of the hypotheses as premises all the other hypotheses logically follow. . . . The establishment of a system as a set of true propositions depends upon the establishment of its lowest-level hypotheses . . ." (*Scientific Explanation*, pp. 12–13 [Selection II in this volume]).

Perhaps this describes physical theory more adequately than did pre-Baconian accounts in terms of simple enumerations, or even post-Millian accounts in terms of ostensibly not-so-simple enumerations. It tells us something about the logic of laws, and what they do in the finished arguments of physicists. H-D accounts do not, however, tell us how laws are proposed in the first place—nor were they intended to. (None the less those who deny real differences between reasons for suggesting H and reasons for accepting it are also inclined sometimes to suppose that scientific discovery *actually proceeds via* the industrious employment of the H-D method.)

Though the H-D account of scientific theories, laws, and hypotheses does not tell us in what kinds of rational contexts laws and hypotheses are suggested, the induction-by-enumeration story did attempt this. It sought to describe good reasons for initially proposing H. The H-D account ought to be silent on this point. The two accounts are not strict alternatives.[5] The induction-by-enumeration account and the H-D account are compatible. Acceptance of the second is no good reason for rejecting the first. A law *might* have been arrived at, or inferred from, little more than an enumeration of particulars (e.g., Boyle's Law in the seventeenth century, Bode's Law in the eighteenth, the Laws of Ampère and Faraday in the nineteenth, and much of meson theory in the twentieth). It could then be built into an H-D system as a higher-order proposition—as indeed has happened with all my examples save the last. So, if there is anything wrong with the older view, H-D accounts do not reveal what this is.

There is something wrong with the older accounts. They are false. Scientists do not always find laws by enumerating and summarizing observables.[6] But this does not strengthen the H-D account of the matter as against the inductive view. There is no H-D account of how "sophisticated generalizations" are *derived*.

If the H-D account were construed as a description of scientific practice it would be misleading.[7] Natural scientists do not "start from" hypotheses. They start from data. And even then not from ordinary commonplace data—but from surprising anomalies. Thus Aristototle

---

[5] As Braithwaite suggests they are when he remarks of a certain "higher-level" hypothesis that it "will not have been established by induction by simple enumeration; it will have been obtained by the hypothetico-deductive method . . ." (op. cit., p. 303).

[6] Thus Braithwaite says: "sophisticated generalizations (such as that about the proton-electron constitution of the hydrogen atom) . . . [were] certainly not derived by simple enumeration of instances . . ." (op. cit., p. 11).

[7] Braithwaite's use of "derived" is thus misleading. So is his announcement (p. 11) that he is going to explain "how we *come to make use* of sophisticated generalizations."

remarks[8] that knowledge begins in astonishment. Peirce makes perplexity the trigger of scientific inquiry.[9] And James and Dewey treat intelligence as the result of mastering problem situations.[10]

By the time a law gets fixed into an H-D system, the *original* scientific thinking is over. The more pedestrian process of deducing observation-statements begins only after the physicist is convinced that the proposed hypothesis will at least explain the data initially requiring explanation. Thus Kepler's assistant could easily work out the consequences of H′ [that all planets travel in elliptical orbits around the sun], and check its validity by seeing whether Mercury, Venus, Earth, Jupiter, and Saturn behaved as H′ predicts. This was possible because of Kepler's reasonable conviction that what H [that Mars' orbit is elliptical] had done for Mars, H′ would do for the other planets. The H-D account is helpful here; it analyses *the argument of a completed research report,* such as Bartsch's report that the consequences of H′ square with the observed positions of the planets. It helps us also to see how the experimentalist elaborates a theoretician's hypotheses. And yet another aspect of science the H-D account illuminates, but its proponents oddly have not stressed it; scientists often dismiss explanations alternative to the one which has won their provisional assent in a way that is almost a model of the H-D method in action. Examples of this are in Ptolemy's *Almagest,* when he rules out a moving earth; in Copernicus' *De Revolutionibus* ..., when he demolishes Ptolemy's lunar theory; in Kepler's *De Motibus Stellae Martis,* when he denies that the planes of the planetary orbits intersect in the centre of the ecliptic instead of (as he proposed) the centre of the sun; and in Newton's *Principia,* when he rejects the idea that the gravitational force law might be of an inverse cube nature. These mirror parts of Mill's *System of Logic,* or Braithwaite's *Scientific Explanation.*

Notwithstanding these merits, however, the H-D analysis leaves undiscussed reasoning which often conditions the discovery of laws.

The induction-by-enumeration story views the important inference as being from observations to the law, from particulars to the general. There is something true about this which the H-D account must ignore. Thus Newton wrote: "the main business of natural philosophy is to argue from phenomena. . . ."[11]

This inductive view ignores what Newton never ignored; the inference is also from *explicanda* to an *explicans.* Why a bevelled

---

[8] *Metaphysica* 982 b 11 ff.
[9] *Collected Papers,* II, Book III, ch. 2, Part III.
[10] Dewey, *How We Think,* pp. 12 ff.
[11] *Principia,* Preface.

mirror shows a spectrum in the sunlight is not explained by saying that all bevelled mirrors display spectra in sunlight. Why Mars moves more rapidly at 270° and 90° than could be expected of circular-uniform motions is not explained by saying that Mars always moves in this manner—or even that all the planets always move in this manner. On the induction-by-enumeration view, these latter might count as laws. But clearly, only when it is explained why bevelled mirrors show spectra in the sunlight, and why planets apparently accelerate at 90°— only then will we have laws of the type suggested: Newton's Laws of Refraction and Kepler's First Law.

So the inductive view rightly suggests that laws are got by inference from data. It wrongly suggests that the law is but a summary of these data, instead of being (what it at least sometimes must be) an explanation of the data.

H-D accounts all agree that physical laws explain data.[12] However, they obscure the initial connection between data and laws. Indeed, they often suggest that the fundamental inference in science is from higher-order hypotheses to observation-statements. This may be a way of setting out reasons for making a prediction after H is formulated and provisionally established. It need not be a way of setting out reasons in favour of proposing H originally. Bartsch could have justified a prediction that Saturn will appear to move faster at 270° and 90° than the hypothesis of its uniform circular motion indicates. Referring to H'and its success with the other planets, he would show how this conclusion about Saturn is entailed by H'. But he would not have set out thus his reasons for entertaining H'initially—if he had any reasons other than that Kepler was convinced that H'was true. Certainly Kepler himself would not have set out thus his reasons for proposing H originally.

Yet the original suggestion of a hypothesis is often a reasonable affair. It is not as dependent on intuition, hunches, and other imponderables as historians and philosophers suppose when they make it the province of genius but not of logic. If the establishment of H through its predictions has a logic, so has the argument which leads to H's proposal initially. To form the first idea of an elliptical planetary orbit, or of constant acceleration, or of universal gravitational attraction does indeed require genius; nothing less than a Kepler, a Galileo, or a Newton. But this need not entail that reflections leading

---

[12] Thus Braithwaite says: "A hypothesis to be regarded as a natural law must be a general proposition which can be thought to *explain* its instances; if the reason for believing the general proposition is solely direct knowledge of the truth of its instances, it will be felt to be a poor sort of explanation of these instances ..." (op. cit., p. 302).

to these ideas are unreasonable, or a-reasonable. Perhaps *only* Kepler, Galileo, and Newton had intellects mighty enough to fashion these notions initially. To concede this is not to concede that their reasons for first entertaining such concepts surpass rational inquiry.

H-D accounts begin with the hypothesis as given, as cooking recipes begin with the trout as given. In an occasional ripple of culinary humour, however, recipes sometimes begin with "First catch your trout". The H-D account describes a recipe physicists often use after catching hypotheses. However, the ingenuity and conceptual boldness which mark the whole history of physics show more clearly in the ways in which scientists *caught* their hypotheses, than in the ways in which they elaborated these once caught.

To study only the verification of hypotheses is to leave a vital part of the story untold—namely, what were the reasons Kepler, Galileo, and Newton had for suggesting their hypotheses initially. In a letter to Fabricius, Kepler underlines this distinction.

Prague, July 4, 1603

Dear Fabricius,
      . . . You believe that I start with imagining some pleasant hypothesis and please myself in embellishing it, examining it only later by observations. In this you are very much mistaken. The truth is that after having built up an hypothesis on the ground of observations and given it proper foundations, I feel a peculiar desire to investigate whether I might discover some natural, satisfying combination between the two. . . .

If any H-D theorist ever sought to give an account of the way in which hypotheses in science are actually discovered, these words are for him.

III

Have any H-D theorists ever thought that they were doing this? Some have. This is connected with their denial of any logical distinction to be made between reasons for proposing H and reasons for accepting it.

Braithwaite writes: "every science *proceeds* . . . by thinking of general hypotheses . . . from which particular consequences are deduced which can be tested by observation . . ."[13] (compare Kepler's letter) and "science proceeds (by the hypothetico-deductive method)"[14]; and again, "Galileo's deductive system was . . . presented as deducible from . . . Newton's Laws of Motion and . . . his Law of Universal Gravitation. . . .".[15] (NB An ingenious theologian could show Galileo's

---

[13] (Op. cit.,) p. ix. (my italics)   [14] Op. cit., p. xi.   [15] Op. cit., p. 18.

system as "deducible from" certain higher-level propositions about God's attributes. What matters is not that it is *deducible* from God's attributes, or Newton's Laws, but that it is *explained by* these Laws. Known planetary positions were deducible by Ptolemy from circular motion, epicycle, deferent, and eccentric. But these positions were not explained via such techniques. This Ptolemy conceded, as did Hipparchus and Apollonius before him, and Thomas and Dante after.)

Rashevsky sees Newton's discovery of universal gravitation as the result of employing the H-D method as a method of inquiry. He writes:

> . . . the scientist . . . studies *in abstracto* all . . . conceivable explanations. Then, by comparing the results of his studies with actual observation, he decides which of the possible explanations apply best. . . . First Newton formulated his general laws of motion, which describe the motion of bodies under the influence of any kind of force. Next he studied the motion under different kinds of central forces. It was then found that the actual motion of planets . . . should occur under the influence of a central force which varies as the inverse square of the distance. The conclusion was thus reached that the force of gravitation varies with distance in this manner.[16]

How one can be misled by H-D accounts of the development of scientific thought, impinges here on the history of physics. On the analysis of this event hangs the plausibility of my position.

An H-D analysis of the law of gravitation, as established in mechanics, would be this one:

1. First the hypothesis H: that between any two particles in the universe exists an attracting force varying inversely as the square of the distance between them ($F = \gamma\, Mm/r^2$).
2. Deduce from this (in accordance with the *Principia*)
   a. *Kepler's* Laws, and
   b. *Galileo's* Laws
3. But particular instances of *a*. and *b*. square with what is observed.
4. Therefore H is, insofar, confirmed.

The H-D account says nothing about the context of reasoning in which H was first puzzled out. If (with Rashevsky) it tries, it goes wrong, as I shall argue. But first I suggest why here the H-D account is prima-facie plausible.

Historians often remark that Newton's serious reflections on this problem began in 1680 when Halley asked him this question: If between a planet and the sun there exists an attraction varying inversely as the square of their distance, what then would be the path of the

---

[16] *Mathematical Thinking in the Social Sciences*, ed. Lazarsfeld, p. 69.

planet? Halley was astonished with the immediate answer: "An ellipse." The astonishment arose not because Newton *knew* the path of a planet, but because it appeared that he had managed to deduce this from the hypothesis of universal gravitation. Halley begged for the proof; but it had been long since lost in the chaos of Newton's untidy room. The promise to work it out anew eventually terminated in the writing of the *Principia* itself. Thus the story unfolds along the lines of the H-D schema: (1) from the suggestion of a hypothesis (whose genesis is a matter of logical indifference, i.e., psychology, or sociology) to (2) the deduction of observation statements (the laws of Kepler and Galileo)—which turn out true, thus (3) establishing the hypothesis.

Another thing which supports the H-D account is this: the *Principia* actually unfolds as the schema requires—from propositions of high generality to those of restricted generality, terminating in observation-statements which are true. Thus Braithwaite observes:

Newton's *Principia* [was] modelled on the Euclidean analogy and pro-fessed to prove [its] later propositions—those which were confirmed by confrontation with experience—by deducing them from original first principles. . . .[17]

Despite this plausibility I long ago became suspicious of this orthodox account. The answer which Newton is reported to have given to Halley is not unique. He could have said "a circle" or "a parabola", and have been equally correct—or equally incorrect. The general answer to Halley's question is: "A conic section". The greatest mathematician of his day is not likely to have dealt with so obviously mathematical a question—requiring to know whether a certain formal demonstration is possible—with an answer which is no more than a single value of the correct answer.

Yet the inference in the reverse direction, that is, the retroduction, *is* unique. Given that the planetary orbits are ellipses, and allowing Huyghen's law of centripetal force, and Kepler's rule (that the square of a planet's mean period of revolution is proportional to the cube of its mean distance from the sun)—from this the law of gravitation can be inferred uniquely. Thus, given the question, "If the planetary orbits are ellipses what form will the force law take?", the unique answer is "an inverse square law".

From the fact of the elliptical orbit, one can (by way of Huyghen's Law and Kepler's third law) *explain* this uniquely by showing it to follow as a matter of course from the less well-known law of universal gravitation.

[17] *Scientific Explanation*, p. 352.

The idea behind these proofs is roughly as follows: Given an egg-shell, elliptical in section (rather than oviform), imagine a marble moving inside that shell (with velocity sufficient to keep it in the maximum elliptical orbit). What force must the egg-shell exert on the marble to keep the latter in this path? Huyghen's weights, when whirled on strings, required a force in the string, and in Huyghen's arm, of $F_{(k)} = r/T^2$ (where r signifies distance, T time, and k is a constant of proportionality). This restraining force was needed to keep the weights from flying away like catapulted projectiles, and something like this force would thus be expected in the egg-shell. But from Kepler's third law we know that $T^2 = r^3$. Hence $F_{(k)} = r/r^3 = 1/r^2$. The force the shell exerts on the marble varies inversely as the square of the distance of the marble from that focus of the ellipse in which the sun rests. This follows by retroductive reasoning. But what *is* this retroductive reasoning whose superiority over the H-D account has been hinted at throughout this paper?

Schematically, it can be set out thus:.

1. Some surprising, astonishing phenomenon p_1, p_2, p_3 ... is encountered.[18]
2. But p_1, p_2, p_3 ... would not be surprising or astonishing if H were true—they would follow as a matter of course from H; H would explain p_1, p_2, p_3 ....
3. Therefore there is good reason for elaborating H—for proposing it as a possible hypothesis from whose assumption p_1, p_2, p_3 ... might be explained.

This presentation is a free development of remarks in Aristotle[19] and Peirce.[20]

How, then, would the discovery of universal gravitation fit into such an account?

1. The surprising, astonishing discovery that all planetary orbits are elliptical was made by Kepler (1605 to 1619).

[18] The astonishment may consist in the fact that p is at variance with accepted *theories*—as, e.g., the discovery of discontinuous emission of radiation by hot black bodies, or the photoelectric effect, the Compton effect, and the continuous β-ray spectrum—or the orbital aberrations of Mercury, the refrangibility of white light, and the high velocities of Mars at 90°. What is important here is *that* the phenomena are encountered as anomalous, not *why* they are so regarded.

[19] *Prior Analytics*, II, 25.

[20] *Collected Papers*, Vol. I, § 188. Peirce amplifies this: "It must be remembered that retroduction, although it is very little hampered by logical rules, nevertheless is logical inference, asserting its conclusion only problematically, or conjecturally, it is true, but nevertheless having a perfectly definite logical form."

2. But such an orbit would not be surprising or astonishing if, in addition to other familiar laws, an inversely varying law of gravitation obtained. Kepler's first law would follow as a matter of course; indeed the hypothesis could even explain why (since the sun is in but one of the foci) the orbits are ellipses on which the planets travel with non-uniform velocity.

3. Therefore there is good reason for elaborating this hypothesis further, for proposing it as that from the assumption of which Kepler's first law might be explained.

This tells us something about the rational context within which H might come to be "caught" in the first place. It begins where all physics begins—with problematic phenomena requiring explanation. It suggests what might be done to hypotheses once proposed, namely, the H-D elaboration. And it points up how much philosophers of science have yet to learn about the kinds of reasons scientists might have for thinking a particular hypothesis may explain initial perplexities—why, e.g., one hypothesis may be preferred over others if it throws the data into patterns within which determinate modes of connection can be perceived. These are the problems which Wittgenstein unearths in the *Philosophical Investigations* and which open up unexplored aspects of scientific research. At least it appears that the ways in which scientists sometimes reason their way towards hypotheses may be as legitimate an area for conceptual inquiry as are the ways in which they sometimes reason their way from hypotheses.

My distrust of the H-D account of Newton's work—which either says nothing about what led Newton to propose universal gravitation, or else mis-tells the whole story—has been reinforced by manuscripts in the Lord Portsmouth collection in the Cambridge University Library. There, in "Additional manuscripts 3968, No. 41, bundle 2", is the following draft in Newton's own hand:

... And in the same year [1665, twenty years before the *Principia*] I began to think of gravity extending to ye orb of the Moon, and (having found out how to estimate the force with which a globe revolving within a sphere presses the surface of the sphere), from Kepler's rule ... I deduced that the forces which keep the planets in their Orbs must be reciprocally as the squares of their distances from the centres about which they revolve. ...

This MS, though familiar to some historians, was unknown to me in writing the preceding. It corroborates my earlier conjecture as to the real reasoning behind Newton's proposal of this hypothesis. ("Deduce", in this passage, is used as when Newton speaks of deducing laws from phenomena—which is just what Aristotle and Peirce would call "retro-duce".) So, Newton knew how to estimate the force of a small globe on the inner surface of a sphere. (To compare this with Halley's question and with my earlier tentative reconstruction, note that such a sphere can be regarded as a degenerate solid ellipse, i.e., where the foci superimpose.) From this, and from Kepler's rule $T^2 = r^3$, Newton retroduced the law of gravitation as that by reference to which these other things would be entailed and, more importantly, would be explained. These were the reasons, the good reasons, which led Newton to think further on universal gravitation. The reasons for accepting this hypothesis as a law are powerfully set out in the *Principia* itself—and they are much more comprehensive than anything which occurred to him at this early age.

My task has been to illuminate an aspect of scientific inquiry neglected by philosophers, namely, the scientists' reasons for considering hypotheses seriously in the first place. Some philosophers, the inductionists (Bacon, Locke, Hume, Mill, Reichenbach), have given a wrong answer to this, suggesting, e.g., that all scientists reason initially from phenomena to hypotheses by variations on "inductio per enumerationem simplicem". They make it sound as if insight and genius have nothing to do with discovery. Other philosophers (Lenzen, Braith-waite, Reichenbach), H-D theorists, say nothing about the matter—but sometimes because they deny any logical differences between the Logic of Discovery and the Logic of Proof. They make it sound as if logic and reason have nothing to do with discovery. Still other H-D thinkers do discuss reasons for entertaining hypotheses initially, but get the issue twisted, putting hypotheses where the surprising phenomena should be. Aristotle, as usual, carves out the important trail here, and Wittgenstein, as usual, lights up the crossroads. More philosophers must venture into these unexplored regions in which the logical issues are often hidden by the specialist work of historians, psychologists, and the scientists themselves. We must attend as much to how scientific hypotheses are caught, as to how they are cooked.

IV

PROSPECTS FOR A
THEORY OF PROJECTION

NELSON GOODMAN

1. A NEW LOOK AT THE PROBLEM

THE problem of confirmation, or of valid projection, is the problem of
defining a certain relationship between evidence or base cases on the
one hand, and hypotheses, predictions or projections on the other.
Since numerous and varied attacks on the problem have brought us no
solution, we may well ask ourselves whether we are still in any way
misconceiving the nature of our task. I think the answer is affirmative:
that we have come to mistake the statement of the required result for
an unduly restricted statement of the means allowed for reaching that
result.

What we want, indeed, is an accurate and general way of saying
which hypotheses are confirmed by, or which projections are validly
made from, any given evidence. Thus each particular case that arises
does concern the relationship of given evidence to entertained
hypotheses. But this does not imply that the only materials available
to us in determining the relationship are the given evidence and the
entertained hypotheses. In other words, while confirmation is indeed
a relation between evidence and hypotheses, this does not mean that
our definition of this relation must refer to nothing other than such
evidence and hypotheses. The fact is that whenever we set about
determining the validity of a given projection from a given base, we
have and use a good deal of other relevant knowledge. I am not
speaking of additional evidence statements, but rather of the record of
past predictions actually made and their outcome. Whether these
predictions—regardless of their success or failure—were valid or not
remains in question; but that some were made and how they turned out
is legitimately available information.

Proper use of such information will admittedly require some care. Surely we cannot subscribe to the naive suggestion that induction is validated simply by its past successes. Every so often someone proclaims that the whole problem is solved just by recognizing that the prediction of future from past cases of a hypothesis is justified by the success of past predictions according to the hypothesis. Critics quickly point out that all the questions that arise about the validity of predicting future cases from past ones arise also about the validity of predicting future successes from past ones. But the fact that legitimately available information has been ineptly used should not lead us to discard it. In our present straits, we cannot afford to deprive ourselves of any honest means that may prove to be helpful.

I think we should recognize, therefore, that our task is to define the relation of confirmation or valid projection between evidence and hypothesis in terms of anything that does not beg the question, that meets our other demands for acceptable terms of explanation, and that may reasonably be supposed to be at hand when a question of inductive validity arises. This will include, among other things, some knowledge of past predictions and their successes and failures. I suppose that seldom, if ever, has there been any explicit proposal to preclude use of such knowledge in dealing with our problem. Rather, a long-standing habit of regarding such knowledge as irrelevant has led us to ignore it almost entirely. Thus what I am suggesting is less a reformulation of our problem than a reorientation: that we regard ourselves as coming to the problem not empty-headed but with some stock of knowledge, or of accepted statements, that may fairly be used in reaching a solution.

Nevertheless, this slight reorientation gives our problem quite a new look. For if we start with past projections as well as with evidence and hypotheses, our task becomes that of defining valid projection—or projectibility—on the basis of actual projections. Clearly this is a typical problem of dispositions. Given the manifest predicate "projected" and certain other information, we have to define the dispositional predicate "projectible." And this, as we have seen, resolves itself into the problem of projecting the predicate "projected". At first, this may be disheartening; for it looks as if we shall have to solve the problem of projection before we can deal with it—as if we must define valid projection before we can validly project "projected". But matters are not really that bad. Our ultimate aim is to define valid projection, or projectibility, in full generality. But this can also be regarded as a specific problem of projectibility: as the problem of projecting the specific predicate "projected", or in other words of defining the specific dispositional predicate "projectible". As I particularly remarked earlier,[1] there is no reason at all why we cannot attempt to deal with a specific problem of dispositions before we have solved the general problem. And in the case of the specific problem of defining the predicate "projectible", the stakes are high; for if we succeed in solving it, we thereby solve the general problem. In effect, the general problem of dispositions has been reduced to the problem of projecting the specific predicate "projected".

The reorientation of our problem may be portrayed in somewhat more figurative language. Hume thought of the mind as being set in motion making predictions by, and in accordance with, regularities in what it observed. This left him with the problem of differentiating between the regularities that do and those that do not thus set the mind in motion. We, on the contrary, regard the mind as in motion from the start, striking out with spontaneous predictions in dozens of directions, and gradually rectifying and channelling its predictive processes. We ask not how predictions come to be made, but how—granting they are made—they come to be sorted out as valid and invalid. Literally, of course, we are not concerned with describing how the mind works but rather with describing or defining the distinction it makes between valid and invalid projections.

2. ACTUAL PROJECTIONS

A hypothesis will be said to be *actually projected* when it is adopted after some of its instances have been examined and determined to be true, and before the rest have been examined. The hypothesis need not be true, or lawlike, or even reasonable; for we are speaking here not of what ought to be projected but of what is in fact projected. Moreover, we are not concerned with the question whether a hypothesis is projected in the tenseless sense that there is some past, present or future time at which it is projected. We are concerned at any given time only with projections that have already been made.

Notice especially that even if all the instances examined up to a given time are favourable, and even if the hypothesis is true, still it may perhaps not be actually projected at that (or any other) time. Actual projection involves the overt, explicit formulation and adoption of the hypothesis—the actual prediction of the outcome of the examination of further cases. That the hypothesis could—or even could legitimately—have been projected at that time is at this stage beside the point. Just here lies the difference between starting from hypotheses and instances alone and starting from actual projections.

A full and exact explanation of actual projection would require much more careful statement of, for example, what is meant by

[1] See the remark in II.3 concerning a small note of comfort [omitted].

adoption of a hypothesis. Obviously, affirmation as certainly true is not demanded, but rather something like affirmation as sufficiently more credible than alternative hypotheses. We could easily embroil ourselves in endless discussion of this and similar questions; but our purposes no more call for detailed answers to such questions than the development of ordinary confirmation theory calls for precise explanation of how evidence is acquired or of just what is involved in the acceptance of observation statements. There all we need do is indicate roughly what we mean by observation or evidence statements, and then proceed to the question of confirmation, assuming that some statements have been taken as evidence statements. The utility of determining that a hypothesis is confirmed by such statements will indeed depend upon their being genuinely accepted evidence statements; but our definition of the confirmation relation is largely independent of this consideration. Similarly, we need here only a summary sketch of what is meant by saying that a hypothesis is actually projected. We can then proceed to our definitional task, assuming that certain hypotheses are taken to have been projected at certain times. The utility of decisions based upon applications of our definition will, again, depend upon whether these projections have been made in fact; but definition of the relation between the projected and the projectible is, again, largely independent of this consideration.[2]

In what follows I shall make frequent use of certain convenient terms that call for brief explanation. Whether or not a hypothesis is actually projected at a given time, such instantiations of it as have already been determined to be true or false may be called respectively its *positive* and its *negative* instances or cases at that time. All the remaining instances are *undetermined* cases. For example, if the hypothesis is

All emeralds are green

and *e* is an emerald, then

Emerald *e* is green

is a positive case when *e* has been found to be green, a negative case

---

[2] In other words, if we have determined that statements E, E', etc. stand to hypothesis H in the relationship specified by an adequate definition of confirmation, still the question whether H is a confirmed hypothesis will depend on whether E, E', etc. are actually evidence statements. Similarly, if we have determined that statements P, P' etc. stand to hypothesis K in the relationship specified by an adequate definition of projectibility, still the question whether K is a projectible hypothesis will depend on whether P, P', etc. are actually projected hypotheses. But see IV.4 below.

when *e* has been found not to be green, and an undetermined case when *e* has not yet been found either to be green or not to be green. The emeralds named in the positive cases constitute the *evidence class* for the hypothesis at the time in question, while the emeralds not named in any of the positive or negative cases constitute the *projective class* for the hypothesis at that time. A hypothesis for which there are some positive or some negative cases up to a given time is said to be *supported* or to be *violated* at that time. A violated hypothesis is false; but a false hypothesis may at a given time be unviolated. If a hypothesis has both positive and negative cases at a given time, it is then both supported and violated; while if it has no cases determined as yet, it is neither. A hypothesis without any remaining undetermined cases is said to be *exhausted.*

Now according to my terminology, adoption of a hypothesis constitutes actual projection only if at the time in question the hypothesis has some undetermined cases, some positive cases, and no negative cases. That is to say, I shall not speak of a hypothesis as being actually projected at any time when it is exhausted, unsupported, or violated. Obviously, adoption of an exhausted hypothesis involves nothing that we want to call projection. And convenience seems best served by denying the term "projection" to the adoption of a hypothesis without favourable direct evidence or in the face of direct counter-evidence. Thus while a given hypothesis may undergo projection, violation, and exhaustion, the projection must antedate the violation and the exhaustion.

When all the undetermined cases of a hypothesis are future cases, its projection is a prediction. Very often, however, undetermined cases may be past cases; and here we have a projection that is not a prediction. Of course, the *determination* of an undetermined case is always later than the projection in question; but such a case may nevertheless be a statement of what has happened prior to that projection. To predict the outcome of the examination of a statement is not tantamount to predicting the (perhaps past) event described by that statement. Since pragmatism has sometimes fostered confusion concerning this point,[3] we should take particular care to remember,

---

[3] Some versions of pragmatism vacillate deftly between truism and patent falsehood, claiming the impregnability of the one and the importance of the other. It is urged that the truth and significance of a hypothesis lie in the accuracy of its predictions. Does this mean that all that counts is whether the hypothesis is true of the future? This is utterly absurd; for it makes the already violated statement "All emeralds are bleen" true if all emeralds not examined before *t* are green. ['Bleen' applies to things examined before t just in case they are blue and to other things just in case they are green. ed.] Does the doctrine mean, then, that the only way of testing a hypothesis in the future is by tests in the future? This

for example, that a hypothesis may remain unviolated at a given time even though some of its past-instance-statements are in fact false; for the violation of a hypothesis consists rather in one of its instances having been *already* determined to be false.

What we have to work with at any given time, then, is a record of projections of a mass of heterogeneous hypotheses at various times. Some of these hypotheses have been violated since the time when they were projected. Others have successfully passed such further tests as they have undergone; but among these are some hypotheses that, since they have by now had all their instances examined and determined to be true, are exhausted and can no longer be projected. Some of the hypotheses projected are false. Some are bizarre. And some are at odds with others. Such is our raw material.

Obviously, not all the hypotheses that are projected are lawlike or legitimately projectible; and not all legitimately projectible hypotheses are actually projected. Hence we come to the task of defining projectibility—of projecting the predicate "projected" to the predicate "projectible". This problem is complex in more ways than one. It calls for elimination as well as expansion. We face the twofold task of ruling out actually projected hypotheses that are not to be countenanced as projectible, and of bringing in legitimately projectible hypotheses that have not been actually projected—the twofold problem of projected unprojectibles and unprojected projectibles.

3. RESOLUTION OF CONFLICTS

We may concentrate at present upon simple universal hypotheses in categorical or hypothetical form—that is, upon hypotheses ascribing a certain predicate either to everything in the universe of discourse or to everything to which a certain other predicate applies. Moreover, projectibility at a time must be our first concern; any question of defining temporally unqualified projectibility will have to wait.

The obvious first step in our weeding-out process is to eliminate all projected hypotheses that have since been violated. Such hypotheses, as

is absurdly true. Since a hypothesis is true only if true for all its cases, it is true only if true for all its future and all its undetermined cases; but equally, it is true only if true for all its past and all its determined cases. The pragmatist may perhaps be insisting rather that all we can learn even about past cases is by means of future experience; but this again is correct only if it amounts to saying, quite needlessly, that all we can learn in the future, even about past cases, is what we can learn in the future.

I am suggesting not that pragmatism is utterly wrong or empty but that it must be careful to distinguish its theses from wrong pronouncements to the effect that truth for future cases is sufficient for the truth of a hypothesis, and also from empty pronouncements to the effect that true hypotheses are true and that future tests are future.

already remarked, can no longer be projected, and are thus henceforth unprojectible. On similar grounds, all hypotheses having no remaining unexamined instances are likewise to be ruled out. However, neither the violated nor the exhausted hypotheses are thereby denied to have been projectible at an earlier time.

Not nearly so obvious are the further steps to be taken in order to eliminate projected hypotheses that, even though neither violated nor exhausted, are nevertheless unlawlike. Suppose, for example, that we are now at the time in question in the example of the preceding lecture, when all emeralds examined have been green; and suppose that the hypothesis that all emeralds are grue is projected. ['Grue' applies to things examined before t just in case they are green and to other things just in case they are blue. ed.] How are we to exclude it? We cannot simply assume that no such projection is ever actually made. Such illegitimate hypotheses are in fact adopted at times; and if I laboured under any blissful delusion to the contrary, you could readily dispel it by arbitrarily adopting one.

Projections of this sort, however, will often *conflict* with other projections. If the hypothesis that all emeralds are green is also projected, then the two projections disagree for unexamined emeralds. In saying these projections thus conflict, we are indeed assuming that there is some unexamined emerald to which only one of the two consequent-predicates applies; but it is upon just this assumption that the problem arises at all. Yet how are we to devise a rule that will make the proper choice between these conflicting projections? We have noted that "green" and "grue" seem to be quite symmetrically related to each other. Are we any better off now than before to formulate the distinction between them?

The answer, I think, is that we must consult the record of past projections of the two predicates.[4] Plainly "green", as a veteran of earlier and many more projections than "grue", has the more impressive biography. The predicate "green", we may say, is much better *entrenched* than the predicate "grue".

We are able to draw this distinction only because we start from the record of past actual projections. We could not draw it starting merely from hypotheses and the evidence for them. For every time that "green" either was actually projected or—so to speak—could have been projected, "grue" also might have been projected; that is to say, whenever such a hypothesis as

[4] A predicate "Q" is said to be projected when a hypothesis such as "All P's are Q's" is projected.

All so-and-sos are green

was supported, unviolated, and unexhausted, the hypothesis

All so-and-sos are grue

was likewise supported, unviolated, and unexhausted.[5] Thus if we count all the occasions when each hypothesis was in this sense available for projection, the two predicates have equal status. The significant difference appears only if we consider just those occasions when each predicate was actually projected.

After having declared this so emphatically, I must immediately modify it in one way. The entrenchment of a predicate results from the actual projection not merely of that predicate alone but also of all predicates coextensive with it. [Predicates are coextensive if and only if they apply to all and only the same things. ed.] In a sense, not the word itself but the class it selects is what becomes entrenched, and to speak of the entrenchment of a predicate is to speak elliptically of the entrenchment of the extension of that predicate. On the other hand, the class becomes entrenched only through the projection of predicates selecting it; entrenchment derives from the use of language. But differences of tongue, use of coined abbreviations, and other variations in vocabulary do not prevent accrual of merited entrenchment.[6] Moreover, no entrenchment accrues from the repeated projection of a word except where the word has the same extension each time.

One principle for eliminating unprojectible projections, then, is that a projection is to be ruled out if it conflicts with the projection of a much better entrenched predicate. Conflicts may, of course, occur between projections of two predicates that are almost equally well or ill entrenched; but such conflicts are to be resolved in other ways and

[5] The interpretation of "could have been projected" introduced here is further discussed below, in the first paragraph of Section 4. Suppose that all occurrences of "green" up to t and all later occurrences of "blue" are taken as 'tokens' of a single word. The name of that word—i.e. the syntactic predicate applying to all and only these occurrences—will indeed be ill entrenched. But each occurrence of the word will fortify the entrenchment of each of the others if and only if all are coextensive. Briefly, the entrenchment of a word does not depend upon the entrenchment of its name. Hence while the problem of projectibility may arise at any syntactic level, my treatment is applicable at all levels and does not, as has sometimes been charged, merely push the problem up from each level to the one above.

[6] And all coextensive *replicas* of a predicate inscription or utterance (all coextensive 'tokens' of the same predicate 'type') will have equal entrenchment, determined by the total number of projections of all these replicas and all other utterances coextensive with them. On the other hand, the entrenchment of an utterance will not be increased by the projection of replicas of the utterance that are not coextensive with it.

do not concern us here.[7] Our principle is inoperative where there is reasonable doubt about one predicate being more solidly entrenched than the other; it takes effect only where the difference is great enough to be obvious. Our primitive relation is that obtaining between any two predicates such that the first is much better entrenched than the second.

Like Hume, we are appealing here to past recurrences, but to recurrences in the explicit use of terms as well as to recurrent features of what is observed. Somewhat like Kant, we are saying that inductive validity depends not only upon what is presented but also upon how it is organized; but the organization we point to is effected by the use of language and is not attributed to anything inevitable or immutable in the nature of human cognition. To speak very loosely, I might say that in answer to the question what distinguishes those recurrent features of experience that underlie valid projections from those that do not, I am suggesting that the former are those features for which we have adopted predicates that we have habitually projected.

My proposal by no means amounts to ruling unfamiliar predicates out of court. In the first place, entrenchment and familiarity are not the same. An entirely unfamiliar predicate may be very well entrenched, as we have seen, if predicates coextensive with it have often been projected; and another way a new predicate can acquire entrenchment will be explained presently. Again, a very familiar predicate may be rather poorly entrenched, since entrenchment depends upon frequency of projection rather than upon mere frequency of use. But in the second place, any wholesale elimination of unfamiliar predicates would result in an intolerable stultification of language. New and useful predicates like "conducts electricity" and "is radioactive" are always being introduced and must not be excluded simply because of their novelty. So far our rule legislates against such predicates only to the extent of eliminating projections of them that conflict with projections of much better entrenched predicates. Not predicates but certain projected hypotheses are being eliminated; and in each case the elimination is based upon specific comparison with an overriding

---

[7] Some conflicts between projections of equally well entrenched predicates may be resolved through conflict of one or both with projections of much better entrenched predicates; others will be resolved by means to be outlined in Section 5 below [omitted]. But in many other cases the decision must await further evidence—a crucial experiment. Our task is not to resolve all conflicts between hypotheses, but only those where a question of legitimacy, or validity, is involved. To 'eliminate' a hypothesis as unprojectible obviously does not involve rejecting it as untrue; for while all consequences of a projectible hypothesis that is accepted as true must themselves be accepted as true, many of them (e.g. those that are unsupported or exhausted) will be unprojectible.

hypothesis, not merely upon general grounds of the youth or oddity of the predicate projected. In framing further rules, we must continue to be on guard against throwing out all that is new along with all that is bad. Entrenched capital, in protecting itself, must yet allow full scope for free enterprise.

On several scores, then, our present approach is altogether different from any mere dismissal of unfamiliar predicates. But an objection of a quite different sort might now be raised. Are we not trusting too blindly to a capricious Fate to see to it that just the right predicates get themselves comfortably entrenched? Must we not explain why, in cases of conflict like those illustrated, the really projectible predicate happens to have been the earlier and more often projected? And in fact wasn't it projected so often *because* its projection was so often obviously legitimate, so that our proposal begs the question? I think not. To begin with, what I am primarily suggesting is that the superior entrenchment of the predicate projected is in these cases a sufficient even if not necessary indication of projectibility; and I am not much concerned with whether the entrenchment or the projectibility comes first. But even if the question is taken as a genetic one, the objection seems to me ill-founded. In the case of new predicates, indeed, the legitimacy of any projection has to be decided on the basis of their relationship to older predicates; and whether the new ones will come to be frequently projected depends upon such decisions. But in the case of our main stock of well-worn predicates, I submit that the judgment of projectibility has derived from the habitual projection, rather than the habitual projection from the judgment of projectibility. The reason why only the right predicates happen so luckily to have become well entrenched is just that the well-entrenched predicates have thereby become the right ones.

If our critic is asking, rather, why projections of predicates that have become entrenched happen to be those projections that will turn out to be *true*, the answer is that we do not by any means know that they will turn out to be true. When the time comes, the hypothesis that all emeralds are green may prove to be false, and the hypothesis that all are grue prove to be true. We have no guarantees. The criterion for the legitimacy of projections cannot be truth that is as yet undetermined. Failure to recognize this was responsible, as we saw, for some of the worst misconceptions of the problem of induction.

4. PRESUMPTIVE PROJECTIBILITY

The principle used above for resolving conflicts now needs to be developed into a more explicit and general rule. In what follows, I shall use "antecedent" and "consequent" for, respectively, the predicate of the antecedent and the predicate of the consequent of a conditional hypothesis. Two hypotheses are unequal in entrenchment if one has a better entrenched antecedent than the other and a no-less-well entrenched consequent, or has a better-entrenched consequent and a no-less-well entrenched antecedent. Two hypotheses conflict if neither follows from the other (and the fact that both are supported, unviolated, and unexhausted) and they ascribe to something two different predicates such that only one actually applies.

Our rudimentary principle may first be strengthened in an important way. How are we to deal with an undesirable hypothesis such as H_1

All emeralds are grue,

if it is projected when no legitimate conflicting hypothesis happens to be projected? We may still rule out H_1 on the ground that it conflicts with a non-projected hypothesis—e.g. K

All emeralds are green

—that has a no-less-well entrenched antecedent-predicate and a much better entrenched consequent-predicate, and is supported and unviolated. In effect, this is to say that H_1 conflicts with a hypothesis, containing suitably entrenched predicates, that was not projected but that could have been projected. "Could have been projected" is a non-toxic locution here, used only to say that at the time in question the hypothesis is supported, unviolated and unexhausted.[8] Now we particularly noted earlier that the entrenchment of a predicate has to be determined solely on the basis of *actual* projections; but once the entrenchment of the predicates concerned has been determined, we are free to make reference to hypotheses that, though actual,[9] are not actually projected but that merely, in the precise sense just defined,

[8] It must be borne in mind that a hypothesis can be projected only when it is unexhausted; hence when we assume for purposes of an illustration that a given hypothesis is or could be projected at a given time, we assume that it then has instances yet to be determined. In the case of K above, its being unexhausted follows from the requirement that it conflict with H_1. By the usage explained above, hypotheses actually projected at a given time are included among those that could have been projected at that time. That a hypothesis could have been projected does not, however, imply that it could legitimately have been projected.

[9] A hypothesis or other statement is actual, tenselessly speaking, if uttered or inscribed at any time—past, present, or future. A hypothesis may thus be actual without ever having been projected up to a given time. Indeed, there may well be actual hypotheses that could be projected at various times but are not projected at any time. Some, for example, may be uttered only after they have been violated or exhausted, or only before any of their instances have been examined, or only in the course of their denial.

could have been projected. Thus we no longer need to depend upon an appropriate hypothesis having actually been projected in order to eliminate an illegitimate conflicting one.

Let us now try framing a general rule and then consider how it applies to further cases. Since only supported, unviolated, and unexhausted hypotheses are projectible, we may confine our attention to these for the present. Among such hypotheses, H will be said to override H' if the two conflict and if H is the better entrenched and conflicts with no still better entrenched hypothesis.[10] Our rule reads: A hypothesis is *projectible* if all conflicting hypotheses are overridden, *unprojectible* if overridden, and *non-projectible* if in conflict with another hypothesis and neither is overridden. Thus, for example, H_1 is overridden by K, and so is unprojectible, when all emeralds examined before t are found to be grue and hence green.[11]

Suppose, however, the predicate "grund" applies to all things examined up to a certain time t that are green and to all things not so examined that are round; and suppose that at some time not later than t, when all emeralds examined have been found to be green, H_2

All emeralds are grund

is projected. How are we to deal with this unwelcome hypothesis in the absence of conflict with K? Of course, if all examined emeralds have also been found to be square, then H_2 will be overridden by H_3

All emeralds are square.

But if all emeralds examined before t have been found to be green but either none has been examined for shape or some have been found to be square and others not square, then H_3 is either unsupported or violated and so cannot override H_2. Here, however, H_2 conflicts with the equally well entrenched hypothesis H_4

All emeralds are grare,

(where a thing is grare if either green and examined before t, or not so

---

[10] So stated, this covers only hierarchies of at most three supported, unviolated, unexhausted, and successively better entrenched and conflicting hypotheses. Since only marked differences in degree of entrenchment are taken into account, no hierarchy will have many members. But hierarchies of more than three members can be covered if necessary by making the definition more general so that a hypothesis is overridden if it is the bottom member of a hierarchy that has an even number of members, that is maximal in that it cannot be extended upward, and minimal in that each hypothesis conflicts only with adjacent ones.

[11] Specifications of the available evidence are often elliptical in this discussion. In the present case, for example, we tacitly assume also that some emeralds have been examined before t, while some things other than emeralds may or may not have been found to be green or of some other colour.

examined and square) so that both H_2 and H_4 are nonprojectible.[12] That is, they are not projectible or unprojectible at the time in question. They can neither be welcomed as projectible nor dismissed as unprojectible; and thus, with the evidence as stated, the choice of H_1 over both H_2 and H_4 is validated. But nonprojectibility does not in general imply illegitimacy. Even the best entrenched conflicting hypotheses are nonprojectible when further evidence is needed to decide between them.[13]

Suppose, though, all emeralds examined before t have been both green and round. Under these circumstances, since H_3 is violated and such hypotheses as H_4 are overridden by H_5

All emeralds are round,

H_2 escapes competent conflict and qualifies as projectible. And plainly, projection of H_2 is harmless where the evidence thus makes projectible two well entrenched hypotheses, H_5 and K

All emeralds are green,

such that H_2 follows from their conjunction. This is *not* to say that consequnces of projectible hypotheses are always projectible; for some such consequences are unsupported or exhausted. But a consequence of a projectible hypothesis meets two of the requirements for projectibility: it is unviolated, and all conflicting hypotheses are overridden. And thus H_2, since also supported and unexhausted by the evidence given, is projectible.

Still, are we content to say that H_2 is projectible in this case? Lingering reluctance to do so arises, it seems, from confusing two senses of "projectible". In one sense, a hypothesis is projectible if support normally makes it credible. In another sense, a hypothesis is projectible only when the actual evidence supports and makes it credible.[14] In the first sense, K is projectible. In the second sense, intended throughout most of what follows, K is not projectible when deprived, by

---

[12] When some emeralds have been found to be square and others round, we can retreat from these two hypotheses to the weaker hypothesis "All emeralds are square or round", which does not conflict with them but is projectible whereas they are not. If statistical hypotheses are taken into account, H_2 may be *un*projectible, being overridden by some hypothesis concerning shape distribution among emeralds; but the treatment of statistical hypotheses is a complicated matter requiring redefinition of support, violation, conflict, and so on.

[13] Differences in *degree* of projectibility among nonprojectible, and other, hypotheses will be considered in the following section [omitted].

[14] In a third sense, a hypothesis is projectible only if projectible in both these senses. Robert Schwartz is planning a paper on some of the several varieties of projectibility.

evidence that violates or exhausts it or leaves it in conflict with hypotheses that are not overridden, of its normal capacity to derive credibility from support. On the other hand H_2, though normally not projectible, may be relieved, by evidence that neither violates nor exhausts it but overrides all conflicting hypotheses, of its normal incapacity to derive credibility from support. In sum, just as a normally projectible hypothesis may lose projectibility under unfavourable evidence, so a hypothesis not normally projectible may gain projectibility under sufficiently favourable evidence.

Besides hypotheses having troublesome consequents, we must also deal with those having troublesome antecedents.[15] Let the predicate "emeruby" apply to emeralds examined for colour before t and to rubies not examined before t; and as before, let us suppose that all emeralds examined for colour prior to time t are green. Thus at a time not later than t, all emerubies examined for colour have been green. Yet clearly at this time a projection of H_6

All emerubies are green

is quite as invalid as is a projection of H_1 or H_2. Of course, if at the time in question some rubies have been examined for colour and all so examined found to be red, then H_6 is overridden by the conflicting hypothesis H_7

All rubies are red.

But what if no rubies have been examined for colour? If, say, all sapphires examined have been blue, H_6 will be nonprojectible as the result of conflict with the no-less-well entrenched hypothesis

All sapphirubies are blue.

And indeed if we have found anything, say the Eiffel tower, of some colour other than green, say black, H_6 will conflict with some such hypothesis as

All Eifferubies are black.

[15] Earlier, considering consequents alone, I have spoken of the entrenchment of a predicate as depending on past projections of the predicate—i.e. upon occurrences as consequent of projected hypotheses. The entrenchment of an antecedent similarly depends upon its occurrences as antecedent of projected hypotheses. The entrenchment of a given predicate as antecedent and as consequent may not always be equal; but in saying that the consequent of one hypothesis is, for example, much better entrenched than the consequent of another, I am always speaking of the comparative entrenchment of the two predicates *as consequents*. And likewise, in the case of antecedents, what is relevant is their entrenchment *as antecedents*.

Suppose, though, that our evidence is confined to just the examined green emeralds—that, in effect, nothing else whatever has been examined for colour. In this case, since even the sweeping hypothesis

All things are green

will be projectible, its consequences—such as H_6—will be harmless.

Finally, as Donald Davidson has noted,[16] some hypotheses are misbegotten with respect to both antecedent and consequent. Consider H_8

All emerubies are gred.

If the evidence consists solely of green emeralds examined before t, this hypothesis is overridden by H_6. However, if evidence consisting solely of red rubies examined before t is added, then H_8 becomes projectible; for the formerly overriding hypothesis H_6 is now itself overridden by H_7. Furthermore, in this case H_8 follows from the two projectible hypotheses K and H_7.

No new consideration is required to show that

All emerubies are grund,

while not projectible if before t either no emeralds or rubies have been examined for shape or else some emeralds or rubies have been found not to be round, is projectible if all examined emeralds are green and all examined rubies round.

The effectiveness of our rule is increased when we take into account an aspect of entrenchment that we have so far ignored for the sake of simplicity. Let us, first, say that a predicate "P" is a parent of a given predicate "Q" if among the classes that "P" applies to is the extension of "Q";[17] for example, the predicate "army division" is a parent of the predicate "soldier in the 26th division". Now a novel predicate may inherit entrenchment from a parent predicate. Compare, for instance, the predicate "marble in bag B", applying to marbles in a bag just found, with the predicate "marble in zig A", applying to marbles in some quite helter-skelter selection. Suppose that each predicate is occurring for the first time as the antecedent of a projected hypothesis. Their direct or earned entrenchment is negligible and equal, but the former is the more comfortably settled by inheritance. Its parent predicate "bagful of marbles" has occurred as antecedent of many more

---

[16] In 'Emeroses by Other Names', *Journal of Philosophy,* 63 (1966), 778–80.

[17] A predicate, unlike a person, may have any number of parents. Note also that a parent predicate of "Q" is a parent of every predicate coextensive with "Q".

projections than has any comparable parent of the predicate "marble in zig A". The inherited entrenchment of two predicates of about equal earned entrenchment is gauged by comparing the better entrenched among the parents of each. This could often call for difficult and delicate judgments except that we are concerned here as earlier only with differences gross enough to be easily discerned. It must be particularly noted, furthermore, that comparison of the inherited entrenchment of two predicates is in point only if neither has much greater earned entrenchment than the other. Earned entrenchment, so to speak, establishes the major levels of entrenchment, and only within these does inherited entrenchment effect a subsidiary grading. Thus a predicate is much better entrenched than another if the former either has much greater earned entrenchment than the latter or has about equal earned and much greater inherited entrenchment.

Our rule is now quite powerful, yielding the proper decision in a wide variety of cases while allowing for introduction of acceptable new predicates. Furthermore, although we began with actual projections, the rule obviously covers all hypotheses, whether projected or not; that is, a hypothesis not actually projected may be projectible according to the rule and may override other hypotheses. In effect, our rule offers us the following definitions: a hypothesis is *projectible* when and only when it is supported, unviolated, and unexhausted, and all such hypotheses that conflict with it are overridden; *nonprojectible* when and only when it and a conflicting hypothesis are supported, unviolated, unexhausted, and not overridden; and *unprojectible* when and only when it is unsupported, violated, exhausted, or overridden.

These formulae, though, are only provisional, and the projectibility here defined is at best *presumptive projectibility*. The sorting into three categories is gross and tentative. Hypotheses assigned to the same category may differ greatly in *degree* of projectibility; and the degree of projectibility of a given hypothesis may be affected by indirect evidence.

V

THE CONCEPT OF CONFIRMING
EVIDENCE

RUDOLF CARNAP

WE have earlier distinguished three semantical concepts of confirmation: (i) the classificatory concept of confirmation, the concept of confirming evidence, (ii) the comparative concept ('more or equally confirmed'), and (iii) the quantitative concept, the concept of degree of confirmation. The first of these three concepts is the simplest; the second is more complicated but also more efficient; the third is still more efficient, provided an adequate explicatum of this kind can be found. Our discussions do not take up the problems of these three concepts in the order just mentioned, which is the order of increasing complexity, but rather in the opposite order. We have first dealt with the regular c-functions (in the two preceding chapters); they—or rather, some of them—come into consideration as explicata for the quantitative concept of confirmation. [A regular c-function is one that satisfies the axioms of the probability calculus.] Only afterward, in the preceding sections of this chapter, did we study the problem of the comparative concept and propose the relation $\mathfrak{MC}$ as an explicatum for it. The discussion of this problem was postponed for the following reason. Although the definition itself of the concept $\mathfrak{MC}$ is in purely comparative, non-quantitative terms, that is, it does not refer to the c-functions, nevertheless the conditions of adequacy for the comparative concept do refer to the c-functions. Therefore it seemed advisable, from the heuristic point of view, to take up the study of the problem of the comparative concept only after a theory of the regular c-functions had been constructed. For the same reason the discussion of the simplest concept, the classificatory concept, was postponed.

We distinguish two forms of the classificatory concept of confirming evidence. The general form is relative to some evidence e. 'i confirms h

From *Logical Foundations of Probability* by Rudolf Carnap (Univ. of Chicago Press, 2nd edn., 1962), pp. 462–4, 468–81. Copyright 1950, 1962 by The University of Chicago. By permission of The University of Chicago Press for the author. (There are some minor omissions.)

on the basis of *e*' is understood in the following sense: *i* is an additional item of evidence which, if added to the prior evidence *e*, contributes positively to the confirmation of the hypothesis *h*. In particular, the concept is applicable to the following situation: *e* represents the prior evidence (that is, the evidence available before the results *i* are found); *i* describes new observational results, for instance, results of experiments made in order to test the hypothesis *h*. We shall use the symbol '$\mathfrak{C}$' for any explicatum of this classificatory concept that might be considered. Thus an explicatum of the above statement will be symbolized by '$\mathfrak{C}(h,i,e)$' ('*h is confirmed by i on the basis e*'). The second form of the concept means simply that *i* is confirming evidence for *h* so to speak absolutely; that is, without reference to any prior factual evidence *e*. More exactly speaking, it refers to that special case of the first concept, where no prior factual evidence is available, in other words, where *e* is the tautology '*t*'. We might say in this case that *i* is *initially* (or a priori) *confirming evidence* for *h*. For an explicatum of this second concept we shall use the symbol '$\mathfrak{C}_0$'. Thus, if a function $\mathfrak{C}$ is given, we define:

$$(1) \qquad \mathfrak{C}_0(h,i) =_{\mathrm{Df}} \mathfrak{C}(h,i,t).$$

('$\mathfrak{C}$' and '$\mathfrak{C}_0$' are not symbols of the object-languages $\mathfrak{L}$, but predicates in the metalanguage like '$\mathfrak{MC}$', '$\mathfrak{Gr}$', etc.)

We began the study of the problem of an explication for the comparative concept by investigating the relation which must hold between any adequate explicatum $\mathfrak{MC}$ and the regular $\mathfrak{c}$-functions. We shall now do the same for the classificatory concept. Suppose we had a regular $\mathfrak{c}$-function $\mathfrak{c}$ which we regarded as an adequate explicatum of the quantitative concept. How could we express with its help the classificatory concept of confirming evidence? This concept means that the degree of confirmation of *h* is increased by the addition of *i* to *e*; hence it is expressible in terms of $\mathfrak{c}$ as follows:

$$(2) \qquad \mathfrak{c}(h,e \bullet i) > \mathfrak{c}(h,e).$$

(This condition implies that *e* and *e* $\bullet$ *i* are non-L[logically]-false, because otherwise $\mathfrak{c}$ would not have values for the sentences in question.) Therefore we shall say that a triadic relation *R* among sentences, considered as an explicatum for the classificatory concept, is *in accord with* a given $\mathfrak{c}$-function $\mathfrak{c}$ under the following condition:

(3) *R* is *in accord with* $\mathfrak{c} =_{\mathrm{Df}}$ for any sentences *h*, *i*, and *e*, if *R(h,i,e)*,

then

$$c(h,e \bullet i) > c(h,e) \, ,$$

in other words, i is *positively relevant* to h on e with respect to c.

For $\mathfrak{C}_0$, 't' takes the place of e. Thus here the condition (2) is replaced by:

(4) $c(h,i) > c(h,t) \, ,$

in other words, i is initially positive to h.

[remainder of section omitted]

HEMPEL'S ANALYSIS OF THE CONCEPT OF CONFIRMING EVIDENCE

In this and the next sections we shall discuss investigations made by Carl G. Hempel concerning confirmation in general and especially the classificatory concept. The following discussion is chiefly based on an article of his published in two parts in *Mind* 1945 ([Studies]; references in the following are to this article [Selection I in this vol.]); some of his technical results had been published previously ([Syntactical], 1943). The first-mentioned article gives a clear and illuminating exposition of the whole problem situation concerning confirmation and the distinction between the classificatory, the comparative, and the quantitative concepts of confirmation. A number of points in this problem complex are here clarified for the first time. For instance, Hempel's distinction between the pragmatical concept of the confirmation of a hypothesis by an observer and the logical (semantical) concept of the confirmation of a hypothesis on the basis of an evidence sentence is important; likewise his distinction of the three phases in the procedure of testing a given hypothesis (op. cit., p. 114): making observations, confronting the hypothesis with the observation report, accepting or rejecting the hypothesis. These distinctions are valuable tools for clarifying the situation for many discussions and controversies at the present time concerning confirmation, the foundations of empiricism, verifiability, and related problems.

The main part of Hempel's article concerns the problem of an explication for the classificatory concept of confirmation. We shall now discuss his views in detail. His explicandum is as follows: a sentence (or a class of sentences, or perhaps an individual) represents confirming (corroborating, favourable) evidence or constitutes a confirming instance for a given hypothesis. In his general discussion and in the examples, no reference is made to any *prior* evidence. Thus

Hempel's explicandum corresponds to our dyadic relation $\mathfrak{C}_0(h,i)$ ('h is confirmed by i') rather than to the triadic relation $\mathfrak{C}(h,i,e)$ ('h is confirmed by i on the basis of the prior evidence e'). Therefore we shall in the following compare the explicata discussed by Hempel with $\mathfrak{C}_0$.

Hempel starts with a critical discussion of an explicatum which seems widely accepted (op. cit., pp. 9 ff.); he quotes the following passages by Jean Nicod as a clear formulation for it: "Consider the formula or the law: *A entails B*. How can a particular proposition, or more briefly, a fact, affect its probability? If this fact consists of the presence of B in a case of A, it is favourable to the law '*A entails B*'; on the contrary, if it consists of the absence of B in a case of A, it is unfavourable to this law. It is conceivable that we have here the only two direct modes in which a fact can influence the probability of a law. ... Thus, the entire influence of particular truths or facts on the probability of universal propositions or laws would operate by means of these two elementary relations which we shall call *confirmation* and *invalidation*" ([Induction], p. 219). Hempel refers here also to R. M. Eaton's discussion on "Confirmation and Infirmation" ([Logic], chap. iii), which is based on Nicod's conception. Thus, according to Nicod's criterion, the fact that the individual b is both M ·and M', or the sentence '$Mb \blacksquare M'b$' describing this fact, is confirming evidence for the law '$(x)(Mx \supset M'x)$'. Hempel discusses this criterion in detail, and I agree entirely with his views. As he points out, the criterion is applicable only to a quite special, though important, form of hypothesis. But even if restricted to this form, the criterion does not constitute a necessary condition; in other words, it is clearly too narrow (in the sense of [the previous section]). Hempel shows that it is not in accord with the Equivalence Condition for Hypotheses (see below, H8.22). For instance, '$Mb \blacksquare M'b$' is confirming evidence, according to Nicod's criterion, for the law stated above, but not for the L-equivalent law '$(x)(\sim M'x \supset \sim Mx)$'. This is an instance of what Hempel calls the *paradox of confirmation*. He discusses this paradox in detail and reveals its main sources (op. cit., pp.13–21). Nicod's criterion may be taken as a sufficient condition for the concept of confirming evidence if it is restricted to laws of the form mentioned with only *one* variable. That in the case of laws with several variables it is not even sufficient is shown by Hempel with the help of the following counter-example (op. cit., p. 13 n.), which is interesting and quite surprising. Let the hypothesis be the law '$(x)(y)[\sim(Rxy \blacksquare Ryx) \supset (Rxy \blacksquare \sim Ryx)]$'. [Incidentally, by an unfortunate misprint in the footnote mentioned, the second conjunctive component in the antecedent was omitted.] Now the fact described by 'Rab ■ $\sim Rba$' fulfils both the antecedent and the consequent in the law; hence this fact should be taken as a confirming case according to Nicod's criterion. However, since the law stated is L-equivalent to '$(x)(y)Rxy$', the fact mentioned is actually disconfirming.

Hempel proposes (p. 22) to take the concept of confirming evidence not, like Nicod, as a relation between an object or fact and a sentence, but as a semantical relation—or, alternatively, a syntactical (i.e., purely formal) relation—between two sentences, as we do with $\mathfrak{C}_0$ (and $\mathfrak{c}$). A language system L is presupposed. The primitive predicates in L designate directly observable properties or relations. An observation sentence is a basic sentence (atomic sentence or negation) in L. An observation report in the narrower sense is a class or conjunction of a finite number of observation sentences (op. cit., p. 23); an observation report in the wider sense is any nongeneral sentence. We shall henceforth use the term in the wider sense. [Hempel uses the wider sense in the more technical paper [Syntactical], p. 126. In the text of [Studies] he uses the narrower sense, but he mentions the wider sense in footnotes (pp. 108, 111) and declares that the narrower sense was used in the text only for greater convenience of exposition and that all results, definitions, and theorems remain applicable if the wider sense is adopted. Thus our use of the wider sense is justified; it will facilitate the construction of some examples.] Hempel admits also contradictory sentences as observation reports (p. 103, footnote 1); however, we shall exclude them, in accord with our general requirement that the evidence referred to by any confirmation concept be non-L-false. (This requirement was later accepted by Hempel [Degree], p. 102; our exclusion here will not affect the results of the subsequent discussion of Hempel's views.) Hempel restricts the evidence e referred to by the concept of confirmation to observation reports, but the hypothesis h may be any sentence of the language L. The structure of L is similar to that of our systems $\mathfrak{L}$ except that L does not contain a sign of identity.

Hempel makes (op. cit., pp. 97 ff.) a critical examination of another explicatum of the concept of confirming evidence, which is often used at least implicitly and which at first glance appears as quite plausible. This explicatum, which Hempel calls the *prediction-criterion* of confirmation, is based on the consideration that it is customary to regard a hypothesis as confirmed if a prediction made with its help is borne out by the facts. This consideration suggests the following definition: An observation report $\mathfrak{K}_i$ confirms the hypothesis $h = {}_{\mathrm{Df}} \mathfrak{K}_i$ can be divided into two mutually exclusive subclasses $\mathfrak{K}_{i1}$ and $\mathfrak{K}_{i2}$ such that $\mathfrak{K}_{i2}$ is not empty, and every sentence of $\mathfrak{K}_{i2}$ can be logically deduced from (i.e., is L-implied by) $\mathfrak{K}_{i1}$ together with h but not from

$\mathfrak{K}_{i1}$ alone. Hempel shows that this concept is indeed a sufficient condition for the explicatum sought, but not a necessary condition; in other words, it is not too wide, but it is clearly too narrow. The chief reason is the obvious fact that most scientific hypotheses do not simply express a conditional connection between observable properties but have a more general and often more complex form. This is illustrated by the simple example of the sentence '$(x)[(y)R_1xy \supset (\exists z) R_2xz]$' in an infinite universe, where R_1 and R_2 are observable relations. If we take any instance of this universal sentence, say with 'b' for 'x', then we see that the antecedent (i.e., '$(y)R_1by$') is not L-implied by any finite class of observation sentences, and that the consequent (i.e., '$(\exists z)R_2bz$') does not L-imply any observation sentence. This shows that it is "a considerable over-simplification to say that scientific hypotheses and theories enable us to derive predictions of future experiences from descriptions of past ones" (p. 100). The logical connection which a scientific hypothesis establishes between observation reports is in general not merely of a deductive kind; it is rather a combination of deductive and nondeductive steps. The latter are inductive in one wide sense of this word; Hempel calls them 'quasi-inductive'.

After these discussions of Nicod's criterion and the prediction-criterion resulting in the rejection of both explicata as too narrow, Hempel proceeds to the positive part of his discussion. He states a number of general conditions for the adequacy of any explicatum for the concept of confirming evidence (pp. 102 ff.); we shall discuss them in the present section. Then he defines his own explicatum and shows that it fulfils the conditions of adequacy; this will be discussed in the next section. Hempel's *conditions of adequacy* are as follows ('H' is here attached to his numbers); the evidence e is always an observation report as explained earlier, while the hypothesis h may be any sentence of the language L. [See pp. 35–37 this vol.] .

(H8.1)   *Entailment Condition:* If h is entailed by e (i.e., $\vdash e \supset h$), then e confirms h.

(H8.2)   *Consequence Condition:* If e confirms every sentence of the class $\mathfrak{K}_i$ and h is a consequence of (i.e., L-implied by) $\mathfrak{K}_i$, then e confirms h.

The following two more special conditions follow from H8.2.

(H8.21)   *Special Consequence Condition:* If e confirms h, then it also confirms every consequence of h (i.e., sentence L-implied by h).

(H8.22)   *Equivalence Condition for Hypotheses:* If h and h' are L-equivalent and e confirms h then e confirms h'.

(H8.3) *Consistency Condition:* The class whose elements are *e* and all the hypotheses confirmed by *e* is consistent (i.e., not L-false).

The following two more special conditions follow from H8.3.

(H8.31) If *e* and *h* are incompatible (i.e., L-exclusive, *e* ∎ *h* is L-false), then *e* does not confirm *h*.

(H8.32) If *h* and *h'* are incompatible (i.e., L-exclusive), then *e* does not confirm both *h* and *h'*.

(H8.4) *Equivalence Condition for Observation Reports* (op. cit., p. 110 n.): If *e* and *e'* are L-equivalent and *e* confirms *h*, then *e'* confirms *h*.

Now we shall examine these conditions of adequacy stated by Hempel. We interpret these conditions as referring to the concept of initial confirming evidence as explicandum; we shall soon come back to the question whether Hempel has not sometimes a different explicandum in mind. Thus we shall apply the conditions to $\mathfrak{C}_0$; but when we accept one of them, we shall state not only a condition (b) for $\mathfrak{C}_0$, but first a more general condition (a) for $\mathfrak{C}$; (b) is then a special case of (a) with '*t*' for '*e*'. It is presupposed for (a) that *e* ∎ *i* is non-L-false, because otherwise $\mathfrak{c}(h, e \blacksquare i)$ would have no value and hence the subsequent condition (2) could not be applied; and it is presupposed for (b) that *e* is not L-false. Our statements of conditions will have the same numbers as Hempel's but with 'C' instead of 'H'. For this discussion we remember that we found that $\mathfrak{C}$ is the same as positive relevance and $\mathfrak{C}_0$ the same as initial positive relevance; therefore we shall make use of the results concerning relevance concepts stated in the preceding chapter. Our examination will be based on the view that any adequate explicatum for the classificatory concept of confirmation must be in accord with at least one adequate explicatum for the quantitative concept of confirmation; in other words, a relation $\mathfrak{C}_0$ proposed as explicatum cannot be accepted as adequate unless there is at least one $\mathfrak{c}$-function $\mathfrak{c}$, which is an adequate explicatum for probability$_1$, such that, if $\mathfrak{C}_0(h, i)$ then

(1) $$\mathfrak{c}(h, i) > \mathfrak{c}(h, t) .$$

Analogously, it is necessary for the adequacy of a proposed explicatum $\mathfrak{C}$ that there is at least one adequate $\mathfrak{c}$ such that, if $\mathfrak{C}(h, i, e)$, then

(2) $$\mathfrak{c}(h, e \blacksquare i) > \mathfrak{c}(h, e) .$$

In examining Hempel's statements of conditions of adequacy or our subsequent statements, we shall regard such a statement as valid if there is at least one explicatum $\mathfrak{C}_0$ (or $\mathfrak{C}$) which is adequate in the sense just explained, i.e., in accord with an adequate $\mathfrak{c}$-function, and which satisfies the statement generally, i.e., for any sentences as arguments.

The *entailment condition* H8.1 may appear at first glance as quite plausible. And it is indeed valid in ordinary cases. However, it does not hold in some special cases as we shall see by the subsequent counter-examples. Therefore we restate it in the following qualified form.

(C8.1) *Entailment Condition.* Let h be either a sentence in a finite system or a nongeneral sentence in the infinite system.

a. If $\vdash e \bullet i \supset h$ and not $\vdash e \supset h$, then $\mathfrak{C}\,(h,i,e)$.

b. If $\vdash i \supset h$ and h is not L-true, then $\mathfrak{C}_0(h,i)$.

The following theorem shows that the entailment condition in the modified form C8.1 is valid.

T87-1.

a. Any instance of the relation $\mathfrak{C}$ which is required by C8.1a is in accord with every regular $\mathfrak{c}$-function.

Proof. Let $\vdash e \bullet i \supset h$ and not $\vdash e \supset h$. It was presupposed that $e \bullet i$ is not L-false. Therefore, for every regular $\mathfrak{c}$, $\mathfrak{c}\,(h,e \bullet i) = 1$ and $\mathfrak{c}(h,e) < 1$. Thus this instance of $\mathfrak{C}$ is in accord with $\mathfrak{c}$.

b. Any instance of $\mathfrak{C}_0$ required by C8.1b is in accord with every regular $\mathfrak{c}$-function. (From (a), with 't' for e.)

In C8.1a, we have excluded the case that $\vdash e \supset h$. This restriction is necessary, because in this case $\mathfrak{c}\,(h,e) = 1 = \mathfrak{c}\,(h,e \bullet i)$; hence $\mathfrak{c}$ is not increased. For the same reason, the case that h is L-true must be excluded in C8.1b.

. . .

The *equivalence conditions* for hypotheses (H8.22) and for observation reports (H8.4) are obviously valid, because the corresponding principles hold for all regular $\mathfrak{c}$-functions. For $\mathfrak{C}$, the former condition can be generalized; the hypotheses h and h' need only be L-equivalent with respect to e, i.e., $\vdash e \supset (h \equiv h')$.

The *consequence condition* H8.2 and the special consequence condition H8.21 are not valid, as we shall see. In his discussion of H8.21, Hempel refers (p. 105, n. 1) to William Barrett ([Dewey], p. 312), whose view that "not every observation which confirms a sentence need also confirm all its consequences" is obviously in contradiction to the consequence condition. Barrett supports his view by pointing to "the simplest case: the sentence 'C' is an abbreviation of '$A \bullet B$', and the observation O confirms 'A', and so 'C', but is irrelevant to 'B', which is a consequence of 'C'". This situation can indeed occur, as we shall see; thus Barrett is right in rejecting the consequence condition. Now Hempel points out that Barrett, in the phrase "and so 'C'" just quoted, seems to presuppose tacitly the *converse consequence condition:* if e confirms h, then it confirms also any sentence of which h is a consequence. Hempel shows correctly that a simultaneous requirement of both the consequence condition and the converse consequence condition would immediately lead to the absurd result that any observation report e confirms any hypothesis h (because e confirms e, hence $e \bullet h$, hence h). Since he accepts the consequence condition, he rejects the converse consequence condition. On the other hand, Barrett, accepting the latter, rejects the former. Each of the two incompatible conditions has a certain superficial plausibility. Which of them is valid? The answer is, neither.

In our investigation of the possible relevance situations for two hypotheses we found the following results, which hold for all regular $\mathfrak{c}$-functions. It is possible that, on the same evidence e, which may be factual or tautological, i is positive to h but negative to $h \lor k$, although the latter is L-implied by the former. This is possible not only if i is negative to k but also if i is irrelevant or even positive to k. We have indicated there a general procedure for constructing cases of this kind, and given a numerical example. This shows that *the consequence condition is not valid*, that is, not in accord with any regular $\mathfrak{c}$-function. We have further found that it is possible that i is positive to h but negative to $h \bullet k$, although the latter L-implies the former. This is possible even if i is positive to k. Here likewise a general construction procedure has been indicated and a numerical example given. [The procedures and examples to which Carnap alludes in this paragraph are discussed in secs. 70-1 of his *Logical Foundations of Probability.* ed.] This shows that *the converse consequence condition is not valid.*

A remark made by Hempel in his discussion of Barrett is interesting because it throws some light on the reasoning which led Hempel to the consequence condition. Hempel quotes Barrett's statement that "the degree of confirmation for the consequence of a sentence cannot be less than that of the sentence itself". This statement is correct; it does indeed hold for every regular $\mathfrak{c}$-function. Hempel agrees with this principle but regards it as incompatible with a renunciation of the special consequence condition, "since the latter may be considered simply as the correlate, for the non-gradated [i.e., classificatory] relation of confirmation, of the former principle which is adapted to the concept of degree of confirmation". This seems to show that here Hempel has in mind as explicandum the following relation: 'the degree of confirmation of h on i is greater than r', where r is a fixed value, perhaps 0 or $1/2$. This interpretation seems indicated also by another remark which Hempel makes in support of the consequence condition: "An observation report which confirms certain hypotheses would invariably be qualified as confirming any consequence of those hypotheses. Indeed: any such consequence is but an assertion of all or part of the combined content of the original hypotheses and has therefore to be regarded as confirmed by any evidence which confirms the original hypotheses" (p. 103). This reasoning may appear at first glance quite plausible; but this is due, I think, only to the inadvertent transition to the explicandum mentioned above. This relation, however, is not the same as our original explicandum, the classificatory concept of confirmation as used, for instance, by a scientist when he says something like this: 'The result of the experiment just made supplies confirming evidence for my hypothesis'; Hempel's general discussions give the impression that he too is originally thinking of this explicandum, when he refers to favourable and unfavourable data, both of which are regarded as relevant and distinguished from irrelevant data, and when he speaks of given evidence as strengthening or weakening a given hypothesis. The difference between the two explicanda is easily seen as follows. Let r be a fixed value. The result that the degree of confirmation of h after the observation i is $q > r$ does not by itself show that i furnishes a positive contribution to the confirmation of h; for it may be that the prior degree of confirmation of h (i.e., before the observation i) was already q, in which case i is irrelevant; or it may have been even greater than q, in which case i is negative. [Example. Let h be '$P_1 b \lor P_2 b$', and i '$P_3 a$'. Take $r = 1/2$. For many $\mathfrak{c}$-functions $\mathfrak{c}(h,i) = \mathfrak{c}(h,t) = 3/4$. Therefore i is (initially) irrelevant to h, although $\mathfrak{c}(h,i) > 1/2$.] And, the other way round, the result that the posterior degree of confirmation of h is higher than the prior one does not necessarily make it higher than r (unless $r = 0$). Thus we see that the essential criterion for the concept of confirming evidence must take into account not simply the posterior degree of confirmation but rather a comparison between this and the prior one.

The consistency condition H8.3 is not valid; it seems to me not even plausible. The special condition H8.31, requiring compatibility of the hypothesis with the evidence, is certainly valid. We restate it here in the general form as Compatibility Condition:

(C8.31) *Compatibility Condition.*

a. If i and h are L-exclusive with respect to e, that is, if $e \blacksquare i \blacksquare h$ is L-false, then not $\mathfrak{C}(h,i,e)$.

b. If i and h are L-exclusive, that is, if $i \blacksquare h$ is L-false, then not $\mathfrak{C}_0(h,i)$.

The following theorem shows that C8.31 is valid, no matter on which $\mathfrak{c}$-function or class of $\mathfrak{c}$-functions $\mathfrak{C}$ is based.

T87-2.

a. If a relation $\mathfrak{C}$ holds in any instance excluded by C8.31a, then it is not in accord with any regular $\mathfrak{c}$-function.

Proof. Let $e \blacksquare i \blacksquare h$ be L-false. Then, for every regular $\mathfrak{c}$, $\mathfrak{c}\,(h,e \blacksquare i)$ = 0, hence not $> \mathfrak{c}\,(h,e)$.

b. If a relation $\mathfrak{C}_0$ holds in any instance exluded by C8.31b, then it is not in accord with any regular $\mathfrak{c}$-function. (From (a), with 't' for e.)

On the other hand, the second special condition H8.32 seems to me invalid. Hempel himself shows that a set of physical measurements may confirm several quantitative hypotheses which are incompatible with each other (p. 106). This seems to me a clear refutation of H8.32. Hempel discusses possibilities of weakening or omitting this requirement, but he decides at the end to maintain it unchanged, without saying how he intends to overcome the difficulty which he has pointed out himself. Perhaps he thinks that he may leave aside this difficulty because the results of physical measurements cannot be formulated in the simple language L to which his analysis applies. However, it seems to me that there are similar but simpler counterexamples which can be formulated in our systems $\mathfrak{L}$ and in Hempel's system L. For instance, let i describe the frequency of a property M in a finite population, and h and h' state two distinct values m and m' for the frequency of M in a sample of s individuals belonging to the population, such that the relative frequencies m/s and m'/s are both near to the relative frequency of M in the population as stated in i. Then i confirms both h and h', although they are incompatible with each other.

Example. Let i be a statistical distribution for M and non-M with respect to 10,000 individuals with the cardinal number 8,000 for M. Let h be a statistical distribution with respect to 100 of these individuals with the cardinal number 80 for M, and similarly h' with respect to the same individuals and with the cardinal number 79. Note that a statistical distribution for a finite class has the form of a disjunction of conjunctions and does not contain variables or the sign of identity; therefore it occurs also in L and it is an observation report (in the wider sense). Let e be either the tautology 't' or a factual sentence irrelevant to h and to h' (on 't' and on i). Then for many c-functions (presumably including all adequate ones) $c\,(h,e \bullet i) >$ $c(h,e)$ and $c\,(h',e \bullet i) > c\,(h',e)$. (These are cases of the direct inductive inference.) Thus i is positively relevant and hence constitutes confirming evidence for both h and h'.

Hempel mentions in this context still another condition, which might be called the *Conjunction Condition:* if e confirms each of two hypotheses, then it also confirms their conjunction (p. 106). Hempel seems to accept this condition; he regards any violation of it as "intuitively rather awkward". However, this condition is not valid for our explicandum; we have found earlier that i may be positive both to h and to k but negative to $h \bullet k$ (this was mentioned above as a refutation of the converse consequence condition). And it is not valid for the second explicandum either, no matter which value we choose for r.

What may be the reasons which have led Hempel to the consistency conditions H8.32 and H8.3? He regards it as a great advantage of any explicatum satisfying H8.3 "that it sets a limit, so to speak, to the strength of the hypotheses which can be confirmed by given evidence", as was pointed out to him by Nelson Goodman. This argument does not seem to have any plausibility for *our* explicandum, because a weak additional evidence can cause an increase, though a small one, in the confirmation even of a very strong hypothesis. But it is plausible for the second explicandum mentioned earlier: the degree of confirmation exceeding a fixed value r. Therefore we may perhaps assume that Hempel's acceptance of the consistency condition is due again to an inadvertent shift to the second explicandum. This assumption seems corroborated by the following result. Although H8.32 is not valid for our explicandum, it is valid for the second explicandum if we take for r $1/2$ or any greater value ($<$1). For if h and h' are L-exclusive, then it is impossible that $c\,(h,i)$ and $c\,(h',i)$ both exceed $1/2$, because the sum of those two c-values is $c\,(h \vee h',i)$ (according to the special addition theorem), and hence cannot exceed 1.

HEMPEL'S DEFINITION OF CONFIRMING EVIDENCE

On the basis of his analysis of the problem of an explication of the concept of confirming evidence, Hempel proceeds to construct the definition of a dyadic relation *Cf* between sentences, which he proposes as an explicatum. We shall briefly state the series of definitions, using our terminology and notation and omitting minor details not relevant for our discussion. We add again 'H' to the numbers in the latter article and call the first definition 'H9.0'. e is any molecular sentence, h any sentence of Hempel's language system L earlier indicated (similar to $\mathfrak{L}$ but without a sign of identity).

(H9.0) The *development* of h for a finite class C of individual constants $=_{\mathrm{Df}}$ the sentence formed from h by the following transformations: (1) every universal matrix $(i_k)\,(\mathfrak{M}_k)$ is replaced by the conjunction of the substitution instances of its scope $\mathfrak{M}_k$ for all in in C; (2) every existential matrix $(\exists\,i_k)(\mathfrak{M}_k)$ is replaced by the disjunction of the substitution instances of its scope $\mathfrak{M}_k$ for all in in C. (If h contains no variables, then its development is h itself.)

(H9.1) *Cfd(e,h)*, *e directly confirms* h = $_{\mathrm{Df}}$ e L-implies the development of h for the class of those in which occur essentially in e (i.e., which occur in every sentence L-equivalent to e).

(H9.2) *Cf(e,h)*, *e confirms* h = $_{\mathrm{Df}}$ h is L-implied by a class of sentences each of which is directly confirmed by e.

Example. Let e be '$Pa_1 \blacksquare Pa_2 \blacksquare \ldots \blacksquare Pa_{10}$', l '$(x)Px$', and h 'Pa_{12}'. Then *Cfd(e,l)*; and, since $\vdash l \supset h$, *Cf(e,h)*; but not *Cfd(e,h)*.

(H9.3) *e disconfirms* h $=_{\mathrm{Df}}$ e confirms non-h.

(H9.4) *e* is *neutral* with respect to h $=_{\mathrm{Df}}$ e neither confirms nor disconfirms h.

Now let us see whether the concept Cf defined by H9.2 seems adequate as an explicatum for our explicandum, the concept of confirming evidence. Hempel shows that Cf satisfies all his conditions of adequacy earlier stated. While he takes this fact as an indication of adequacy, it will make us doubtful, since we found that some of the requirements are invalid.

It follows from our refutation of the special consequence condition H8.21 and the special consistency condition H8.32 that no R can possibly fulfil all of the following four conditions:

(i) R is not clearly too wide,
(ii) R is not clearly too narrow,
(iii) R satisfies H8.21,
(iv) R satisfies H8.32.

For if (ii) and (iii) are fulfilled, then our counterexamples to H8.21 lead to cases where R holds but the explicandum does clearly not hold; hence (i) is not fulfilled. And if (i) and (iv) are fulfilled, then our counterexamples to H8.32 lead to cases which are excluded by H8.32 but in which the explicandum clearly holds; hence (ii) is not fulfilled.

Since Hempel has shown that his explicatum *Cf* satisfies all his requirements, among them H8.21 and H8.32, *Cf* must be either clearly too wide or clearly too narrow or both. I am not aware of any cases in which *Cf* holds but the explicandum does clearly not hold. Thus we may assume, unless and until somebody finds counterinstances, that *Cf* is not clearly too wide. However, it is clearly too narrow; we shall see, indeed, that *Cf* is limited to some quite special kinds of cases of the explicandum. The result that a proposed explicatum is found too narrow constitutes a much less serious objection than the result that it is too wide. In the former case the proposed concept may still be useful; it may be an adequate explicatum for a subkind of the explicandum within a limited field. It seems that this is the case with *Cf*.

We shall now consider the four most important kinds of inductive reasoning and examine, for each of them, under what conditions *Cf* holds. In the following discussion the population is assumed to be finite. Individuals not referred to in the evidence *e* are called new individuals. 'rf' means relative frequency. (In (1) and (2) we restrict the present discussion, for the sake of simplicity, to a hypothesis *h* concerning one individual.)

1. *Direct inference. e* is a statistical distribution to the effect that the rf of a property in the population, say, the primitive property *P*, has the value *r; h* is '*Pb*', where *b* belongs to the population.

1a. Let *r* be 1; that is, all individuals in the population are known to be *P*. Then *Cf* holds, but this case is trivial because *e* L-implies *h*.

1b. Let $0 < r < 1$. *Cf* does *not* hold. However, if *r* is close to 1, most people would regard *e* as confirming evidence for *h*. This holds even for both explicanda: (i) $\mathfrak{c}$ is increased by adding *e* to '*t*'; (ii) $\mathfrak{c}(h,e)$ exceeds the fixed value *q*, say 1/2.

2. *Predictive inference. e* is a statistical distribution to the effect that the rf of a property, say, *P*, in a given sample is *r; h* is the singular prediction '*Pd*', where *d* is a new individual.

2a. Let *r* be 1; that is, all individuals in the observed sample have been found to be *P*. Then *Cf* holds (see the above example following H9.2).

2b. Let $0 < r < 1$. *Cf* does *not* hold. However, if *r* is close to 1, most people would regard *e* as confirming evidence for *h*, in the sense of either explicandum (as in 1b). (For any adequate $\mathfrak{c}$-function, in the case of a sufficiently large sample $\mathfrak{c}(h,e)$ is close or equal to *r*.)

Example. Let e and h be as in the earlier example following (H9.2) and i '$\sim Pa_{11}$'. (i is negative to h on e). Then not $Cf(e \cdot i,h)$.

2c. Let the evidence contain, in addition to e with $r = 1$, irrelevant data on additional individuals. Then Cf does *not* hold.

Example. Let e and h be as above, and i' be '$P_2 a_{11}$'. (i' is irrelevant to h on e.) Then not $Cf(e \cdot i',h)$. However, for every adequate $\mathfrak{c}$, $\mathfrak{c}(h,e \cdot i') = \mathfrak{c}(h,e)$. Therefore, since e is regarded as confirming evidence for h, $e \cdot i'$ will usually be regarded so too.

3. *Inverse inference.* e is a statistical distribution to the effect that the rf of P in a given sample of a population is r; h is a statistical distribution saying that the rf of P in the population is r'.

3a. Let r and r' be 1, that is, all individuals in the sample and in the population are stated to be P. Here $Cf(e,h)$ holds, and even $Cfd(e,h)$ (see $Cfd(e,l)$ in the example following H9.2).

3b. Let $0 < r < 1$. Then Cf holds for *no* value of r'. However, for r' equal or near to r, many people, though not all, would regard e as confirming evidence for h.

4. *Universal inductive inference.* Let h be a universal sentence, say '$(x)Mx$', and e be a conjunction of sentences concerning the individuals of a given sample not containing negative instances. (If 'b' occurs essentially in e, it is called a positive instance for h if e L-implies 'Mb', a negative instance if e L-implies '$\sim Mb$', and a neutral instance if it is neither a positive nor a negative instance.)

4a. Let e contain only positive instances. Then Cf and even Cfd hold. (This case is the same as 3a.)

4b. Let e contain both positive and neutral instances. Then Cf does *not* hold.

Example. Let l, e, and i' be as previously. Then not $Cf(e \cdot i',l)$. However, many will regard i' as irrelevant to l on e, that is, $\mathfrak{c}(l,e \cdot i')$ $= \mathfrak{c}(l,e)$. Since now e is regarded as confirming l, that is, $\mathfrak{c}(h,e) >$ $\mathfrak{c}(h,t)$, $\mathfrak{c}(h,e \cdot i')$ is likewise $> \mathfrak{c}(h,t)$. Hence $e \cdot i'$ will be regarded as confirming h.

Thus we see that in each of the kinds of inductive inference just discussed Cf holds only in the special case where the evidence ascribes to *all* individuals essentially occurring in it the property in question. Although this case is of great importance, it is very limited. In the great majority of the cases in which scientists speak of confirming evidence, the rf in e is not 1 or 0 but has an intermediate value. These cases are not covered by Cf. However, Cf can presumably be regarded as an adequate explicatum for the concept of confirming evidence in the special case described.

Hempel's investigations of the problem of confirming evidence supplied the first thoroughgoing and clear analysis of the whole problem complex. As such they remain valuable independently of his attempted solution of the particular problem of finding a nonquantitative explicatum for the concept of confirming evidence. The latter problem is today no longer as important as it was at the time Hempel made his investigations. Some years ago those who worked on these problems expected that, if and when a definition of degree of confirmation were to be constructed, it would be based on a definition of a nonquantitative concept of confirming evidence. However, today it is seen that this is not the case either for Hempel's definition of dc nor for my definition of c^* [Carnap's preferred probability function, ed.], and it is not regarded as probable that it will be the case for other definitions which will be proposed. It appears at present more promising to proceed in the opposite direction, that is, to define a quantitative form of the concept of confirming evidence on the basis of an explicatum for degree of confirmation, for instance, $\mathfrak{C}^*$ (or $\mathfrak{C}_0^*$) based on c^* or analogous concepts based on Hempel's dc or on other explicata for degree of confirmation.

VI

CONFIRMATION AND RELEVANCE

WESLEY C. SALMON

. . .

1. CARNAP AND HEMPEL

As Carnap pointed out in *Logical Foundations of Probability*, the concept of confirmation is radically ambiguous. [See selection V in this vol.] If we say, for example, that the special theory of relativity has been confirmed by experimental evidence, we might have either of two quite distinct meanings in mind. On the one hand, we may intend to say that the special theory has become an accepted part of scientific knowledge and that it is very nearly certain in the light of its supporting evidence. If we admit that scientific hypotheses can have numerical degrees of confirmation, the sentence, on this construal, says that the degree of confirmation of the special theory on the available evidence is high. On the other hand, the same sentence might be used to make a very different statement. It may be taken to mean that some particular evidence—e.g., observations on the lifetimes of mesons—renders the special theory more acceptable or better founded than it was in the absence of this evidence. If numerical degrees of confirmation are again admitted, this latter construal of the sentence amounts to the claim that the special theory has a higher degree of confirmation on the basis of the new evidence than it had on the basis of the previous evidence alone.

The discrepancy between these two meanings is made obvious by the fact that a hypothesis h, which has a rather low degree of confirmation on prior evidence e, may have its degree of confirmation raised by an item of positive evidence i without attaining a high degree of confirmation on the augmented body of evidence $e.i$. In other words,

From *Induction, Probability and Confirmation*, Minnesota Studies in the Philosophy of Science, vol. 6, ed. Grover Maxwell and Robert M. Anderson, Jr., pp. 5–24, 27–36. Copyright © 1975 by the University of Minnesota. By permission of the Univ. of Minnesota Press.

a hypothesis may be confirmed (in the second sense) without being confirmed (in the first sense). Of course, we may believe that hypotheses can achieve high degrees of confirmation by the accumulation of many positive instances, but that is an entirely different matter. It is initially conceivable that a hypothesis with a low degree of confirmation might have its degree of confirmation increased repeatedly by positive instances, but in such a way that the confirmation approaches ¼ (say) rather than 1. Thus, it may be possible for hypotheses to be repeatedly confirmed (in the second sense) without ever getting confirmed (in the first sense). It can also work the other way. A hypothesis h that already has a high degree of confirmation on evidence e may still have a high degree of confirmation on evidence $e.i.$, even though the addition of evidence i does not raise the degree of confirmation of h. In this case, h is confirmed (in the first sense) without being confirmed (in the second sense) on the basis of additional evidence i.

If we continue to speak in terms of numerical degrees of confirmation, as I shall do throughout this paper, we can formulate the distinction between these two senses of the term "confirm" clearly and concisely. For uniformity of formulation, let us assume some background evidence e (which may, upon occasion, be the tautological evidence t) as well as some additional evidence i on the basis of which degrees of confirmation are to be assessed. We can define "confirm" in the first (absolute; nonrelevance) sense as follows:

> D1. Hypothesis h is confirmed (in the absolute sense) by evidence i in the presence of background evidence $e =_{df} c(h,e.i) > b$, where b is some chosen number, presumably close to 1.

This concept is absolute in that it makes no reference to the degree of confirmation of h on any other body of evidence.[1] The second (relevance) sense of "confirm" can be defined as follows:

> D2. Hypothesis h is confirmed (in the relevance sense) by evidence i in the presence of background evidence $e =_{df} c(h,e.i) > c(h,e)$.

---

[1] The term "absolute probability" is sometimes used to refer to probabilities that are not relative or conditional. For example, Carnap's null confirmation $c_0(h)$ is an absolute probability, as contrasted with $c(h,e)$ in which the degree of confirmation of h is relative to, or conditional upon, e. The distinction I am making between the concepts defined in D1 and D2 is quite different. It is a distinction between two different types of confirmation, where one is a conditional probability and the other is a relevance relation defined in terms of conditional probabilities. In this paper, I shall not use the concept of absolute probability at all; in place of null confirmation I shall always use the confirmation $c(h,t)$ on tautological evidence, which is equivalent to the null confirmation, but which is a conditional or relative probability.

This is a relevance concept because it embodies a relation of change in degree of confirmation. Indeed, Carnap's main discussion of this distinction follows his technical treatment of relevance relations, and the second concept of confirmation is explicitly recognized as being identical with the concept of positive relevance.[2]

It is in this context that Carnap offers a detailed critical discussion of Hempel's criteria of adequacy for an explication of confirmation.[3] Carnap shows conclusively, I believe, that Hempel has conflated the two concepts of confirmation, with the result that he has adopted an indefensible set of conditions of adequacy. As Carnap says, he is dealing with two explicanda, not with a single unambiguous one. The incipient confusion is signalled by his characterization of

the quest for general objective criteria determining (A) whether, and—if possible—even (B) to what degree, a hypothesis h may be said to be corroborated by a given body of evidence e. . . . The two parts of this . . . problem can be related in somewhat more precise terms as follows:

(A) To give precise definitions of the two nonquantitative relational concepts of confirmation and disconfirmation; *i.e.* to define the meaning of the phrases 'e confirms h' and 'e disconfirms h'. (When e neither confirms nor disconfirms h, we shall say that e is neutral, or irrelevant, with respect to h.)

(B) (1) To lay down criteria defining a metrical concept "degree of confirmation of h with respect to e," whose values are real numbers . . . .[4]

The parenthetical remark under (A) makes it particularly clear that a relevance concept of confirmation is involved there, while a nonrelevance concept of confirmation is obviously involved in (B).

The difficulties start to show up when Hempel begins laying down conditions of adequacy for the concept of confirmation (A) (as opposed to degree of confirmation (B)). According to the very first condition "entailment is a special case of confirmation". This condition states:

H-8.1 *Entailment Condition.* Any sentence which is entailed by an observation report is confirmed by it.[5]

[2] Carnap, *Logical Foundations*, sec. 86 [Selection V].

[3] These conditions of adequacy are presented in Carl G. Hempel, 'Studies in the Logic of Confirmation,' Mind, 54 (1945), 1-26, 97-121. Reprinted, with a 1964 postscript, in Carl G. Hempel, *Aspects of Scientific Explanation* (New York: Free Press, 1965). [Selection I] Page references in succeeding notes will be to the reprinted version.

[4] Hempel, *Aspects of Scientific Explanation*, p. 6. [pp. 13-14 this vol.]. Hempel's capital letters "H" and "E" have been changed to lower case for uniformity with Carnap's notation.

[5] Ibid., p. 31. [p. 35 this vol.]. Following Carnap, an "H" is attached to the numbers of Hempel's conditions.

If we are concerned with the absolute concept of confirmation, this condition is impeccable, for $c(h,e) = 1$ if e entails h. It is not acceptable, however, as a criterion of adequacy for a relevance concept of confirmation. For suppose our hypothesis h is "$(\exists x)Fx$" while evidence e is "Fa" and evidence i is "Fb". In this case, i entails h, but i does not confirm h in the relevance sense, for $c(h,e.i) = 1 = c(h,e)$.

Carnap offers further arguments to show that the following condition has a similar defect:

>   H-8.3 *Consistency Condition.* Every logically consistent obser-
>   vation report is logically compatible with the class of all the
>   hypotheses which it confirms.[6]

This condition, like the entailment condition, is suitable for the absolute concept of confirmation, but not for the relevance concept. For, although no two incompatible hypotheses can have high degrees of confirmation on the same body of evidence, an observation report can be positively relevant to a number of different and incompatible hypotheses, provided that none of them has too high a prior degree of confirmation on the background evidence e. This happens typically when a given observation is compatible with a number of incompatible hypotheses—when, for example, a given bit of quantitative data fits several possible curves.

The remaining condition Hempel wished to adopt is as follows:

>   H-8.2 *Consequence Condition.* If an observation report confirms
>   every one of a class k of sentences, then it also confirms
>   any sentence which is a logical consequence of k.[7]

It will suffice to look at two conditions that follow from it:[8]

>   H-8.21 *Special Consequence Condition.* If an observation report
>   confirms a hypothesis h, then it also confirms every conse-
>   quence of h.
>   H-8.22 *Equivalence Condition.* If an observation report confirms
>   a hypothesis h, then it also confirms every consequence of
> h.

The equivalence condition must hold for both concepts of confir-
mation. Within the formal calculus of probability (which Carnap's concept of degree of confirmation satisfies) we can show that, if h is equivalent to h', then $c(h,e) = c(h',e)$, for any evidence e whatever.

[6] Ibid., p. 33. [p. 37 this vol.].
[7] Ibid., p. 31. [p. 35 this vol.].
[8] Ibid.

Thus, if h has a high degree of confirmation on $e.i$, h' does also. Likewise, if i increases the degree of confirmation of h, it will also increase the degree of confirmation of h'.

The special consequence condition is easily shown to be valid for the nonrelevance concept of confirmation. If h entails k, then $c(k,e) \geq c(h,e)$; hence, if $c(h,e.i) > b$, then $c(k,e.i) > b$. But here, I think, our intuitions mislead us most seductively. It turns out, as Carnap has shown with great clarity, that the special consequence condition fails for the relevance concept of confirmation. It is entirely possible for i to be positively relevant to h without being positively relevant to some logical consequence k. We shall return in section 3 to a more detailed discussion of this fact.

The net result of the confusion of the two different concepts is that obviously correct statements about confirmation relations of one type are laid down as conditions of adequacy for explications of concepts of the other type, where, upon examination, they turn out to be clearly unsatisfactory. Carnap showed how the entailment condition could be modified to make it acceptable as a condition of adequacy.[9] As long as we are dealing with the relevance concept of confirmation, it looks as if the consistency condition should simply be abandoned. The equivalence condition appears to be acceptable as it stands. The special consequence condition, surprisingly enough, cannot be retained.

Hempel tried to lay down conditions for a nonquantitative concept of confirmation, and we have seen some of the troubles he encountered. After careful investigation of this problem, Carnap came to the conclusion that it is best to establish a quantitative concept of degree of confirmation and then to make the definition of the two nonquantitative concepts dependent upon it, as we have done in D1 and D2 above.[10] Given a quantitative concept and the two definitions, there is no need for conditions of adequacy like those advanced by Hempel. The nonquantitative concepts of confirmation are fully determined by those definitions, but we may, if we wish, see what general conditions such as H-8.1, H-8.2, H-8.21, H-8.22, H-8.3 are satisfied. In a 1964 postscript to the earlier article, Hempel expresses general agreement with this approach of Carnap.[11] Yet, he does so with such equanimity that I wonder whether he, as well as many others, recognize the profound and far-reaching consequences of the fact that the relevance concept of confirmation fails to satisfy the special consequence condition and other closely related conditions (which will be discussed in section 3).

[9] Carnap, *Logical Foundations,* p. 473. [p. 86 this vol.].
[10] Ibid., p. 467. [cf. p. 80 this vol.].
[11] Hempel, *Aspects of Scientific Explanation*, p. 50.

2. CARNAP AND POPPER

Once the fundamental ambiguity of the term "confirm" has been pointed out, we might suppose that reasonably well-informed authors could easily avoid confusing the two senses. Ironically, even Carnap himself did not remain entirely free from this fault. In the preface to the second edition of *Logical Foundations of Probability* (1962), he acknowledges that the first edition was not completely unambiguous. In the new preface, he attempts to straighten out the difficulty.

In the first edition, Carnap had distinguished a triplet of confirmation concepts:[12]

1. Classificatory—*e* confirms *h*.
2. Comparative—*e* confirms *h* more than *e'* confirms *h'*.
3. Quantitative—the degree of confirmation of *h* on *e* is *u*

In the second edition, he sees the need for two such triplets of concepts.[13] For this purpose, he begins by distinguishing what he calls "concepts of firmness" and "concepts of increase of firmness". The concept of confirmation we defined above in D1, which was called an "absolute" concept, falls under the heading "concepts of firmness". The concept of confirmation we defined in D2, and called a "relevance" concept, falls under the heading "concepts of increase of firmness". Under each of these headings, Carnap sets out a triplet of classificatory, comparative, and quantitative concepts:

I. Three Concepts of Firmness

I-1. *h* is firm on the basis of *e*. $c(h,e) > b$, where b is
                                                    some fixed number.
I-2. *h* is firmer on *e* than is *h'* on *e'*. $c(h,e) > c(h',e')$.
I-3. The degree of firmness of *h* on *e* is *u*. $c(h,e) = u$.

To deal with the concepts of increase of firmness, Carnap introduces a simple relevance measure $D(h,i) =_{df} c(h,i) - c(h,t)$. This is a measure of what might be called "initial relevance", where the tautological evidence *t* serves as background evidence. The second triplet of concepts is given as follows:

II. Three Concepts of Increase of Firmness

II-1. *h* is made firmer by *i*. $D(h,i) > 0$.
II-2. The increase in firmness of *h* due to *i* is greater than the
      increase of firmness of *h'* due to *i'*. $D(h,i) > D(h',i')$.

---

[12] Carnap, *Logical Foundations*, sec. 8.
[13] Carnap, *Logical Foundations*, 2nd edn, pp. xv-xvi.

II-3. The amount of increase of firmness of h due to i is w.

$$D(h,i) = w.$$

Given the foregoing arrays of concepts, any temptation we might have had to identify the absolute (nonrelevance) concept of confirmation with the original classificatory concept, and to identify the relevance concept of confirmation with the original comparative concept, while distinguishing both from the original quantitative concept of degree of confirmation, can be seen to be quite mistaken. What we defined above in D1 as the absolute concept of confirmation is clearly seen to coincide with Carnap's new classificatory concept I-1, while our relevance concept of confirmation defined in D2 obviously coincides with Carnap's other new classificatory concept II-1. Carnap's familiar concept of degree of confirmation (probability$_1$) is obviously his quantitative concept of firmness I-3, while his new quantitative concept II-3 coincides with the concept of degree of relevance. Although we shall not have much occasion to deal with the comparative concepts, it is perhaps worth mentioning that the new comparative concept II-2 has an important use. When we compare the strengths of different tests of the same hypothesis we frequently have occasion to say that a test that yields evidence i is better than a test that yields evidence i'; sometimes, at least, this means that i is more relevant to h than is i'—i.e., the finding i would increase the degree of confirmation of h by a greater amount than would the finding i'.

It is useful to have a more general measure of relevance than the measure D of initial relevance. We therefore define the relevance of evidence i to hypothesis h on (in the presence of) background evidence e as follows:[14]

D3. $R(i,h,e) = c(h,e.i) - c(h,e)$.

Then we can say:

D4. i is positively relevant to h on $e =_{df} R(i,h,e) > 0$.
   i is negatively relevant to h on $e =_{df} R(i,h,e) < 0$.
   i is irrelevant to h on $e =_{df} R(i,h,e) = 0$.

Hence, the classificatory concept of confirmation in the relevance sense can be defined by the condition $R(i,h,e) > 0$. Using these relevance

---

[14] Carnap introduces the simple initial relevance measure D for temporary heuristic purposes in the preface to the second edition. In ch. 6 he discusses both our relevance measure R and Keynes's relevance quotient $c(h,e.i)/c(h,e)$, but for his own technical purposes he adopts a more complicated relevance measure $r(i,h,e)$. For purposes of this paper, I prefer the simpler and more intuitive measure R, which serves as well as Carnap's measure r in the present context. Since this measure differs from that used by Carnap in ch. 6 of *Logical Foundations*, I use a capital "R" to distinguish it from Carnap's lower-case symbol.

concepts, we can define a set of concepts of confirmation in the relevance sense as follows:

> D5. i confirms h given e =$_{df}$ i is positively relevant to h on e.
>
> i disconfirms h given e =$_{df}$ i is negatively relevant to h on e.
>
> i neither confirms nor disconfirms h given e =$_{df}$ i is irrelevant to h on e.

Having delineated his two triplets of concepts, Carnap then acknowledges that his original triplet in the first edition was a mixture of concepts of the two types; in particular, he had adopted the classificatory concept of increase of firmness II-1, along with the comparative and quantitative concepts of firmness I-2 and I-3. This fact, plus some misleading informal remarks about these concepts, led to serious confusion.[15]

As Carnap further acknowledges, Popper called attention to these difficulties, but he fell victim to them as well.[16] By equivocating on the admittedly ambiguous concept of confirmation, he claimed to have derived a contradiction within Carnap's formal theory of probability$_1$. He offers the following example:

> Consider the next throw with a homogeneous die. Let x be the statement 'six will turn up'; let y be its negation, that is to say, let $y = \bar{x}$; and let z be the information 'an even number will turn up'.
>
> We have the following absolute probabilities:
>
> $p(x) = 1/6; p(y) = 5/6; p(z) = 1/2.$
>
> Moreover, we have the following relative probabilities:
>
> $p(x,z) = 1/3; p(y,z) = 2/3.$
>
> We see that x is supported by the information z, for z raises the probability of x from 1/6 to 2/6 = 1/3. We also see that y is undermined by z, for z lowers the probability of y by the same amount from 5/6 to 4/6 = 2/3. Nevertheless, we have $p(x,z) < p(y,z)$.[17]

From this example, Popper quite correctly draws the conclusion that there are statements x, y, and z such that z confirms x, z disconfirms y, and y has a higher degree of confirmation on z than x has. As Popper points out quite clearly, this result would be logically inconsistent *if* we were to take the term "confirm" in its nonrelevance sense. It would be self-contradictory to say,

> The degree of confirmation of x on z is high, the degree of confirmation of y on z is not high, and the degree of confirmation of y on z is higher than the degree of confirmation of x on z.

[15] Carnap, *Logical Foundations*, 2nd edn, pp. xvii–xix.
[16] Ibid., p. xix, fn.
[17] Popper, *The Logic of Scientific Discovery*, p. 390.

The example, of course, justifies no such statement; there is no way to pick the number b employed by Carnap in his definition of confirmation in the (firmness) sense I-1 according to which we could say that the degree of confirmation of x on z is greater than b and the degree of confirmation of y on z is not greater than b. The proper formulation of the situation is:

> The evidence z is positively relevant to x, the evidence z is negatively relevant to y, and the degree of confirmation of x on z is less than the degree of confirmation of y on z.

There is nothing even slightly paradoxical about this statement.

Popper's example shows clearly the danger of equivocating between the two concepts of confirmation, but it certainly does not show any inherent defect in Carnap's system of inductive logic, for this system contains both degree of confirmation $c(h,e)$ and degree of relevance $r(i,h,e)$. The latter is clearly and unambiguously defined in terms of the former, and there are no grounds for confusing them.[18] The example shows, however, the importance of exercising great care in our use of English language expressions in talking about these exact concepts.

3. THE VAGARIES OF RELEVANCE

It can be soundly urged, I believe, that the verb "to confirm" is used more frequently in its relevance sense than in the absolute sense. When we say that a test confirmed a hypothesis, we would normally be taken to mean that the result was positively relevant to the hypothesis. When we say that positive instances are confirming instances, it seems that we are characterizing confirming evidence as evidence that is positively relevant to the hypothesis in question. If we say that several investigators independently confirmed some hypothesis, it would seem sensible to understand that each of them had found positively relevant evidence. There is no need to belabour this point. Let us simply assert that the term "confirm" is often used in its relevance sense, and we wish to investigate some of the properties of this concept. In other words, let us agree for now to use the term "confirm" solely in its relevance sense (unless some explicit qualification indicates otherwise), and see what we will be committed to.

It would be easy to suppose that, once we are clear on the two senses of the term *confirm* and once we resolve to use it in only one of these senses in a given context, it would be a simple matter to tidy up our usage enough to avoid such nasty equivocations as we have already

---

[18] Carnap, *Logical Foundations*, sec. 67.

discussed. This is not the case, I fear. For, as Carnap has shown by means of simple examples and elegant arguments, the relevance concept of confirmation has some highly counterintuitive properties.

Suppose, for instance, that two scientists are interested in the same hypothesis h, and they go off to their separate laboratories to perform tests of that hypothesis. The tests yield two positive results, i and j. Each of the evidence statements is positively relevant to h in the presence of common background information e. Each scientist happily reports his positive finding to the other. Can they now safely conclude that the net result of both tests is a confirmation of h? The answer, amazingly, is no! As Carnap has shown, two separate items of evidence can each be positively relevant to a hypothesis, while their conjunction is negative to that very same hypothesis. He offers Example 1.[19]

Example 1. Let the prior evidence e contain the following information. Ten chess players participate in a chess tournament in New York City; some of them are local people, some from out of town; some are junior players, some are seniors; some are men (M), some are women (W). Their distribution is known to be as follows:

	Local players	Out-of-towners
Juniors	M, W, W	M, M
Seniors	M, M	W, W, W

Table 1

Furthermore, the evidence e is supposed to be such that on its basis each of the ten players has an equal chance of becoming the winner, hence $1/10$ . . . It is assumed that in each case [of evidence that certain players have been eliminated] the remaining players have equal chances of winning.

Let h be the hypothesis that a man wins. Let i be the evidence that a local player wins; let j be the evidence that a junior wins. Using the equi-probability information embodied in the background evidence e, we can read the following values directly from Table 1:

$$\begin{aligned}
c(h,e) &= 1/2 & c(h,e.i) &= 3/5 & R(i,h,e) &= 1/10 \\
& & c(h,e.j) &= 3/5 & R(j,h,e) &= 1/10 \\
& & c(h,e.i.j) &= 1/3 & R(i.j,h,e) &= -1/6
\end{aligned}$$

Thus, i and j are each positively relevant to h, while the conjunction $i.j$ is negatively relevant to h. In other words, i confirms h and j confirms h but $i.j$ disconfirms h.

The set-up of Example 1 can be used to show that a given piece

[19] Ibid., pp. 382–3. Somewhat paraphrased for brevity.

of evidence may confirm each of two hypotheses individually, while that same evidence disconfirms their conjunction.[20]

Example 2. Let the evidence e be the same as in example 1. Let h be the hypothesis that a local player wins; let k be the hypothesis that a junior wins. Let i be evidence stating that a man wins. The following values can be read directly from Table 1:

$$c(h,e) \quad = 1/2 \quad c(h,e.i) \quad = 3/5 \ \mathrm{R}(i,h,e) \quad = \quad 1/10$$
$$c(k,e) \quad = 1/2 \quad c(k,e.i) \quad = 3/5 \ \mathrm{R}(i,k,e) \quad = \quad 1/10$$
$$c(h.k,e) = 3/10 \ c(h.k,e.i) = 1/5 \ \mathrm{R}(i,h.k,e) = -1/10$$

Thus, i confirms h and i confirms k, but i disconfirms $h.k$.

In the light of this possibility it might transpire that a scientist has evidence that supports the hypothesis that there is gravitational attraction between any pair of bodies when at least one is of astronomical dimensions and the hypothesis of gravitational attraction between bodies when both are of terrestrial dimensions, but which disconfirms the law of universal gravitation! In the next section we shall see that this possibility has interesting philosophical consequences.

A further use of the same situation enables us to show that evidence can be positive to each of two hypotheses, and nevertheless negative to their disjunction.[21]

Example 3. Let the evidence e be the same as in Example 1. Let h be the hypothesis that an out-of-towner wins; let k be the hypothesis that a senior wins. Let i be evidence stating that a woman wins. The following values can be read directly from Table 1:

$$c(h,e) \qquad = 1/2 \qquad c(h,e.i) \qquad = 3/5 \qquad \mathrm{R}(i,h,e) \qquad = \quad 1/10$$
$$c(k,e) \qquad = 1/2 \qquad c(k,e.i) \qquad = 3/5 \qquad \mathrm{R}(i,k,e) \qquad = \quad 1/10$$
$$c(h \lor k,e) = 7/10 \quad c(h \lor k,e.i) = 3/5 \quad \mathrm{R}(i,h \lor k,e) = -1/10$$

Thus, i confirms h and i confirms k, but i nevertheless disconfirms $h \lor k$.

Imagine the following situation:[22] a medical researcher finds evidence confirming the hypothesis that Jones is suffering from viral pneumonia and also confirming the hypothesis that Jones is suffering from bacterial pneumonia—yet this very same evidence disconfirms the hypothesis that Jones has pneumonia! It is difficult to entertain such a state of affairs, even as an abstract possibility.

---

[20] Ibid., pp. 394–5.
[21] Ibid., p. 384.
[22] This example is adapted from ibid., p. 367.

These three examples illustrate a few members of a large series of severely counterintuitive situations that can be realized:

    i.   Each of two evidence statements may confirm a hypothesis, while their conjunction disconfirms it. (Example 1.)

    ii. Each of two evidence statements may confirm a hypothesis, while their disjunction disconfirms it. (Example 2a, Carnap, *Logical Foundations*, p. 384.)

    iii. A piece of evidence may confirm each of two hypotheses, while it disconfirms their conjunction. (Example 2.)

    iv. A piece of evidence may confirm each of two hypotheses, while it disconfirms their disjunction. (Example 3.)

This list may be continued by systematically interchanging positive relevance (confirmation) and negative relevance (disconfirmation) throughout the preceding statements. Moreover, a large number of similar possibilities obtain if irrelevance is combined with positive or negative relevance. Carnap presents a systematic inventory of all of these possible relevance situations.[23]

In section 1, we mentioned that Hempel's special consequence condition does not hold for the relevance concept of confirmation. This fact immediately becomes apparent upon examination of statement iv above. Since h entails $h \lor k$, and since i may confirm h while disconfirming $h \lor k$, we have an instance in which evidence confirms a statement but fails to confirm one of its logical consequences. Statement ii, incidentally, shows that the converse consequence condition, which Hempel discusses but does not adopt,[24] also fails for the relevance concept of confirmation. Since $h.k$ entails h, and since i may confirm h without confirming $h.k$, we have an instance in which evidence confirms a hypothesis without confirming at least one statement from which that hypothesis follows. The failure of the special consequence condition and the converse consequence condition appears very mild when compared with the much stronger results i-iv, and analogous ones. While one might, without feeling too queasy, give up the special consequence condition—the converse consequence condition being unsatisfactory on the basis of much more immediate and obvious considerations—it is much harder to swallow possibilities like i-iv without severe indigestion.

4. DUHEM AND RELEVANCE

According to a crude account of scientific method, the testing of a hypothesis consists in deducing observational consequences and seeing

[23] Ibid., secs. 69, 71.
[24] Hempel, *Aspects of Scientific Explanation*, pp. 32–3. [p. 36 this vol.].

whether or not the facts are as predicted. If the prediction is fulfilled we have a positive instance; if the prediction is false the result is a negative instance. There is a basic asymmetry between verification and falsification. If, from hypothesis h, an observational consequence o can be deduced, then the occurrence of a fact o' that is incompatible with o (o' entails $\sim o$) enables us to infer the falsity of h by good old modus tollens. If, however, we find the derived observational prediction fulfilled, we still cannot deduce the truth of h, for to do so would involve the fallacy of affirming the consequent.

There are many grounds for charging that the foregoing account is a gross oversimplification. One of the most familiar, which was emphasized by Duhem, points out that hypotheses are seldom, if ever, tested in isolation; instead, auxiliary hypotheses a are normally required as additional premises to make it possible to deduce observational consequences from the hypothesis h that is being tested. Hence, evidence o' (incompatible with o) does not entail the falsity of h, but only the falsity of the conjunction $h.a$. There are no deductive grounds on which we can say that h rather than a is the member of the conjunction that has been falsified by the negative outcome. To whatever extent auxiliary hypotheses are invoked in the deduction of the observational consequence, to that extent the alleged deductive asymmetry of verification and falsification is untenable.

At this point, a clear warning should be flashed, for we recall the strange things that happen when conjunctions of hypotheses are considered. Example 2 of the previous section showed that evidence that disconfirms a conjunction $h.a$ can nevertheless separately confirm each of the conjuncts. Is it possible that a *negative* result of a test of the hypothesis h, in which auxiliary hypotheses a were also involved, could result in the *confirmation* of the hypothesis of interest h and in a *confirmation* of the auxiliary hypotheses a as well?

It might be objected, at this point, that in the Duhemian situation o' is not merely negatively relevant to $h.a$; rather,

(1) o' entails $\sim (h.a)$.

This objection, though not quite accurate, raises a crucial question. Its inaccuracy lies in the fact that h and a together do not normally entail o'; in the usual situation some initial conditions are required along with the main hypothesis and the auxiliary hypotheses. If this is the case, condition (1) does not obtain. We can deal with this trivial objection to (1), however, by saying that, since the initial conditions are established by observation, they are to be taken as part of the background evidence e which figures in all of our previous investigations of relevance relations. Thus, we can assert that, in the presence of background evidence e, o can be derived from $h.a$. This allows us to reinstate condition (1).

Unfortunately, condition (1) is of no help to us. Consider the situation in Example 4.

Example 4. The evidence e contains the same equiprobability assumptions as the evidence in Example 1, except for the fact that the distribution of players is as indicated in the following table:

	Local players	Out-of-towners
Juniors	W	M, M
Seniors	M, M	M, W, W, W, W

Table 2

Let h be the hypothesis that a local player wins; let k be the hypothesis that a junior wins. Let i be evidence stating that a man wins. In this case, condition (1) is satisfied; the evidence i is logically incompatible with the conjunction $h.k$. The following values can be read directly from the Table:

$c(h,e)$ = 0.3	$c(h,e.i)$ = 0.4	$R(i,h,e)$ = 0.1
$c(k,e)$ = 0.3	$c(k,e.i)$ = 0.4	$R(i,k,e)$ = 0.1
$c(h.k,e)$ = 0.1	$c(h.k,e.i)$ = 0	$R(i,h.k,e)$ = −0.1

This example shows that evidence i, even though it conclusively refutes the conjunction $h.k$, nevertheless confirms both h and k taken individually.

Here is the situation. Scientist Smith comes home late at night after a hard day at the lab. "How did your work go today, dear?" asks his wife.

"Well, you know the Smith hypothesis, h_8, on which I have staked my entire scientific reputation? And you know the experiment I was running today to test my hypothesis? Well, the result was negative."

"Oh, dear, what a shame! Now you have to give up your hypothesis and watch your entire reputation go down the drain!"

"Not at all. In order to carry out the test, I had to make use of some auxiliary hypotheses."

"Oh, what a relief—saved by Duhem! Your hypothesis wasn't refuted after all," says the philosophical Mrs. Smith.

"Better than that," Smith continues, "I actually confirmed the Smith hypothesis."

"Why that's wonderful, dear," replies Mrs. Smith, "you found you could reject an auxiliary hypothesis, and that in so doing, you could establish the fact that the test actually confirmed your hypothesis? How ingenious!"

"No," Smith continues, "it's even better. I found I had confirmed the auxiliary hypotheses as well!"

This is the Duhemian thesis reinforced with a vengeance. Not only does a negative test result fail to refute the test hypothesis conclusively—it may end up confirming both the test hypothesis and the auxiliary hypotheses as well.

It is very tempting to suppose that much of the difficulty might be averted if only we could have sufficient confidence in our auxiliary hypotheses. If a medical researcher has a hypothesis about a disease which entails the presence of a certain micro-organism in the blood of our favourite victim Jones, it would be outrageous for him to call into question the laws of optics as applied to microscopes as a way of explaining failure to find the bacterium. If the auxiliary hypotheses are well enough established beforehand, we seem to know where to lay the blame when our observational predictions go wrong. The question is how to establish the auxiliary hypotheses in the first place, for if the Duhemian is right, no hypotheses are ever tested in isolation. To test any hypothesis, according to this view, it is necessary to utilize auxiliary hypotheses; consequently, to establish our auxiliary hypotheses a for use in the tests of h, we would need some other auxiliary hypotheses a' to carry out the tests of a. A vicious regress threatens.

A more contextual approach might be tried.[25] Suppose that a has been used repeatedly as an auxiliary hypothesis in the *successful* testing of other hypothesis j, k, l, etc. Suppose, that is, that the conjunctions $j.a$, $k.a$, $l.a$, etc., have been tested and repeatedly confirmed—i.e., all test results have been positively relevant instances. Can we say that a has been highly confirmed as a result of all of these successes? Initially, we might have been tempted to draw the affirmative conclusion, but by now we know better. Examples similar to those of the previous section can easily be found to show that evidence positively relevant to a conjunction of two hypotheses can nevertheless be negative to each conjunct.[26] It is therefore logically possible for each confirmation of a conjunction containing a to constitute a disconfirmation of a—and indeed a disconfirmation of the other conjunct as well in each such case.

[25] This paper was motivated by Grünbaum's questions concerning this approach. See his "Falsifiability and Rationality" to be published in a volume edited by Joseph J. Kockelmans (proceedings of an international conference held at Pennsylvania State University).

[26] Carnap, *Logical Foundations*, pp. 394–5, 3b, is just such an example.

There is one important restriction that applies to the case in which new observational evidence refutes a conjunction of two hypotheses, namely, hypotheses that are incompatible on evidence $e.i$ can have, at most, probabilities that add to one. If $e.i$ entails $\sim (h.k)$

$$c(h,e.i) + c(k,e.i) \leqslant 1.$$

Since we are interested in the case in which i is positively relevant to both h and k, these hypotheses must also satisfy the condition

$$c(h,e) + c(k,e) < 1.$$

We have here, incidentally, what remains of the asymmetry between confirmation and refutation. If evidence i refutes the conjunction $h.k$, that fact places an upper limit on the sum of the probabilities of h and k relative to $e.i$. If, however, evidence i confirms a conjunction $h.k$ while disconfirming each of the conjuncts, there is no lower bound (other than zero) on the sum of their degrees of confirmation on i.

In this connection, let us recall our ingenious scientist Smith, who turned a refuting test result into a positive confirmation of both his pet hypothesis h_8 and his auxiliary hypotheses a. We see that he must have been working with a test hypothesis or auxiliaries (or both) which had rather low probabilities. We might well question the legitimacy of using hypotheses with degrees of confirmation appreciably less than one as auxiliary hypotheses. If Smith's auxiliairies a had decent degrees of confirmation, his own hypothesis h_8 must have been quite improbable. His clever wife might have made some choice remarks about his staking an entire reputation on so improbable a hypothesis. But I should not get carried away with dramatic license. If we eliminate all the unnecessary remarks about staking his reputation on h_8, and regard it rather as a hypothesis he finds interesting, then its initial improbability may be no ground for objection. Perhaps every interesting general scientific hypothesis starts its career with a very low prior probability. Knowing, as we do, that a positively relevant instance may disconfirm both our test hypothesis and our auxiliairies, while a negative instance may confirm them both, there remains a serious, and as yet unanswered, question how any hypothesis ever can become either reasonably well confirmed or reasonably conclusively disconfirmed (in the absolute sense). It obviously is still an open question how we could ever get any well-confirmed hypotheses to serve as auxiliaries for the purpose of testing other hypotheses.

Suppose, nevertheless, that we have a hypothesis h to test and some auxiliairies a that will be employed in conducting the test and that somehow we have ascertained that a has a higher prior confirmation than h on the initial evidence e:

$c(a,e) > c(h,e)$.

Suppose, further, that as the result of the test we obtain negative evidence o' which refutes the conjunction $h.a$, but which confirms both h and a. Thus, o' entails $\sim (h.a)$ and

$c(h,e.o') > c(h,e)$ $c(a,e.o') > c(a,e)$.

We have already seen that this can happen (example 4). But now we ask the further question, is it possible that the posterior confirmation of h is greater than the posterior confirmation of a? In other words, can the negative evidence o' confirm both conjuncts and do so in a way that reverses the relation between h and a? A simple example will show that the answer is affirmative.

Example 5. The Department of History and Philosophy of Science at Polly Tech had two openings, one in history of science and the other in philosophy of science. Among the 1000 applicants for the position in history, 100 were women. Among the 2000 applicants for the position in philosophy, 100 were women. Let h be the hypothesis that the history job was filled by a woman; let k be the hypothesis that the philosophy job was filled by a woman. Since both selections were made by the use of a fair lottery device belonging to the inductive logician in the department,

$c(h,e) = .1$
$c(k,e) = .05$
$c(h,e) > c(k,e)$.

Let i be the evidence that the two new appointees were discovered engaging in heterosexual intercourse with each other in the office of the historian. It follows at once that

$c(h.k,e.i) = 0$
$c(h,e.i) + c(k,e.i) = 1$

i.e., one appointee was a woman and the other a man, but we do not know which is which. Since it is considerably more probable, let us assume, that the office used was that of the male celebrant; we assign the values

$c(h,e.i) = .2$ $c(k,e.i) = .8$

with the result that

$$c(h,e.i) < c(k,e.i).$$

This illustrates the possibility of a reversal of the comparative relation between the test hypothesis and auxiliaries as a result of refuting evidence. It shows that a's initial superiority to h is no assurance that it will still be so subsequent to the refuting evidence. If, prior to the negative test result, we had to choose between h and a, we would have preferred a, but after the negative outcome, h is preferable to a.

There is one significant constraint that must be fulfilled if this reversal is to occur in the stated circumstances. If our auxiliary hypotheses a are initially better confirmed than our test hypothesis h, and if the conjunction $h.a$ is refuted by evidence o' that is positively relevant to both h and a, and if the posterior confirmation of h is greater than the posterior confirmation of a, then the prior confirmation of a must have been less than $1/2$. For,

$$c(h,e.o') + c(a,e.o') \leqslant 1$$

and

$$c(h,e.o') > c(a,e.o').$$

Hence,

$$c(a,e.o') < 1/2.$$

Moreover,

$$c(a,e) < c(a,e.o').$$

Therefore,

$$c(a,e) < 1/2.$$

It follows that if a is initially more. probable than h and also initially more probable than its own negation $\sim a$, then it is impossible for a refuting instance o' which confirms both h and a to render h more probable than a. Perhaps that is some comfort. If our auxiliaries are more probable than not, and if they are better established before the test than our test hypothesis h, then a refuting test outcome which confirms both h and a cannot make h preferable to a.

But this is not really the tough case. The most serious problem is whether a refutation of the conjunction $h.a$ can render h more probable than a by being positively relevant to h and negatively relevant to a, even when a is initially *much* more highly confirmed than h. You will readily conclude that this is possible; after all of the weird outcomes we have discussed, this situation seems quite prosaic. Consider the following example:

Example 6. Let

e = Brown is an adult American male
h = Brown is a Roman Catholic
k = Brown is married

and suppose the following degrees of confirmation to obtain:

$c(h,e) = .3$
$c(k,e) = .8$
$c(h.k,e) = .2.$

Let i be the information that Brown is a priest—that is, an ordained clergyman of the Roman Catholic, Episcopal, or Eastern Orthodox church. Clearly, i refutes the conjunction $h.k$, so

$c(h.k,e.i) = 0.$

Since the overwhelming majority of priests in America are Roman Catholic, let us assume that

$c(h,e.i) = .9$

and since some, but not all, non-Roman Catholic priests marry, let

$c(k,e.i) = .05.$

We see that i is strongly relevant to both h and k; in particular, it is positively relevant to h and negatively relevant to k. Moreover, while k has a much higher degree of confirmation than h relative to the prior evidence $e,$ h has a much higher degree of confirmation than k on the posterior evidence $e.i.$ Thus, the refuting evidence serves to reverse the preferability relation between h and k.

. . .

5. ANALYSIS OF THE ANOMALIES

There is, of course, a striking contrast between the "hypotheses" and "evidence" involved in our contrived examples, on the one hand, and the genuine hypotheses and evidence to be found in actual scientific practice, on the other. This observation might easily lead to the charge that the foregoing discussion is not pertinent to the logic of actual scientific confirmation, as opposed to the theory of confirmation constructed by Carnap on highly artificial and oversimplified languages.

This irrelevance is demonstrated by the fact, so the objection might continue, that the kinds of problems and difficulties we have been discussing simply do not arise when real scientists test serious scientific hypotheses.

This objection, it seems to me, is wide of the mark. I am prepared to grant that such weird possibilities as we discussed in previous sections do not arise in scientific practice; at least, I have no concrete cases from the current or past history of science to offer as examples of them. This is, however, a statement of the problem rather than a solution. Carnap has provided a number of examples that, on the surface at least, seem to make a shambles of confirmation; why do they not also make a shambles of science itself? There can be no question that, for example, one statement can confirm each of two other statements separately while at the same time disconfirming their disjunction or conjunction. If that sort of phenomenon never occurs in actual scientific testing, it must be because we know something more about our evidence and hypotheses than merely that the evidence confirms the hypotheses. The problem is to determine the additional factors in the actual situation that block the strange results we can construct in the artificial case. In this section, I shall try to give some indications of what seems to be involved.

The crux of the situation seems to be the fact that we have said very little when we have stated merely that a hypothesis h has been confirmed by evidence i. This statement means, of course, that i raises the degree of confirmation of h, but that *in itself* provides very little information. It is by virtue of this paucity of content that we can go on and say that this same evidence i confirms hypothesis k as well, without being justified in saying anything about the effect of i upon the disjunction or the conjunction of h with k.

This state of affairs seems strange to intuitions that have been thoroughly conditioned on the extensional relations of truth-functional logic. Probabilities are not extensional in the same way. Given the truth-values of h and k we can immediately ascertain the truth-values of the disjunction and the conjunction. The degrees of confirmation ("probability values") of h and k do not, however, determine the degree of confirmation of either the disjunction or the conjunction. This fact follows immediately from the addition and multiplication rules of the probability calculus:

(2) $c(h \vee k, e) = c(h, e) + c(k, e) - c(h.k, e)$
(3) $c(h.k, e) = c(h, e) \times c(k, h.e) = c(k, e) \times c(h, k.e)$.

To determine the probability of the disjunction, we need, in addition to the values of the probabilities of the disjuncts, the probability of the conjunction. The disjunctive probability is the sum of the probabilities of the two disjuncts if they are mutually incompatible in the presence of evidence e, in which case $c(h.k,e) = 0$.[27] The probability of the conjunction, in turn, depends upon the probability of one of the conjuncts alone and the conditional probability of the other conjunct given the first.[28] If

(4) $c(k,h.e) = c(k,e)$

the multiplication rule assumes the special form

(5) $c(h.k,e) = c(h,e) \times c(k,e)$

in which case the probability of the conjunction is simply the product of the probabilities of the two conjuncts. When condition (4) is fulfilled, h and k are said to be independent of one another.[29] Independence, as thus defined, is obviously a relevance concept, for (4) is equivalent to the statement that h is irrelevant to k, i.e, $R(h,k,e) = 0$.

We can now see why strange things happen with regard to confirmation in the relevance sense. If the hypotheses h and k are mutually exclusive in the presence of e (and a fortiori in the presence of $e.i$), then

(6) $c(h \lor k,e) = c(h,e) + c(k,e)$
(7) $c(h \lor k,e.i) = c(h,e.i) + c(k,e.i)$

so that if

(8) $c(h,e.i) > c(h,e)$ and $c(k,e.i) > c(k,e)$

it follows immediately that

(9) $c(h \lor k,e.i) > c(h \lor k,e)$.

Hence, in this special case, if i confirms h and i confirms k, then i must confirm their disjunction. This results from the fact that the relation between h and k is the same in the presence of $e.i$ as it is in the presence of e alone.[30]

[27] The condition $c(h.k,e) = 0$ is obviously sufficient to make the probability of the disjunction equal to the sum of the probabilities of the disjuncts, and this is a weaker condition than e entails $\sim (h.k)$. Since the difference between these conditions has no particular import for the discussion of this paper, I shall, in effect, ignore it.

[28] Because of the commutativity of conjunction, it does not matter whether the probability of h conditional only on e or the probability of k conditional only on e is taken. This is shown by the double equality in formula (3).

[29] Independence is a symmetric relation; if h is independent of k then k will be independent of h.

[30] To secure this result it is not necessary that $c(h.k,e) = c(h.k,e.i) = 0$; it is sufficient to have $c(h.k,e) = c(h.k,e.i)$, though obviously this condition is not necessary either.

If, however, h and k are not mutually exclusive on evidence e we must use the general formulas

(10) $c(h \vee k, e) = c(h, e) + c(k, e) - c(h.k, e)$
(11) $c(h \vee k, e.i) = c(h, e.i) + c(k, e.i) - c(h.k, e.i)$.

Now, if it should happen that the evidence i drastically alters the relevance of h to k in just the right way our apparently anomalous results can arise. For then, as we shall see in a moment by way of a concrete (fictitious) example, even though condition (8) obtains—i.e., i confirms h and i confirms k—condition (9) may fail. Thus, if

(12) $c(h.k, e.i) > c(h.k, e)$

it may happen that

(13) $c(h \vee k, e.i) < c(h \vee k, e)$

i.e., i disconfirms $h \vee k$. Let us see how this works.

Example 7. Suppose h says that poor old Jones has bacterial pneumonia, and k says that he has viral pneumonia. I am assuming that these are the only varieties of pneumonia, so that $h \vee k$ says simply that he has pneumonia. Let evidence e contain the results of a superficial diagnosis as well as standard medical background knowledge about the disease, on the basis of which, we can establish degrees of confirmation for h, k, $h.k$, and $h \vee k$. Suppose, moreover, that the probability on e that Jones has both viral and bacterial pneumonia is quite low, that is, that people do not often get them both simultaneously. For the sake of definiteness, let us introduce some numerical values. Suppose that on the basis of the superficial diagnosis it is 98 per cent certain that Jones has one or the other form of pneumonia, but the diagnosis leaves it entirely uncertain which type he has. Suppose, moreover, that on the basis of e there is only a 2 per cent chance that he has both. We have the following values:

$$c(h, e) \quad = .50 \qquad c(k, e) \quad = .50$$
$$c(h \vee k, e) = .98 \qquad c(h.k, e) = .02.$$

These values satisfy the addition formula (2). Suppose, now, that there is a certain test which indicates quite reliably those rare cases in which the subject has both forms of pneumonia. Let i be the statement that this test was administered to Jones with a positive result, and let this result make it 89 per cent certain that Jones has both types. Assume, moreover, that the test rarely yields a positive result if the patient has only one form of pneumonia (i.e., when the positive result occurs for a patient who does not have both types, he usually has neither type). In particular, let

$$c(h,e.i) = .90, \quad c(k,e.i) = .90, \quad c(h.k,e.i) = .89$$

from which it follows that

$$c(h \vee k,e.i) = .91 < c(h \vee k,e) = .98.$$

The test result i thus confirms the hypothesis that Jones has bacterial pneumonia and the hypothesis that Jones has viral pneumonia, but it disconfirms the hypothesis that Jones has pneumonia!

It achieves this feat by greatly increasing the probability that he has both. This increase brings about a sort of clustering together of cases of viral and bacterial pneumonia, concomitantly decreasing the proportion of people with only one of the two types. The effect is easily seen diagrammatically in Figure VI.1. Even though the rectangles in 2-b are larger than those in 2-a, those in 2-b cover a smaller total area

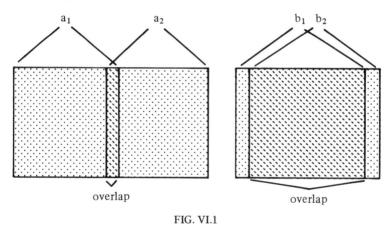

FIG. VI.1

on account of their very much greater degree of overlap. Taking the rectangles to represent the number of cases of each type, we see graphically how the probability of each type of pneumonia can increase simultaneously with a decrease in the overall probability of pneumonia. The evidence i has significantly altered the relevance relation between h and k. Using the multiplication formula (3), we can establish that

$$c(k,h.e) = .04 \qquad c(k,h.e.i) \cong .99$$
$$R(h,k,e) = -0.46 \qquad R(h,k,e.i) \cong .09.$$

In the presence of e alone, h is negatively relevant to k; in the presence of i as well, h becomes positively relevant to k. There is nothing outlandish in such changes of relevance in the light of additional evidence. This case thus exemplifies condition (13) by satisfying condition (12).

A similar analysis enables us to understand how an item of evidence can confirm each of two hypotheses, while disconfirming—indeed, even while conclusively refuting—their conjunction. If hypotheses h and k are independent of each other in the presence of evidence $e.i$ and also in the presence of e alone, the following relations obtain:

(14) $c(h.k,e) = c(h,e) \times c(k,e)$
(15) $c(h.k,e.i) = c(h,e.i) \times c(k,e.i)$

so that if

(16) $c(h,e.i) > c(h,e)$ and $c(k,e.i) > c(k,e)$

it follows immediately that

(17) $c(h.k,e.i) > c(h.k,e)$.

Hence, in this special case, if i confirms h and i confirms k, then i must confirm $h.k$.

A different situation obtains if h and k are not independent on both e and $e.i$; in that case we must use the general formulas

(18) $c(h.k,e) = c(h,e) \times c(k,h.e)$
(19) $c(h.k,e.i) = c(h,e.i) \times c(k,h.e.i)$.

Even given that condition (16) still obtains, so that

(20) $c(k,e.i) > c(k,e)$

it is still possible that

(21) $c(k,h.e.i) < c(k,h.e)$[31]

---

[31] To establish the compatibility of (20) and (21), perhaps a simple example, in addition to the one about to be given in the text, will be helpful. Let

    e = X is a man. i = X is American.
    h = X is very wealthy. k = X vacations in America.

Under this interpretation, relation (20) asserts: It is more probable that an American man vacations in America than it is that a man (regardless of nationality) vacations in America. Under the same interpretation, relation (21) asserts: It is less probable that a very wealthy American man will vacation in America than it is that a very wealthy man (regardless of nationality) will vacation in America. The interpretation of formula (20) seems like an obviously true statement; the interpretation of (21) seems likely to be true owing to the apparent tendency of the very wealthy to vacation abroad. There is, in any case, no contradiction in assuming that every very wealthy American man vacations on which makes it possible, in turn, that

(22) $c(h.k,e.i) < c(h.k,e)$.

Since, according to (20) and (21),

(23) $c(k,e.i) - c(k,e) = R(i,k,e) > 0$
(24) $c(k,h.e.i) - c(k,h.e) = R(i,k,h.e) < 0$

the possibility of i confirming each of two hypotheses while disconfirming their conjunction depends upon the ability of h to make a
difference in the relevance of i to k. We said above, however, that the
occurrence of the strange confirmation phenomena depends upon the
possibility of a change in the relevance of the hypotheses to one
another in the light of new evidence. These characterizations are,
however, equivalent to one another, for the change in relevance of i to
k brought about by h is equal to the change in relevance of h to k
brought about by i, that is,

(25) $R(h,k,e) - R(h,k,e.i) = R(i,k,e) - R(i,k,h.e)$.[32]

We can therefore still maintain that the apparently anomalous confirmation situation arises from the ability of new evidence to change
relations of relevance between the hypotheses, as was suggested by our
initial examination of the general addition and multiplication rules (2)
and (3).

Let us illustrate the conjunctive situation with another concrete
(though fictitious) example.

Example 8. Suppose that the evidence e tells us that two radioactive
atoms A and B decay, each ejecting a particle, and that the probability
in each case is 0.7 that it is an alpha particle, 0.2 that it is a negative
electron, and 0.1 that it is a positive electron (positron). Assume that
the two emissions are independent of one another. Let h be the statement that atom A emits a negative electron; let k be the statement

the French Riviera, while every very wealthy man from any other country
vacations in America.
[32] This equality can easily be shown by writing out the relevance terms
according to their definitions as follows:
$R(h,k,e) =_{df} c(k,h.e) - c(k,e)$
$R(h,k,e.i) =_{df} c(k.h.e.i) - c(k,e.i)$
$R(h,k,e) - R(h,k,e.i) = c(k,h.e) - c(k,e) - c(k,h.e.i) + c(k,e.i)$ (*).
$R(i,k,e) =_{df} c(k,e.i) - c(k,e)$
$R(i,k,h.e) =_{df} c(k,h.e.i) - c(k,h.e)$
$R(i,k,e) - R(i,k,h.e) = c(k,e.i) - c(k,e) - c(k,h.e.i) + c(k,h.e)$ (**).
The right-hand sides of equations (*) and (**) obviously differ only in the
arrangement of terms.

that atom B emits a negative electron. We have the following probabilities:

$$c(h,e) = .2, \quad c(k,e) = .2, \quad c(h.k,e) = .04.$$

Let i be the observation that the two particles approach one another and annihilate upon meeting. Since this occurrence requires the presence of one positive and one negative electron, i entails $\sim (h.k)$. At the same time, since a negative electron must have been present, and since it is just as probable that it was emitted by atom A as atom B, we have

$$c(h,e.i) = .5 \quad \text{and} \quad c(k,e.i) = .5.$$

Hence, evidence i, which refutes the conjunction of the two hypotheses, confirms each one of them.[33]

This occurs because the evidence i makes the hypotheses h and k, which were independent of one another on evidence e alone, into mutually exclusive and exhaustive alternatives, i.e.,

$$c(k,h.e) - c(k,e) = R(h,k,e) = 0$$
$$c(k,h.e.i) - c(k,e.i) = R(h,k,e.i) = -.5.$$

Hypotheses that were totally irrelevant to each other in the absence of evidence i become very strongly relevant in the presence of i. Again, there is nothing especially astonishing about such a change in relevance as a result of new evidence.

Since, as we have seen, all the trouble seems to arise out of a change in the relevance of one hypothesis to the other as a result of new evidence, the most immediate suggestion might be to choose hypotheses h and k whose mutual relevance relations will not change in the light of the new evidence i. We have noted that this constancy of relevance is guaranteed if we begin with hypotheses that are mutually exclusive on evidence e; they remain mutually exclusive on any augmented evidence $e.i$. But when we use the conjunction of a test hypothesis h with auxiliary hypotheses a in order to attempt a test of h, we certainly do not want h and a to be mutually exclusive–that is, we do not want to be in the position of knowing that we must reject our test hypothesis h if we are prepared to accept the auxiliaries a, even without the addition of any new evidence i. It would be more reasonable to insist that the auxiliary hypotheses a should themselves be neutral (irrelevant, independent) to the test hypothesis h. If that

---

[33] This case constitutes a counterexample to the Hempel consistency condition H-8.3 discussed in sec. 2 above.

condition is satisfied, we can accept the auxiliary hypotheses *a* and still keep an entirely open mind regarding *h*. We cannot, however, demand that *h* and *a* remain irrelevant to one another after the new evidence *i* has been obtained. The interesting test situation is that in which, given *e, h.a* entails some observational consequence *o*. If a result *o'* occurs which is incompatible with *o*, then our hypotheses *h* and *a*, which may have been independent in the presence of *e* alone, are mutually exclusive in the light of the new evidence *o'*. Thus, the very design of that kind of test requires hypotheses whose mutual relevance relations are bound to change in the face of new evidence. Several of our examples (5—positions at Polly Tech; 6—celibacy among priests; 8—electron-positron annihilation) show exactly what can happen when new evidence renders independent hypotheses mutually incompatible.

6. CONCLUSIONS

The crude hypothetico-deductive account of scientific inference, according to which hypotheses are confirmed by deducing observational consequences which are then verified by observation, is widely recognized nowadays as an oversimplification (even leaving aside the Duhemian objections). One can hardly improve upon Russell's classic example. From the hypothesis, "Pigs have wings", in conjunction with the observed initial condition, "Pigs are good to eat", we can deduce the consequence, "Some winged things are good to eat." Upon observing that such winged creatures as ducks and turkeys are good to eat, we have a hypothetico-deductive confirmation of the hypothesis, "Pigs have wings".[34] I am inclined to agree with a wide variety of authors who hold that something akin to a Bayesian schema must be involved in the confirmation of scientific hypotheses. If this is correct, it is entirely possible to have positive hypothetico-deductive test results that do not confirm the hypothesis (i.e., that do not add anything to its degree of confirmation on prior evidence). To emphasize this point, Reichenbach aptly described the crude hypothetico-deductive inference as an instance of "the fallacy of incomplete schematization".[35] Recognition of the basic inadequacy of the hypothetico-deductive schema does no violence to the logic of science; it only shows that the methods of science are more complex than this oversimplified schema.

Acknowledging the fact that positive hypothetico-deductive instances may not be confirming instances, I have been discussing the

[34] Bertrand Russell, "Dewey's New 'Logic'", in Paul Arthur Schilpp, ed., *The Philosophy of John Dewey* (New York: Tudor, 1939), p. 149.
[35] Hans Reichenbach, *The Theory of Probability* (Berkeley and Los Angeles: University of California Press, 1949), p. 96.

logic of confirmation—that is, I have been investigating the conclusions that can be drawn from the knowledge that this or that evidence confirms this or that hypothesis. By and large, we have found this logic to be poverty-ridden. Although evidence i confirms hypotheses h and k, we have found that we cannot infer that i confirms $h.k$. Evidence i may in fact confirm $h.k$, but to draw that conclusion from the given premises would be another instance of the fallacy of incomplete schematization. Indeed, our investigations have revealed exactly what is missing in the inference. In addition to knowing that i is positively relevant to h and positively relevant to k, we must know what bearing i has on the relevance of h to k. If this is known quantitatively, and if the degrees of relevance of i to h and to k are also known quantitatively, we can ascertain the relevance of i to $h.k$ and to $h \vee k$. Without this quantitative knowledge, we cannot say much of anything. The moral is simple: even if we base our qualitative concept of confirmation (in the relevance sense) upon a quantitative concept of degree of confirmation, the resulting qualitative concept is not very serviceable. It is too crude a concept, and it doesn't carry enough information to be useful. In order to make any substantial headway in understanding the logic of evidential support of scientific hypotheses, we must be prepared to work with at least crude estimates of quantitative values of degree of confirmation and degree of relevance. Then, in contexts such as the discussion of the Duhemian problem, we must bring the more sophisticated concepts to bear if we hope to achieve greater clarity and avoid logical fallacies. In detailing the shortcomings of the qualitative concept of confirmation, we have, in a way, shown that this sort of confirmation theory is a shambles, but we have done no more violence to the logic of science than to show that it embodies more powerful concepts.

If we are willing, as Carnap has done, to regard degree of confirmation (in the nonrelevance sense) as a probability—that is, as a numerical functor that satisfies the probability calculus—then we can bring the structure of the quantitative probability concept to bear on problems of confirmation. With this apparatus, which gives us the power of Bayes's theorem, we can aspire to a much fuller understanding of relations of confirmation (in both the absolute and the relevance senses).

We can also provide an answer to many who have claimed that confirmation is not a probability concept. Confirmation in the relevance sense is admittedly not a probability; as we have insisted, it is not to be identified with high probability. A quantitative concept of degree of relevance can nevertheless be defined in terms of a concept of degree of confirmation. Degree of relevance, as thus defined, is not a probability; it obviously can take on negative values, which degree of probability cannot do. It is a probability concept, however, in the sense that it is explicitly defined in terms of degree of confirmation which is construed as a probability concept. Thus, even though degree of confirmation in the relevance sense cannot be construed as degree of probability, this fact is no basis for concluding that the concept of probability is an inadequate or inappropriate tool for studying the logic of evidential relations between scientific hypotheses and observational evidence. Moreover, it provides no basis whatever for rejecting the notion that high probabilities as well as high content are what we want our scientific hypotheses eventually to achieve on the basis of experimental testing.

VII
RELEVANT EVIDENCE

CLARK GLYMOUR

SCIENTISTS often claim that an experiment or observation tests certain hypotheses within a complex theory but not others. Relativity theorists, for example, are unanimous in the judgement that measurements of the gravitational red shift do not test the field equations of general relativity; psychoanalysts sometimes complain that experimental tests of Freudian theory are at best tests of rather peripheral hypotheses; astronomers do not regard observations of the positions of a single planet as a test of Kepler's third law, even though those observations may test Kepler's first and second laws. Observations are regarded as relevant to some hypotheses in a theory but not relevant to others in that same theory. There is another kind of scientific judgement that may or may not be related to such judgements of relevance: determinations of the accuracy of the predictions of some theories are not held to provide tests of those theories, or, at least, positive results are not held to support or confirm the theories in question. There are, for example, special relativistic theories of gravity that predict the same phenomena as does general relativity, yet the theories are regarded as mere curiosities.[1]

Prima facie, such judgements either may be conventional and properly explained entirely by sociological factors, or else they may have an underlying rationale and so may be explained as applications of general principles of scientific inference. At least with regard to the first kind of judgements, that is, those which are explicitly judgements of relevance, three different philosophical views are common: (1) the hypothetico-deductive method provides an obvious and well-understood rationale for such discriminations; (2) one or another system of inductive logic provides a rationale for such discriminations;

From *Journal of Philosophy* 72 (1975), pp. 403–20, 424–6. By permission of the author and the Managing Editor, The Journal of Philosophy.

[1] See, for example, Ya. B. Zeldovich and I. D. Novikov, *Relativistic Astrophysics* (Chicago: University Press, 1971), pp. 66–71.

and (3) there is no rationale for the judgements in question, and they must really be entirely the result of convention.[2] All three opinions are, I believe, quite wrong; there are principles that explain and provide a rationale for scientific judgements of relevance, but they are not exactly hypothetico-deductive principles nor are they principles of a probabilistic kind. The principles that provide a rationale for judgements of relevance also provide a partial rationale for other central features of scientific method; notably, they also explain why some theories are not supported by determinations of the accuracy of predictions derived from them. One consequence is that, although theories may be underdetermined by all possible evidence of a specified kind, they need not be so radically or so easily underdetermined as some writers, including myself,[3] have thought.

Consider the first of the above positions: One might suppose that some hypotheses in a theory are, in conjunction with initial conditions, *essential* to the deduction of a sentence that is decidable by experiment or observation. Such hypotheses would then be tested by the appropriate experiments or observations whereas other hypotheses in the theory—those not essential to the deduction—would not be so tested. An account of this kind is satisfactory only if the notion of an "essential" hypothesis can be made precise; and there are good reasons to believe that such a clarification is not trivial and perhaps not even possible, for the difficulties in making precise the notion of essential hypotheses are exactly those which meet any attempt to provide a criterion of cognitive significance of the kind long sought by the positivists. The positivists proposed to divide the predicates of a theory into two disjoint classes, one of which would comprise the "observation terms" of the theory. A sentence in the language of the theory was to be deemed significant if it was testable, and testability was to be defined solely in terms of the consequence relation holding between, on the one hand, sentences, or classes of sentences, in the language of

---

[2] For the third position, see Kaplan, *infra*; the view is certainly suggested by many of Quine's remarks, but I find it nowhere explicitly in his writings. The second position is perhaps the most popular: cf. C. I. Lewis, *An Analysis of Knowledge and Valuation* (La Salle, Ill.: Open Court, 1946); H. Reichenbach, *Experience and Prediction* (Chicago: University Press, 1938); R. C. Jeffrey, "Probability and Falsification", unpublished; I can cite no texts for the first view, but philosophers at the University of Chicago and at Indiana University, where earlier versions of this paper were read, urged it. I am indebted to them for their criticism, and to the National Science Foundation for support of research. I owe special thanks to Richard Jeffrey and to Carl Hempel for reading and criticizing drafts of this essay.
[3] "Theoretical Realism and Theoretical Equivalence", in R. Buck and R. Cohen, eds., *Boston Studies in the Philosophy of Science*, vol. VIII (Boston: Reidel, 1971).

the theory, and, on the other hand, sentences whose only nonlogical terms were observational. Every attempt to provide such a criterion has failed, and the catalogue of failures is familiar.[4] But if we could specify in precise logical terms what it is for a hypothesis, in conjunction with initial conditions, to be essential to the deduction of an experimentally decidable sentence, then taking the observation terms to be those nonlogical terms occurring in the experimentally decidable sentence or in the statement of initial conditions, we would have an account of testability of the kind the positivists required. We must expect that all the technical sorts of objections that told against empiricist criteria of cognitive significance would tell against any attempt to give a hypothetico-deductive account of epistemic relevance. Some of those who were themselves once part of the positivist tradition saw this connection fairly clearly and drew very strong holist conclusions from the failure of significance criteria. David Kaplan[5] reports that when Carnap was presented with a class of counter-examples (devised by Kaplan) to his last attempt at a significance criterion "he reflected that he had been quite wrong for about 30 years, and that his critics who had been arguing that theories must be accepted or rejected as a whole (he mentioned at least Quine and Hempel) were very likely correct." And Hempel, at the end of his negative review of attempts at empiricist significance criteria, proposed that theories be evaluated in terms of their clarity and precision, and by such holist canons as simplicity, explanatory and predictive power, and the extent to which they have, as a whole, been confirmed by experience.

Which brings us to the second position. Hempel's own qualitative theory of confirmation[6] has the property that, if e is an evidence statement and p any sentence, consistent with e, that is not a logical consequence of a sentence all of whose nonlogical terms occur in e, then e confirms neither p nor the negation of p. But most of the evidence for complex theories is stated in terms that use only fragments of the vocabularies of the theories. For example, the positions of the planets on the celestial sphere supports Kepler's laws, but this evidence is stated in terms of times, ascensions, and declinations: the notions of a period of an orbit, a mean distance from the sun, and so on, do not occur in the statement of such evidence. Accordingly, despite the fact that his intent was to give an account of epistemic

---

[4] Cf. Hempel, "Empiricist Criteria of Cognitive Significance: Problems and Changes", in *Aspects of Scientific Explanation* (New York: Free Press, 1965).

[5] "Homage to Carnap", in Buck and Cohen, op. cit., pp. xlvi-xlvii.

[6] "Studies in the Logic of Confirmation", in *Aspects of Scientific Explanation*, op. cit. [Selection I.]

relevance,[7] Hempel's theory cannot explain why such evidence provides support for the theory as a whole or for particular hypotheses within the theory. Quantitative theories of confirmation using logical measure functions—Carnap's m^* for example—do better, but they share some of the limitations of Hempel's system; for example, if a hypothesis and an evidence statement share no nonlogical vocabulary, then the second generally cannot confirm or disconfirm the first.

Several contemporary accounts of scientific inference suppose it to proceed by the formation of conditional probabilities by means of Bayes's theorem in the theory of probability. That is, it is assumed that there are prior probabilities assigned to all hypotheses in question, and the new or posterior probability of (or degree of belief in) a hypothesis h on new evidence e is just the conditional probability of h on e (and whatever old evidence there may be). Richard Jeffrey has generalized this strategy so that it need not be assumed that the evidence statement, e, is certain.[8] A test that results in evidence e is taken to be relevant to hypothesis h if and only if the posterior probability of h, that is, its conditional probability on e, is different from the prior probability of h. Analyses of this sort may perhaps be made consistent with the sorts of judgements of relevance described at the outset, but I think we should doubt that they explain such judgements or provide a rationale for them. In order to determine the conditional probability of h on e by Bayes's rule we must know the prior probabilities of h and of e, and we must know the conditional probability of e on h. Frequentists maintain that such prior probabilities are objective frequencies; more particularly, Reichenbach proposed that the prior probability of a theory or hypothesis be taken as the frequency of success in a suitable reference class of theories of the same kind as the theory in question. He gave, unfortunately, no account of how the success of past theories might, without circularity, be determined, nor did he indicate with any concrete examples just how the required groupings might be effected. Reichenbach himself seems to have understood his account as a proposal for future practice: "Should we some day reach a stage in which we have as many statistics on theories as we have today on cases of disease and subsequent death . . . the choice of the reference class for the probability of theories would seem as

---

[7] See ibid, p. 5/6. Hempel was, of course, aware of the difficulty and entertained remedies. One remedy, the converse consequence condition, he rightly rejected, and subsequent attempts to revive it [cf. B. Brody, "Confirmation and Explanation", *Journal of Philosophy,* LXV, 10 (16 May 1968): 282–9] have not proved fruitful.

[8] *The Logic of Decision* (New York: McGraw Hill, 1965), ch. 11.

natural as that of the reference class for the probability of death."[9]
Whatever the merits or difficulties with the proposal, one thing is clear:
it cannot provide a rationale for those detailed judgements of relevance
which scientists now make and have long been making, nor can it
explain the great agreement scientists in the same field show about such
matters. For we simply do not have statistics of the kind Reichenbach
envisioned, nor do we have any idea of what their values would be or
even of how to collect them.

Subjective probability theorists, who regard the probabilities of
hypotheses as measures of our degrees of belief in them, are not
affected by such criticism. But of course, on a strict subjectivist view,
the assignments of prior probabilities are quite arbitrary so long as
they accord with the requirements of the theory of probability. If,
then, judgements of relevance are to be explained ultimately in terms
of prior probability distributions, and those distributions are without
rationale, the judgements of relevance will also be without rationale.[10]
The bare subjectivist account seems to be a version of the third position
above: judgements of relevance are conventional.

The conventionalist view would presumably attribute the agreement
about relevance to such factors as the education of graduate students:
young scientists are told by old scientists what is relevant to what. All
relativity texts say that certain experiments do not test certain
hypotheses because that was what all relativity textbook writers were
taught. There are two difficulties: these suppositions do not explain
how judgements of relevance came to be established in the first place,
and they do not explain how it is that, with very little controversy,
judgements of relevance are made in new cases. The latter fact,
especially, suggests that, if scientific education determines scientific
judgements about the relevance of evidence to theory, it must do so
by teaching, explicitly or tacitly, principles and not merely cases. On
the other hand, the conventionalist view has for its support the fundamental consideration that no plausible principles are known that would

---

[9] *Theory of Probability* (Berkeley: Univ. of California Press, 1949). This
passage is taken from S. Luckenbach, *Probabilities, Problems and Paradoxes*
(Encino, Calif.: Dickenson, 1972), p. 44.

[10] The standard Bayesian response to criticisms that turn on the arbitrariness
of prior probabilities is by appeal to stable estimation theorems; i.e., to proofs
that, under certain conditions whatever the prior distributions may be, the
posterior distributions will be nearly the same given sufficient evidence. [Cf.
Edwards, Lindman, and Savage, "Bayesian Statistical Inference for Psychological
Research", *Psychological Review*, LXX (1963).] But I know of no such theorems
for the kind of case under consideration, that is, when the evidence statements are
confined to a proper sublanguage of the language in which the hypotheses may be
formulated.

warrant the discrimination in question. I shall try to remove that support.

II

It is widely thought that, save in exceptional circumstances, universal hypotheses are supported or confirmed by their positive instances. If the hypothesis contains anomalous predicates—"grue", for example— then it will fail to be confirmed by positive instances, and, likewise, if the hypothesis is entailed by some well-confirmed theory, and a positive instance of the hypothesis is inconsistent with that theory, then the instance may serve to reduce our reasons to believe the hypothesis. But, barring circumstances such as these, we expect that universal hypotheses will be confirmed by their positive instances, and, in particular, we expect that a quantitative hypothesis stated as an equation will be confirmed by a set of values for the magnitudes[11] occurring in the hypothesis if the set is a solution to the equation. Now the trouble is that our experiments, observations, and measurements do not appear to provide us with positive instances of the hypotheses of our theories; in the quantitative case, for example, the magnitudes we determine by experiment or observation are generally not those, or not all of those, which occur in our theories concerning the phenomena observed.

Scientists seem to know very well how to get values of magnitudes occurring in their theories from values of magnitudes determined experimentally. Their strategy is to use hypotheses of the very theory to be tested to compute values of other magnitudes from experimentally determined magnitudes. To take a very simple example, suppose our theory consists of the single hypothesis that, for any sample of gas, so long as no gas is added to or removed from the sample, the product of the pressure and volume of the gas is proportional to the temperature of the gas. In other terms, under the given conditions

$$PV = kT$$

where k is an undetermined constant. Suppose further that we have means for measuring P, V, and T, but no means for measuring k. Then the hypothesis may be tested by obtaining two sets of values for P,

---

[11] I shall use the terms 'magnitude' or 'quantity' either to signify abstract objects, e.g., the type of the token 'kinetic energy', or else to signify properties under a description. The important point is that for my purposes 'mean kinetic energy' and 'temperature' must count as different quantities even though temperature is mean kinetic energy.

V, and T, using the first set of values together with the very hypothesis to be tested to determine a value for k

$$k = \frac{PV}{T}$$

and using the value k thus obtained together with the second set of values for P, V, and T either to instantiate or to contradict the hypothesis.

In the example the very hypothesis to be tested was used to determine, from experiment, a value for a quantity occurring in it, and the determination was very simple. Cases of this kind abound in scientific literature,[12] but in general the situation is considerably more complicated. Typically, the theory in question will contain a great many hypotheses, and a given experiment or collection of experiments may fail to measure values of more than one quantity in the theory. To determine a value for one of the latter quantities the use of several hypotheses in the theory may be required, and the determination may proceed through the computation of values for intermediate quantities, or combinations of such. Such a determination or computation may be represented by a finite graph. The initial, or zero-level, nodes of the graph will be experimentally determined quantities; n-level nodes will be quantities or combinations of quantities such that, for each n-level node, some hypothesis of the theory determines a unique value of that node from suitable values of all the $(n-1)$-level nodes with which it is connected. The graph will have a single maximal element, and that element will be a single quantity. We permit that two connected or unconnected nodes may correspond to the same quantity or combination of quantitites. I will call such a graph a *computation*.

The graph associated with the computation of the constant in the ideal-gas law is obvious, but it may not be clear what happens in a more complicated case. Let us consider a theory developed in a recent psychological paper;[13] since our considerations are almost entirely structural, we need not concern ourselves with much of the detail regarding the interpretation—which happens to be complicated—of the quantitites occurring in the theory. The theory consists of the following set of linear equations, together with their consequences (with respect to real algebra):

[12] For example, some of Jean Perrin's tests of equations of the kinetic theory are exactly of the kind illustrated. Perrin had, for instance, to use one of the equations to be tested to determine a value for a constant (Avogadro's number) it contained.

[13] J. Jinks and D. Fulker, "Comparison of the Biometrical, Genetical MAVA and Classical Approaches to the Analysis of Human Behavior", *Psychological Bulletin*, LXXIII, 5 (May 1970). The equations given are taken from p. 316.

$$(1) \quad A_1 = E_1$$
$$(2) \quad B_1 = G_1 + G_2 + E_2$$
$$(3) \quad A_2 = E_1 + E_2$$
$$(4) \quad B_2 = G_1 + G_2$$
$$(5) \quad A_3 = G_1 + E_1$$
$$(6) \quad B_3 = G_2 + E_2$$

The As and Bs are supposed to be quantities that we know how to estimate experimentally. Suppose then that we do an experiment that gives us values for the quantities A_1, B_1, A_3, and B_3. Naturally we could use equation (1) to compute a value for E_1 immediately from the experimental value of A_1. But it is also possible to compute a value for E_1 from the values of B_1, A_3, and B_3 in Fig. VII. 1.

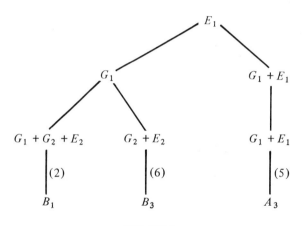

FIG. VII. 1

As we have seen, a given set of data may permit the computation of a value for a quantity in more than one way. If the data are consistent with the theory, then these different computations must agree in the value they determine for the computed quantity, but, if the data are inconsistent with the theory, then different computations of the same quantity may give different results. Further, and most important, what quantities in a theory may be computed from a given set of initial data depends both on the initial data and on the structure of the theory. In the example above we supposed given values for A_1, B_1, A_3, and B_3. These permit us to compute values for E_1 and for G_1, but, as the authors of the paper from which we have taken the equations put it, "two of the parameters, G_2 and E_2, occur only together in the expectations with the same coefficients, and are therefore inseparable. We can therefore estimate only G_1, E_1, and $(G_2 + E_2)$" (ibid., 317). That is, we cannot, with this theory, get values of G_2 and of E_2 with these data. Similar things happen with other sets of possible initial values. If we have values of A_1, B_1, A_2, B_2 only, then we cannot compute values for G_1 or for G_2. If, initially, we have values for A_2, B_2, A_3, B_3 only, then we cannot compute values for any of the quantities that appear on the right-hand side of the preceding equations.

It is clear, then, I hope, how scientists may use hypotheses in their theories for the determination of values of quantities that are not in fact measured or estimated by standard statistical methods. The examples already given suffice, I believe, to show that the strategy is in fact used explicitly in some cases. The question is, to what end is this strategy used? More particularly, if experiment permits the computation of values for all quantities occurring in a hypothesis, and these values accord with the hypothesis, does the positive instance thus obtained support or confirm the hypothesis? The answer cannot always be affirmative. Consider the example just discussed; suppose we determine A_1 by experiment and use the hypothesis:

(1) $A_1 = E_1$

to compute a value for E_1. We then have values for both A_1 and E_1, and these values are in accord with hypothesis (1) and provide a positive instance of that hypothesis. But clearly it would be wrong to think that this instance provides any support for the hypothesis. Intuitively, the difficulty is that the value of E_1 has been determined in such a way that, no matter what the value of A_1, it could not possibly fail to provide a positive instance of the hypothesis. To test a hypothesis we must do something that could result in presumptive evidence against the hypothesis. So a plausible necessary condition for a set I of values of quantities to test hypothesis h with respect to theory T is that there exist computations (using hypotheses in $T \& h$) from I of values for the quantities occurring in h, and there exist a set J of possible values for the same initial quantities such that the same computations from J result in a negative instance of h—that is, the values of the quantities occurring in h which are computed from J must contradict h. Actually, it is not necessary that all the quantities occurring in h be computable from the initial data, for some of them may occur vacuously. For example, to test an equation of the form

$$a(x^2 + y) + bx - ay = 0$$

we do not require a value for y. The quantity y is vacuous in the equation because, given any value v of x for which there exists a value u of y such that (v, u) is a solution to the equation, then (v, z) is also a solution for all possible values, z, of y. The generalization to cases with more quantities is obvious.

There is another useful condition which, for many theories, is equivalent to that just given. Suppose a hypothesis is equivalent to an equation of the form:

$$X(Q_1 \ldots Q_j) = 0$$

where X is some functional form, and where it is understood that two hypotheses are equivalent if every set of values which is a solution of one is a solution of the other and vice versa. Suppose further that a value for every quantity occurring in the hypothesis can be computed (by using hypotheses of a given theory T) from a set of values for experimentally determined quantities $E_1 \ldots E_k$. Now for any quantity Q_i occurring in the hypothesis, the computation for Q_i specifies Q_i as a single-valued function of the quantities whose nodes are immediately connected to the Q_i node in the graph of the computation. Similarly, the quantities at the nth-level nodes are, each of them, specified as single-valued functions of the quantities at the $(n-1)$-level nodes with which they are connected. Thus, ultimately, by composing all these functions, Q_i itself is specified as a single-valued function $f_i(E_1 \ldots E_k)$ of the experimentally determined quantities $E_1 \ldots E_k$. Replacing each Q_i in the hypothesis by $f_i(E_1 \ldots E_k)$ we obtain the equation

$$X(f_1(E_1 \ldots E_k), \ldots, f_j(E_1 \ldots E_k))$$

in which the only quantities are those experimentally determined. We shall say that this equation *represents* the hypothesis for this set of computations. For example, if the hypothesis is (1) above, that is,

$$A_1 = E_1$$

and the only computation is that of E_1 illustrated previously, then the representative of the hypothesis for this computation is

$$A_1 = (A_3 + B_3 - B_1).$$

Now the following is obvious: If the representative of a hypothesis for a set of computations holds identically, that is, if every set of possible values for the quantities occurring in the representative is a solution of the representative, then the computations cannot test the hypothesis, because the necessary condition given before will not obtain. Something more is true. If the functional form X of the hypothesis, and the functions f_i, are composed of operators that determine unique values for all possible sets of values of the quantities they operate on, then the hypothesis will be tested by a set of computations from initial data if the equation representing the hypothesis is not an identity.

We have, in effect, an account of theory testing, and one that naturally evolves from a few elementary observations: *ceteris paribus*, hypotheses are supproted by positive instances, disconfirmed by negative; instances, whether positive or negative, of a hypothesis in a theory are got by using the hypotheses of that theory itself (or, conceivably, some other) to make computations from values got from experiment, observation, or independent theoretical considerations; the computations must be carried out in such a way as to admit the possibility that the resulting instance of the hypothesis tested will be negative. Hypotheses, on this account, are not generally tested or supported or confirmed absolutely, but only *relative to a theory*. The general idea is certainly not new. Herman Weyl,[14] for example, seems to have had it:

The requirements which emerge from our discussion for a correct theory of the course of the world may be formulated as follows:

1. *Concordance*. The definite value which a quantity occurring in the theory assumes in a certain individual case will be determined from the empirical data on the basis of the theoretically posited connections. *Every such determination has to yield the same result* ... Not infrequently a (relatively) direct observation of the quantity in question ... is compared with a computation on the basis of other observations. ...

2. It must in principle always be possible to determine on the basis of observational data the definite value which a quantity occurring in the theory will have in a given individual case. This expresses the postulate that the theory in its explanation of the phenomena, must not contain redundant parts (121/2).

Again, in "Testability and Meaning"[15] Carnap proposed to regard hypotheses as confirmed by observation statements if the hypotheses, or instances of them, could be deduced from premises consisting of the observation statements and certain special hypotheses. The special hypotheses—bilateral reduction sentences—were in effect allegedly

---

[14] *Philosophy of Mathematics and Natural Science* (New York: Atheneum, 1963).

[15] *Philosophy of Science*, III, 4 (October 1936): 419-71; IV, 1 (January 1937): 1-40; reprinted in H. Feigl and M. Brodbeck, *Readings in the Philosophy of Science* (New York: Appleton-Century-Crofts, 1953).

privileged hypotheses of a theory; privileged in being immune from disconfirmation and in being analytic. But the appeal to analytic truth is quite independent of the main idea, namely, to confirm hypotheses by deducing instances of them by means of other hypotheses in the same theory.

III

Before turning to the questions with which we began, some objections to this account of theory testing need to be considered.

One objection is that the foregoing account is an account of testing for quantitative theories only; it does not seem to apply to qualitative theories or to theories construed as deductively closed, axiomatizable sets of first-order sentences. But the account is straightforwardly extended to first-order theories, and thereby to qualitative theories if the logical form of their hypotheses is known.

By a "quantity" we will mean an open atomic formula [e.g., 'x is red,' 'x is larger than y' ed.] By a "value" for a quantity we will mean an atomic sentence [e.g., 'this object is red' ed.] or its negation containing the same predicate constant as the quantity. It certainly must be allowed that, if initial data I (that is, a set of values for quantities) and theory T are consistent, then I discomfirms h with respect to T if T and I together entail $\sim h$ but T alone does not. Conversely, if T and I are consistent and T and I entail h but T alone does not, then I must count as confirming h with respect to T. The more typical and more complicated cases arise when T and I together neither entail nor refute h unless T does so alone. For these cases we may give a quasi-Hempelian analysis:

I confirms h with respect to T if

(i) T and I are consistent with each other and with h.
(ii) There exists a set, call it S, of values for quantities such that there are computations from I of the values in S and, further, such that S entails the development (in Hempel's sense[16]) of h for the individual constants occurring in members of S.
(iii) There exists a set J of possible values for the initial quantities such that the same computations (as in ii) from J give values of the quantities in S that entail the development of the negation of h.

I disconfirms h if I confirms the negation of h.

I should like briefly to note some features of this account. If I is inconsistent with T, then I neither confirms nor disconfirms any

---

[16] Cf. "Studies in the Logic of Confirmation", op. cit. [Selection I]

hypothesis with respect to T; but in that case I may none the less confirm or disconfirm various hypotheses with respect to sub-theories of T. Hempel's consistency and equivalence conditions are satisfied so long as the theory is kept fixed. The same initial data may, however, confirm inconsistent hypotheses with respect to different theories. Because of condition iii, Hempel's special consequence condition is not satisfied, and neither, of course, is the converse consequence condition.

On Hempel's theory, $\sim R(a)$ confirms both $\forall x \sim Rx$ and $\forall x(Rx \supset Bx)$, but, on the account just given, it does not, because no value of $R(x)$ will, by itself, entail the development of the negation of the second hypothesis, and so condition iii is not met. The "paradox" of the ravens arises in the new account just as in Hempel's, but it is at least confined: if initial data Ra, Ba confirm a hypothesis of universal conditional form with respect to theory T, it is not always the case that $\sim Ra, \sim Ba$ also confirm that hypothesis with respect to T. For example, if the hypothesis is $\forall x(Cx \supset Dx)$ and the theory is $\forall x(Rx \supset Cx)$ & $\forall x(Dx \equiv Bx)$, then the first set of initial data, Ra, Ba confirms the hypothesis, but $\sim Ra, \sim Ba$ does not confirm the hypothesis.

Although I think that most of the features of the foregoing account for first-order theories are plausible enough, I shall not defend them now. There are a variety of ways in which the general strategy I have outlined in the previous section might be extended to formalized theories, and the quasi-Hempelian account just given is only one of them. One can, for example, try to preserve the consequence condition by replacing iii with a radically weaker condition, e.g.,

(iii*) If h has a representative for the set of computations in ii, the representative is not a valid formula.

but then one will have to allow that $\sim Ra$ confirms $\forall x(Rx \supset Bx)$. Again, it is straightforward to adapt the general strategy to a Popperian viewpoint, so that hypotheses of universal form may be tested but hypotheses of existential or mixed form never are. The point is that the account *can be* extended to formalized theories, and the extension need not be much less plausible—I think not any less plausible at all—than accounts of confirmation that are confined to "observation" statements.

A serious difficulty, urged by Professor Hempel, is this: typically, the hypotheses of a theory of themselves determine nothing about experimental or observational data; something definite about experimental outcomes can be inferred from the theory—or values of theoretical quantities can be inferred from the data—only if special, empirically untested, assumptions are made. Hempel calls such assumptions "qualifying clauses" or "provisos". One example, alleged by several writers, is that no observable consequences about the motions of heavenly bodies follow from Newton's three laws and the law of universal gravitation unless one makes some assumption about what forces are acting, e.g., that only gravitational forces act between the bodies of the solar system.

There may indeed be many cases in which a theory can be applied to a system only if it is assumed that the system has some property of a kind that is not determined experimentally; even when that is so, however, one must still be able to say what hypotheses in the theory are tested by the experimental results on the supposition that the qualifying clause is met, and our account proposes an answer to that question. Of course, one wants to know something more about when it is reasonable to assume that qualifying clauses are satisfied, and what role they may play in the assessment of a whole theory, but that is beyond our scope at present.

It is not clear to me how often such qualifying clauses are really essential. Consider Newton again. In book III of the *Principia* Newton uses his first two laws to deduce from Kepler's laws that there is a centripetal force acting on the planets in inverse proportion to the square of their distances from the sun. He further shows, using terrestrial experiments and the third law, that this centripetal force between two bodies must be proportional to the product of their masses. Now, as deductivists like Duhem[17] have insisted, these deductions do not result in an instance of the gravitational-force law because that law requires that the gravitational force acting between *any two* bodies be proportional to the product of the masses and inversely proportional to the square of the distance between them; but the total gravitational force acting on any planet must be the sum of the forces due to the sun and to the other bodies in the solar system, and hence the total gravitational force acting on a planet ought not to be inversely proportional to the square of its distance from the sun. Newton's conclusions are inconsistent with his law. Duhem's objection fails entirely, however, if we recognize that Kepler's laws need not be taken as strictly correct initial data, but rather as very good approximations subject to whatever errors there may be in the observations of planetary positions and times. The question then becomes whether the planetary perturbations are sufficiently small that the deviation in

---

[17] Cf. *The Aim and Structure of Physical Theory* (Princeton, N.J.: University Press, 1954), *passim.*

the total force acting on a planet from that calculated by Newton using Kepler's laws is less than the error of the computed result due to error in the initial data. Such a determination in turn requires, besides some idea of the error of the observations, an estimate of the relative masses of the planets to the sun. For any planet with a satellite, the ratio of the planet's mass to the sun's can be estimated from data independent of those used to compute the circumsolar force; Newton is thus able to argue without circularity that the gravitational interaction of the planets is very small in comparison with the solar force.[18]

In effect, the method of testing described in this paper is Newton's method, save that in Newton's case the matter is complicated by the use of empirical laws as initial data and the use of approximations. Not only Newton, but Newtonian scientists of the eighteenth and nineteenth centuries claimed to deduce their laws from the phenomena. Perhaps they overstated their case, but they had, nonetheless, a case to state. The scorn heaped on their method by Duhem is undeserved.

Another objection is that the account is, after all, just the old hypothetico-deductive account. For, if a set of initial data confirms a hypothesis with respect to a theory according to the preceding account, then surely there is a valid deduction of some of the propositions in the initial data set from premises consisting of the rest of the propositions in the initial data set, the hypothesis tested, and the theorems of the theory that are used in the computations. Further, if the data disconfirm the hypothesis, the negation of some proposition in the initial data set must be deducible in an analogous way. And surely H-D theorists would agree that in some contexts only some particular hypothesis or hypotheses from among all those which might appear in such deductions are in fact tested.

It is true, I think, that any test can be converted into a deductive argument in the way suggested; but the converse is not true. Not all deductions of singular statements from putative laws and initial conditions can be transformed into tests. For example, suppose hypothesis h is tested by data I with respect to theory T. For each predicate occurring in h or in T but not occurring in I, choose two new, distinct predicates, and replace each occurrence of each predicate, P say, by the disjunction of the two new predicates associated with

<hr>

[18] This discussion ignores many historical niceties. Newton assumes, for example, that the centre of gravity of the solar system moves inertially, and this assumption, having no experimental support, is presumably just the sort of thing Hempel would call a "proviso". But Newton's argument does not in fact require the assumption. A more careful account of Newton's argument is given in my "Physics and Evidence", to appear in *Pittsburgh Studies in the Philosophy of Science.*

P. Then *h* is changed into a new hypothesis *h**, and *T* is changed into a new theory *T**, and, further, if there is a valid deduction of a proposition in *I* from the rest of *I, h*, and theorems of *T*, then, by the substitution theorem, there is also a valid deduction of that proposition in *I* from the rest of *I, h**, and *T**. But, in general, *I* will not test *h** with respect to *T**. That is exactly as it should be, for no scientist would take evidence to support a theory like *T** when another like *T* was available. The H-D method has us deduce singular statements from laws; the new procedure, in effect, has us deduce *instances* of laws from singular statements and other laws. The two are not the same. I have no doubt that H-D advocates agree that sometimes data test certain hypotheses and not others; what I doubt is that their principles afford any explanation of those judgements.

IV

We still have to consider what the account of theory testing can contribute to the questions with which we began. What grounds can there be for claims to the effect that one or another experiment has no bearing on one or another hypothesis within a theory? In general terms our answer is clear enough: depending on the nature of the experiment or observation and the structure of the theory in question, a given hypothesis may or may not be tested according to the scheme outlined in previous sections. In particular cases, detailing the application of the scheme may be very complex, and the psycho-analytic and relativity examples mentioned at the outset are certainly too complex to discuss here.[19] It is, however, fairly easy to see how the account of theory testing can explain the claim that observations of a single planet do not, of themselves, provide a test of Kepler's third law.

Kepler's first and second laws specify features of the motion of any planetary body moving about the sun. The third law, however, relates features of the orbits of any two bodies; specifically it claims that the ratio of the periods of any two planets equals the 3/2 power of the ratio of their mean distances from the sun. The parameters that uniquely determine the Keplerian orbit at any time can be estimated from several observations of the planet on the celestial sphere; in fact,

---

[19] For a very qualitative application of the strategy to Freudian theory, see my "Freud, Kepler and the Clinical Evidence", in R. Wollheim, ed., *Freud* (New York: Doubleday, 1975). The explanation I should offer of why the field equations of general relativity are not tested by measurements of the gravitational red shift turns on the imprecision of these measurements and closely follows the account given by John Anderson in his *Principles of Relativity Physics* (New York: Academic Press, 1967), ch. 12.

140

CLARK GLYMOUR

three suitably chosen observations suffice for the computations,[20] and a fourth observation of a single planet permits a test of Kepler's first and second laws. But, however many observations we may have of the location of a single planet on the celestial sphere, those are not, by assumption, observations of the location of any *other* planet on the celestial sphere. To test Kepler's third law, we need estimates of the periods and mean distances from the sun of at least two planets. But from the observations of one planet alone we cannot compute, using Kepler's laws and their consequences, the parameters of the orbit of any other planet. We can, of course, compute under those circumstances the *ratio* of the square of the period to the cube of the mean distance from the sun for any planet whatsoever, but only by *using* Kepler's third law itself. So, even if we count such a ratio as one quantity, the representative of Kepler's third law (see p. 133 above) for the requisite computations will be a trivial identity, and hence the third law will not be tested.

The account of theory testing helps to account for a good deal more about scientific methodology. A standard methodological principle is that a theory is better supported by a variety of evidence than by a narrow spectrum of evidence. The substance of the principle is, however, unclear so long as we lack some account of what constitutes relevant variety. One view, which I believe is incorrect, is that what constitutes a relevant variety of evidence for a theory is entirely determined by what other theories happen to be in competition with the first.[21] On the contrary, if, as I have argued, a given piece of evidence may be evidence for some hypothesis in a theory even while it is irrelevant to other hypotheses in that theory, then we surely want our pieces of evidence to be various enough to provide tests of as many different hypotheses in that theory as possible, regardless of what, in historical context, the competing theories may be. There is a further complication. In assessing a theory we are judging how well it is supported with respect to itself, and this reflexive feature of theory testing makes for certain difficulties. If a hypothesis is confirmed by observations and computations using another hypothesis in the theory, then it is always possible that the agreement between hypothesis and evidence is spurious: both the hypothesis tested and some hypothesis used in the computations of the test may be in error, but the errors in

[20] The classic treatment is Gauss, *Theory of the Motion of Heavenly Bodies Moving about the Sun in Conic Sections*. A translation from the Latin is published by Dover, New York, 1963.

[21] For this view see, for example, Peter Achinstein, "Inference to Scientific Laws", in R. Stuewer, ed., *Minnesota Studies in the Philosophy of Science*, vol. v (Minneapolis: Univ. of Minnesota Press, 1970), p. 95.

one hypothesis may be exactly (or exactly enough) compensated for by the errors in the other. Conversely, a true hypothesis may be disconfirmed by observations and computations using other hypotheses in the theory if one or more of the hypotheses used in the computations are incorrect. The only means available for guarding against such errors is to have a variety of evidence, so that as many hypotheses as possible are tested in as many different ways as possible. What makes one way of testing relevantly different from another is that the hypotheses used in the one computation are different from the hypotheses used in the other computation. Part of what makes one piece of evidence relevantly different from another piece of evidence is that some test is possible from the first that is not possible from the second, or that in the two cases there is some difference in the precision of computed values of theoretical quantities.

Kepler's laws again provide a simple example. Kepler did not determine elliptical orbits for planets as simply the best fit for the data; on the contrary, he gave a physical argument for the area rule—his second law—and used the area rule together with the data to infer that the planetary orbits are ellipses. Seventeenth-century astronomers were able to confirm Kepler's first law only by using his second, and they were able to confirm his second only by using his first. Understandably, there remained considerable disagreement and uncertainty as to whether the two laws were correct, or whether the errors in one were compensated for by the errors in the other. Not until the invention of the micrometer and Flamsteed's observations of Jupiter and its satellites, late in the seventeenth century, was a confirmation of Kepler's second law obtained without any assumption concerning the planet's orbit.[22] I doubt that this example is singular; quite the reverse: it seems unlikely to me that the development and testing of any complex modern theory in physics or in chemistry can be understood without some appreciation of the way a variety of evidence serves to separate hypotheses.

. . .

V

There are two theses which have recently gained such wide assent among empiricist philosophers that they deserve to be regarded as new dogmas of empiricism. I have in mind the claim that our theories

[22] Cf. Curtis Wilson, 'From Kepler's Laws, So-called, to Universal Gravitation: Empirical Factors', *Archive for the History of Exact Sciences*, VI (1969): 89–170.

may be underdetermined by all possible evidence, and the further claim that each theory is tested as a whole. Dogmas may of course be true, and, with suitable qualifications, these dogmas are. I should like to conclude by saying something about the qualifications.

For some theories, at some stages of their development, a set of quantities can plausibly be demarcated such that the evidence for or against the theory in question consists of values for these quantities for various systems. When such a demarcation can plausibly be made, it not only makes sense to ask whether the theory is uniquely determined by all possible evidence of the relevant kind, but, further, we can sometimes hope to get an answer to this question. Of course an answer, whether affirmative or negative, says nothing about what sorts of underdetermination may occur if novel kinds of evidence are discovered. For example, the state of absolute rest is undeterminable in Newtonian gravitational theory, but, had the combination of Newtonian theory with Maxwell's electrodynamics proved correct, optical experiments would have permitted a determination of the rest frame.[23] Again for certain models of general relativity it can be shown that no measurements of the quantities peculiar to that theory suffice to determine the global topology of space-time,[24] but, even if our universe is in fact one of these topologically underdetermined universes, it is still possible that other branches of physics—plasma physics for example—might provide evidence and theory sufficient to determine a unique topology.

If we confine consideration to a given kind of evidence, we can inquire whether evidence of that kind uniquely determines a best theory that explains it. Conceivably, all possible such evidence might fail to determine a unique theory for either of two kinds of reasons. First, there might occur two or more theories that are not intertranslatable but all of whose hypotheses are tested positively by the evidence so that every methodological demand met by one theory is met by the other. I know of no plausible candidates for this kind of case, but I see no reason why they should not exist. Second, there might occur two or more theories that differ only in hypotheses that cannot be tested, and, for some reason or other, every plausible theory accounting for the evidence also contains such a hypothesis. There are a great many examples of this kind of case, and analysing when this sort of underdetermination arises is a standard problem in the social sciences.[25]

[23] A discussion of this case is given in M. Friedman, "Foundations of Space-Time Theories", unpublished Ph.D. thesis, Princeton, 1972.
[24] Cf. my "Topology, Cosmology and Convention", *Synthese*, XXIV, 2 (August 1972): 195–218.
[25] Cf. Franklin Fisher, *The Identification Problem in Econometrics* (New York: McGraw-Hill, 1966).

Demonstrating underdetermination is sometimes possible, but it is not as easy as some writers have supposed. Reichenbach,[26] for example, argued that, even in the context of classical physics, the theory of the geometry of space is underdetermined; for, given any geometry, we can suppose it to be the true one and explain the coincidence behaviour of material bodies in terms of this geometry and the action of a "universal force". But, if one sets out actually to write down such a theory, one quickly discovers that it is obtainable only by dividing the Euclidean metric of Newtonian theory into two new quantities, just as Thirring divided the metric field of general relativity into two new quantities. The result is a theory which, on the same evidence, is less well tested than Newtonian theory. We cannot demonstrate underdetermination by substituting for one or more predicates of a theory a combination of new predicates, since the result of the substitution is a theory less well tested than the original.

Early in this century both Duhem and Frege urged that a theory must be tested as a whole. Reductive programs, like Carnap's *Aufbau*, would have avoided holism had they succeeded, but they did not succeed. Later, a number of philosophers, notably Carnap and C. I. Lewis, tried to avoid holism by putting analytic truth to work. They kept in common some version of the claim that, given a collection of analytic truths, or truths by convention, each hypothesis in a theory has its own, independent connections with experience. It is understandable that a new romance with holism should be the concomitant of estrangement from the distinction between analytic truths and synthetic truths.

Part of what has been said or suggested on behalf of holism is false, and part of it is true. It is true that a great part of a theory may be involved in the confirmation of any of its hypotheses, and it is further true that the assessment of any hypothesis in a theory in the face of negative evidence requires the assessment of all hypotheses in that theory. It is false that a piece of evidence is evidence indiscriminately for all hypotheses in a theory or for none of them, and it is false as well that theories must be accepted or rejected as a whole. For positive evidence may fail to provide any support for some hypotheses in a theory—support, that is, with respect to the theory itself—even while confirming other hypotheses. And, if the total evidence is of sufficient variety, evidence inconsistent with a theory may still leave us with a fragment that is best confirmed with respect to itself. If we are lucky, in some axiomatizations of the theory we may even be able to single out a particular axiom that deserves the blame. A naive holism that supposes theory to confront experience as an unstructured, blockish

[26] *The Philosophy of Space and Time* (New York: Dover, 1957).

whole will inevitably be perplexed by the power of scientific argument to distribute praise and to distribute blame among our beliefs.

VIII
CONCEPTS OF EVIDENCE

PETER ACHINSTEIN

1. THREE CONCEPTS

ALAN'S skin has yellowed, so on Monday he sees the doctor, who examines him and declares that he has jaundice, i.e., the visible expression of an increased concentration of bilirubin in the blood (which I shall abbreviate as an i.c.b.). Some tests are made as a result of which on Friday, although Alan's yellowness remains, the doctor declares that Alan does not have an i.c.b. but that his yellow skin was produced by a dye with which he was working. On Friday which of the following propositions, if any, should the doctor affirm?

(i) Alan's yellow skin was evidence of an i.c.b. and still is.

(ii) Alan's yellow skin was but no longer is evidence of an i.c.b.

(iii) Alan's yellow skin is not and never was evidence of an i.c.b.

The doctor might be tempted to assert (i) on the ground that Alan's yellow skin is typically the kind of skin associated with an i.c.b. On the other hand, (ii) might be tempting to say since the doctor now has additional information which makes the original evidence efficacious no longer. Finally, he might be tempted to assert (iii) on the ground that false or misleading evidence is no evidence at all. He might say that Alan's yellow skin is not and never was (real or genuine) evidence of an i.c.b., though on Monday he mistakenly thought it was.

I believe that these three responses represent conflicting tendencies in the way we actually speak about evidence, and that a different but related concept of evidence can be associated with each.

I begin with a notion which I shall call *potential* evidence. The presence of Alan's yellow skin is potential evidence of an i.c.b. since yellow skin of that sort is generally associated with an i.c.b. That 35

From *Mind*, 87 (1978), pp. 22–45. By permission of Basil Blackwell Publisher. The author has incorporated some material from *The Nature of Explanation* (Oxford University Press, 1983), chs. 10–11. He is indebted to the N.S.F. for support of research.

per cent of those sampled in this district said they would vote for the Democratic candidate is potential evidence that roughly 35 per cent of all those voting in the district will vote for him since samples of that size are usually accurate. Without here trying to define this concept let me indicate several of its features.

First, e can be potential evidence that h even if h is false.[1] Secondly, potential evidence is objective in the sense that whether e is potential evidence that h does not depend upon anyone's beliefs about e or h or their relationship. That Alan has yellow skin is potential evidence that he has an i.c.b. even if no one believes that it is or knows or believes that he has yellow skin or an i.c.b. In these two respects potential evidence is akin to the concept Hempel seeks to define in 'Studies in the Logic of Confirmation'[2] and to one Carnap calls the classificatory concept of confirmation which he defines using his theory of probability.[3]

Although Hempel and Carnap in addition allow e as well as h to be false, I am inclined to think that if there is a concept of potential evidence in use it is one that requires e to be true. This, then, is the third feature I attribute to this concept. That Alan has yellow skin is potential evidence that he has an i.c.b. only if he does in fact have yellow skin. The concept that Hempel and Carnap seek to analyse which has no such requirement could be described as 'doubly potential' ('e would be potential evidence that h if e were true'). Finally, although both of these authors allow e to entail h (as a 'limiting' case), I doubt that there is such a concept of evidence in use. The fact that Alan has yellow skin is not evidence that he has skin; it is too good to be evidence.

Can a concept of evidence with these characteristics be defined, and if so will it support proposition (i)? Various definitions of potential

---

[1] In what follows the evidence sentences that will be considered are, or are transformable into, ones of the form

(ϕ) The fact that e (or that e) is evidence that h

in which e and h are sentences. However, when speaking schematically about such evidence sentences I shall follow the usual custom and simply write 'e is evidence that h'. This does not mean that I am subscribing to the view that evidence sentences of form (ϕ) should be construed as relating sentences, or indeed anything at all. This paper will not be concerned with the 'logical form' of ϕ-sentences, although the reader is referred to my 'Causation, Transparency, and Emphasis', *Canadian Journal of Philosophy* v (1975), 1–23, and 'What is an Explanation?', *American Philosophical Quarterly* xiv (1977), 1–15, where such questions about causation and explanation sentences are discussed, the answers to which have a bearing on ϕ-sentences.

[2] Reprinted in Carl G. Hempel, *Aspects of Scientific Explanation* (New York, 1965). [Selection I]

[3] Rudolf Carnap, *Logical Foundations of Probability* (2nd edn., Chicago, 1962), p. xvi. [See Selection V.]

evidence will be examined in later sections, after which this question will be addressed.

I turn now to a second concept, *veridical* evidence, that sanctions proposition (iii) above. e is veridical evidence that h only if e is potential evidence that h and h is true. However, this is not yet sufficient. Suppose that Alan's having yellow skin is potential evidence of an i.c.b. and that Alan in fact has an i.c.b. But suppose that Alan's yellow skin did not result from an i.c.b. but from the chemical dye with which he was working. We would then conclude that his having the yellow skin he does is not (veridical) evidence of an i.c.b. Veridical evidence requires not just that h and e both be true but that e's truth be related in an appropriate manner to h's. Alan does not have the yellow skin he does *because* he has an i.c.b. but because he has been working with a yellow dye. More generally, I shall speak of an *explanatory connection* between e's being true and h's being true and say that

(1) e is veridical evidence that h if and only if e is potential evidence that h, h is true, and there is an explanatory connection between e's being true and h's being true.

Although I shall not try to define the notion of an explanatory connection,* some further comments are in order. The concept of evidence characterized in (1) does not require that h's being true correctly explain e's being true; the converse is also possible. That Jones has a severe chest wound can be veridical evidence that he will die, even though the hypothesis that he will die does not explain the fact that he has a severe chest wound. Rather the reverse explanation is correct: he will die because he has a severe chest wound. Alternatively, there may be some common explanation which correctly explains why both e and h are true. The fact that hydrogen and oxygen combine in a simple ratio by volume may be evidence that nitrogen and oxygen do too. (Gay-Lussac indeed took it to be so.) In this case h does not explain e, nor conversely. Still both h and e are explained by appeal to the fact that the pairs of substances involved are gases and gases combine in simple ratios by volume. (Or at a deeper level both h and e are explained by appeal to Avogadro's hypothesis.)

If we can assume—as I shall do here—that whether there is an explanatory connection between the truth of e and h does not depend on what anyone believes (except, of course, where e and h themselves describe beliefs or intentional actions) then veridical evidence, like

---

* [For such a definition see *The Nature of Explanation*, ch. 10.]

potential evidence, is an objective concept of evidence.[4] Moreover, it is a concept in accordance with which proposition (iii) should be asserted. If Alan does not have an i.c.b. (i.e., h is false) then by (1) the fact that he has yellow skin is not and never was (veridical) evidence that he has an i.c.b.

Turning to a third concept of evidence, we speak not only of something's being evidence that h but also of something's being *so-and-so's* evidence that h. On Monday the doctor's evidence that Alan has an i.c.b. was that Alan has yellow skin. I take this to involve at least the claim that on Monday the doctor believed that Alan's yellow skin is potential evidence of an i.c.b. However, this is not sufficient if on Friday Alan's yellow skin is potential evidence of an i.c.b.; for the fact that Alan has yellow skin is not on Friday the doctor's evidence that Alan has an i.c.b., even if on Friday the doctor believes that it is potential evidence. Accordingly, one might be tempted to say that the fact that Alan has yellow skin is the doctor's evidence that Alan has an i.c.b. only if the doctor believes that this fact is *veridical* evidence of an i.c.b. More generally,

(2) e is X's evidence that h only if X believes that e is veridical evidence that h; i.e., X believes that e is potential evidence that h, that h is true, and that there is an explanatory connection between the truth of h and e.[5]

However, (2) may be too strong in requiring that X believe that h is true and that there is an explanatory connection between h and e. Suppose that on Monday the doctor is unsure about whether Alan has an i.c.b. He thinks it probable but he does not know whether to believe it, so he orders tests. Later when the tests reveal no i.c.b. and Alan indignantly asks the doctor 'what was your evidence that I have an i.c.b.?', the doctor might reply: 'the fact that you have yellow skin'.

---

[4] To make this claim as well as those in the previous paragraph is not to take a stand on a number of debated issues on explanation. One is whether to adopt a contextual or a non-contextual approach. Contextualists can understand the last clause in (1) to mean 'there are (types of) contexts in which one can correctly explain why e is true by appeal to h, or why h is true by appeal to e, etc.', whose truth does not depend on whether anyone in particular believes that one can correctly explain e by appeal to h, etc. Another issue concerns the ontological status of an explanation and of the item explained. In 'What is an Explanation?' (see p. 23 n. 1) and 'The Object of Explanation', in S. Körner, ed., *Explanation* (Oxford, 1975), 1–45, various possible ontological positions are discussed, and (1) can be reformulated to meet the requirements of any of them.

[5] 'X's evidence that h' like 'X's explanation' is ambiguous. It can mean (roughly) 'what X takes to be evidence that h'—as in (2) above—or 'what X takes to be evidence that h *and* is evidence that h', which is a combination of (2) with either 'e is potential evidence that h' or 'e is veridical evidence that h'.

Even if on Monday the doctor was not sure whether to believe that Alan has an i.c.b. at least he believed that this is probable and that it is probable that this explains his yellow skin. Accordingly, (2) might be weakened as follows:

(2′) e is X's evidence that h only if X believes that e is potential evidence that h, that it is probable that h is true, and that it is probable that there is an explanatory connection between the truth of h and e.

Neither (2) nor (2′), however, supplies a sufficient condition. For e to be X's evidence that h it is necessary in addition that

(3) X believes that h is true or probable (and does so) *for the reason that e.*

The fact that Alan is receiving a certain medical treatment T may be (veridical) evidence that he has an i.c.b. (since treatment T is given only to such people). Even if Alan's doctor knows and therefore believes that the fact that Alan is receiving treatment T is (veridical) evidence that he has an i.c.b., this fact is not the *doctor's* evidence that Alan has an i.c.b. His reason for believing this is not that Alan is receiving treatment T. Accordingly, I would add condition (3) to (2) or (2′) to obtain sufficient conditions. (2) and (3) can be said to characterize a strong sense of 'X's evidence', (2′) and (3) a weak one.

Both (2) and (2′) (with (3) added) sanction proposition (ii). When we say that Alan's yellow skin was but no longer is evidence of an i.c.b. we may be understood to be referring to *someone's* evidence, in this case the doctor's. We may mean that on Monday the fact that Alan has yellow skin was the doctor's evidence that Alan has an i.c.b., but on Friday it is no longer so. On Friday due to other facts he has learned the doctor no longer believes (it probable) that Alan has an i.c.b. This concept of evidence is thoroughly subjective. Whether e is X's evidence that h depends entirely on what X believes about e, h, and their relationship, and not on whether in fact e is potential or veridical evidence that h.

This subjectivity means that one cannot draw an inference from the fact that e is X's evidence that h to the claim that e is at least some good reason to believe h, or even for X to believe h. It is commonly supposed that evidence bears some relationship to what it is reasonable to believe. Although this may be expressed in a variety of ways perhaps the following simple formulation will suffice for our purposes:

A Principle of Reasonable Belief. If, in the light of background information b,[6] e is evidence that h, then, given b, e is at least some good reason for believing h.[7]

This principle is satisfied by the two objective concepts of evidence. If, in the light of the background information (b) that yellow skin of that type is generally associated with an i.c.b., the fact that Alan has yellow skin is potential (or veridical) evidence that he has an i.c.b., then, given b, the latter fact is at least some good reason for believing that Alan has an i.c.b. The subjective concept, on the other hand, does not satisfy this principle. The fact that Max has lost ten fights in a row may be *his* evidence that his luck will change and he will win the eleventh. But this fact is not a good reason at all, even for Max, to believe this hypothesis.

To summarize, then, the three concepts of evidence here character-ized provide a way of answering the question of whether the fact that Alan has yellow skin is evidence that he has an i.c.b. It is potential evidence since that kind of skin is typically associated with an i.c.b. It is not veridical evidence since the hypothesis is false and his yellow skin is correctly explained not by his having an i.c.b. but by the fact that he was working with a dye. On Monday but not on Friday it was the doctor's evidence that Alan has an i.c.b., since on Monday but not on Friday the doctor believed that Alan has an i.c.b. for the reason that he has yellow skin which he believed was veridical evidence of an i.c.b.

If potential evidence can be defined, then so can the other two concepts via (1), (2), and (3). Of various definitions of potential evidence that appear in the literature two general types will be discussed here because each by itself is not sufficient but if appro-priately altered and combined the result may be. The first and most popular type defines evidence in terms of probability, the second in terms of explanation.

2. THE PROBABILITY DEFINITIONS

According to one probability definition e is potential evidence that h if and only if the probability of h given e is greater than the prior probability of h:

---

[6] The role of background information here and its relationship to evidence statements will be discussed in section 5.

[7] Note that this is not a principle relating evidence to what anyone is justified in believing. e can be a good reason for believing h even though Smith, say, is not justified in believing h for the reason e (since, e.g., he is not justified in believing e).

(1a) e is potential evidence that h if and only if p(h,e) > p(h).
Or, if b is background information,
  (1b) e is potential evidence that h if and only if p(h, e&b) > p(h,b).

A definition of this sort is offered by many writers.[8] However, despite its widespread acceptance it cannot possibly be correct if 'evidence' and 'probability' are being used as they are in ordinary language or science. For one thing, neither (1a) nor (1b) requires that e be true; and this, as noted earlier, seems to be necessary for evidence. That Alan has yellow skin is not evidence that he has an i.c.b., if he does not have yellow skin. However, even with the addition of a truth-requirement the resulting definition is unsatisfactory. I shall concentrate on (1b), since this is the most prevalent form of the definition, and note three types of counterexamples. The first shows that an increase in probability is not sufficient for evidence, the second and third that it is not necessary.

The first lottery case. Let b be the background information that on Monday 1000 lottery tickets were sold and that John bought 100 and Bill bought 1. Let e be the information that on Tuesday all the lottery tickets except those of John and Bill have been destroyed but that one ticket will still be drawn at random. Let h be the hypothesis that Bill will win. The probability that Bill will win has been increased approximately tenfold over its prior probability. But surely e is not evidence that Bill will win. If anything it is evidence that John will win.

Reverting to the principle of the previous section which relates potential (as well as veridical) evidence to a reason for belief, assume for the sake of argument that in the light of b, e is potential evidence that (h) Bill will win. Then according to the principle of reasonable belief, given b, e is at least some good reason for believing h. But surely it is not. In the light of the background information that on Monday John bought 100 and Bill bought 1 of the 1000 lottery tickets sold, the fact that on Tuesday all of the tickets except those of John and Bill have been destroyed but one ticket will still be drawn at random is not a good reason at all for believing that Bill will win. Someone who believes that Bill will win for such a reason is believing something irrationally.

Events often occur which increase the probability or risk of certain consequences. But the fact that such events occur is not necessarily evidence that these consequences will ensue; it may be no good reason

---

[8] e.g., Carnap, op. cit., p. 463 [Selection V]; Mary Hesse, *The Structure of Scientific Inference* (Berkeley, 1974), p. 134. Richard Swinburne, *An Introduction to Confirmation Theory* (London, 1973), p. 3.

at all for expecting such consequences. When I walk across the street I increase the probability that I will be hit by a 1970 Cadillac; but the fact that I am walking across the street is not evidence that I will be hit by a 1970 Cadillac. When Mark Spitz goes swimming he increases the probability that he will drown; but the fact that he is swimming is not evidence that he will drown.

What these examples show is that for e to be evidence that h it is not sufficient that e increase h's (prior) probability. The next two examples show that it is not even necessary.

The paradox of ideal evidence.[9] Let b be the background information that in the first 5000 spins of this roulette wheel the ball landed on numbers other than 3 approximately 35/36ths of the time. Let e be the information that in the second 5000 spins the ball landed on numbers other than 3 approximately 35/36ths of the time. Let h be the hypothesis that on the 10,001st spin the ball will land on a number other than 3. The following claim seems reasonable:

$$p(h, e\&b) = p(h,b) = 35/36.$$

That is, the probability that the ball will land on a number other than 3 on the 10,001st spin is unchanged by e, which means, according to (1b), that e is not evidence that h. But it seems unreasonable to claim that the fact that the ball landed on numbers other than 3 approximately 35/36ths of the time during the second 5000 spins is not evidence that it will land on a number other than 3 on the 10,001st spin, even though there is another fact which is also evidence for this. More generally, e can be evidence that h even if there is other equally good evidence that h. To be sure, if we have already obtained the first batch of evidence there may be no need to obtain the second. But this does not mean that the second batch is not evidence that h.

The second lottery case. Let b be the background information that there is a lottery consisting of 1001 tickets, one of which will be drawn at random, and by Tuesday 1000 tickets have been sold, of which Alice owns 999. Let e be the information that by Wednesday 1001 lottery tickets have been sold, of which Alice owns 999, and no more tickets will be sold. Let h be the hypothesis that Alice will win. Now, I suggest, e is evidence that h in this case. The information that Alice owns 999 of the 1001 tickets sold and that no more tickets will be sold is evidence that Alice will win. (The principle of reasonable belief, e.g., is clearly satisfied, since, given b, e is a good reason for believing h.) However, notice that in this case $p(h, e\&b) < p(h, b)$. ($p(h, e\&b) =$

---

[9] The expression is Karl Popper's, *Logic of Scientific Discovery* (London, 1959), p. 407, but I am changing his example to suit my purposes here.

999/1001; p(h, b) > 999/1001.)[10] In the case of the 'paradox of ideal evidence', we have a situation in which information is evidence for a hypothesis even though it does not increase the proability of the hypothesis. In the second lottery case, we have a situation in which information is evidence for a hypothesis even though *it lowers the probability of the hypothesis from what it was before.* (In this case, on Tuesday there is evidence that Alice will win, and on Wednesday there is also evidence that Alice will win, which is slightly weaker than Tuesday's evidence.)

It may be replied that in the last two examples e is not evidence that h but only evidence that h is probable. Even if some others might wish to pursue this (dubious) line, it is doubtful that defenders of the increase-in-probability definition can. Let us change the second lottery case a bit by introducing e′ = the information that by Wednesday 1001 tickets have been sold, of which Alice owns 1000, and no more tickets will be sold. Now, since p(h, e′&b) > p(h, b), using definition (1b), increase-in-probability theorists will conclude that e′ is evidence that h. They will not insist here that e′ is evidence only for the hypothesis that h is probable. How could they then insist that e in the second lottery case is evidence only for the hypothesis that h is probable? (The probabilities conferred on h by e and e′ are only marginally different, and both, though less than 1, are extremely high.)

In the light of these three examples perhaps it will be agreed that 'e is evidence that h' cannot be defined simply as 'e increases h's probability'. But it may be contended that a related concept can be so defined, viz. 'e increases the evidence that h'. Thus,

e increases the evidence that h if and only if p(h, e&b) > p(h,b). However, increasing the evidence that h is not the same as increasing the probability of h. To increase the evidence that h is to start with information which is evidence that h and add to it something which is also evidence that h or at least is so when conjoined with previous information. But to do this it is neither sufficient nor necessary to increase h's probability. The first lottery example shows that it is not sufficient, while the paradox of ideal evidence shows that it is not necessary. In the first lottery example there is no increase in evidence that Bill will win, since in the first place there is no evidence that he will win, and the combined new and old information is not evidence that he will win, even though the probability that he will win has increased. In the paradox of ideal evidence there is an increase in

[10] The latter inequality holds assuming that p(Alice will buy the remaining ticket on Wednesday) > 0. p(h,b) = 999/1001 + m/n(1/1001), where m/n = the probability that Alice will buy the remaining ticket on Wednesday.

evidence that the ball will land on a number other than 3 on the 10,001st spin, but there is no increase in the probability of this hypothesis.

At this point a second definition of evidence in terms of probability might be offered, viz.

(2) e is potential evidence that h if and only if $p(h,e) > k$ (where k is some number, say $1/2$).

Some writers, indeed, claim that the concept of evidence (or confirmation) is ambiguous and that it can mean either (1) or (2).[11] One of these meanings is simply that given e, h has a certain (high) probability.

This proposal has the advantage of being able to handle both the first and second lottery cases and the paradox of ideal evidence. In the first lottery case, although the probability that Bill will win is increased by e, the probability that Bill will win, given e and b, is not high. (It is $1/101$.) Therefore, by (2), e&b is not evidence that Bill will win. On the other hand it is evidence that John will win, since p(John will win, e&b) = $100/101$. And this is as it should be. In the second lottery case we judge that the information given is evidence that Alice will win (despite the fact that the probability that Alice will win is lower than before). Such a judgement is justified on the basis of (2), since p(Alice will win, e) = $999/1001$.

The paradox of ideal evidence is also avoided by (2) since the fact that (e) the ball landed on numbers other than 3 approximately 35/36ths of the time during the second 5000 spins makes the probability very high that it will land on a number other than 3 on the 10,001st spin. In this case $p(h,e) > k$, and therefore, by (2), e is evidence that h, even though p(h, e&b) = p(h,b).

However, (3) is beset by a major problem of its own.

The Wheaties case (or the problem of irrelevant information).[12] Let e be the information that this man eats the breakfast cereal Wheaties. Let h be the hypothesis that this man will not become pregnant. The probability of h given e is extremely high (since the probability of h is extremely high and is not diminished by the assumption of e). But e is not evidence that h. To claim that the fact that this

---

[11] See Carnap, op. cit., pp. xv–xx; Wesley C. Salmon, 'Confirmation and Relevance', in G. Maxwell and R. Anderson, Jr., eds., *Minnesota Studies in the Philosophy of Science*, vol. 6 (Minneapolis, 1975), p. 5 [Selection VI]; Hesse, op. cit., pp. 133–4.

[12] Salmon, *Statistical Explanation and Statistical Relevance*, uses a similar example against the D-N model of explanation, but not as an argument against (2).

man eats Wheaties is evidence that he will not become pregnant is to make a bad joke at best.

Such examples can easily be multiplied. The fact that Jones is drinking Whiskey (praying to God, taking vitamin C, etc.) to get rid of his cold is not evidence that he will recover within a week, despite the fact that people who have done these things do generally recover within a week (i.e., despite the fact that the probability of recovering in this time, given these remedies, is very high). It may well be for this reason that some writers prefer definition (1) over (2). On (1) e in the present examples would not be evidence that h because $p(h,e) = p(h)$, i.e., because e is probabilistically irrelevant for h. I would agree that the reason that e is not evidence that h is that e is irrelevant for h, but this is not mere probabilitistic irrelevance (as will be argued later).

A defender of (2) might reply that in the Wheaties example we can say that the probability of h given e is high only because we are assuming as background information the fact that no man has ever become pregnant; and he may insist that this background information be incorporated into the probability statement itself by writing '$p(h, e\&b) > k$'. In section 5 contrasting views about the role of background information with respect to probability (and evidence) statements will be noted, only one of which insists that such information always be incorporated into the probability statement itself. However, even if the latter viewpoint is espoused the Wheaties example presents a problem for (2) if we agree that information that is irrelevant for h can be added to information that is evidence that h without the result being evidence that h.

Suppose that b is evidence that h and that $p(h,b) > k$. There will be some irrelevant e such that $p(h, e\&b) = p(h,b)$, yet e\&b is not evidence that h. Thus let h be the hypothesis that this man will not become pregnant. Let b be the information that no man has ever become pregnant, and let e be the information that this man eats Wheaties. We may conclude that $p(h, e\&b) > k$, which, as demanded above, incorporates b into the probability statement. But although b is evidence that h we would be most reluctant to say that e\&b is too.[13]

Wesley Salmon[14] has claimed that the notion of evidence that

---

[13] An analogous problem arises for those who defend the D-N model of explanation. Kinetic theory entails the ideal gas law, but so does kinetic theory conjoined with laws from economic theory. Not wishing to say that this enlarged set explains the ideal gas law, the D-N theorist requires an elimination of the irrelevant laws in the D-N explanans.

[14] 'Bayes' Theorem and the History of Science', in R. Stuewer, ed., *Minnesota Studies in the Philosophy of Science*, vol. 5.

confirms a hypothesis can be understood in terms of Bayes's theorem of probabilities, a simple form of which is

$$p(h,e) = \frac{p(h) \times p(e,h)}{p(e)}.$$

According to this theorem, to determine the probability of h on e we must determine three quantities: the initial probability of h ($p(h)$), the 'likelihood' of h on e ($p(e,h)$), and the initial probability of e ($p(e)$). Salmon criticizes a view of evidence which says that if a hypothesis entails an observational conclusion e which is true, then e is evidence that h. This view, he points out, considers only one of the probabilities above, viz. $p(e,h) = 1$. To determine whether e is evidence that h one must also consider the initial probabilities of h and e.

This may be a valid criticism but it does not avoid the previous problems. Suppose that Bayes's theorem is used to determine the 'posterior' probability of h, i.e., $p(h,e)$, by reference to the initial probabilities of h and of e and the likelihood of h on e. We must still determine what, if anything, this has to do with whether e is evidence that h. If definitions (1) or (2) are used to determine this we confront all of the previous difficulties even though we have used Bayes's theorem in calculating $p(h,e)$. Thus let e be the information that this man eats Wheaties, and h be the hypothesis that this man will not become pregnant. Assume the following probabilities, which do not seem unreasonable: $p(h) = 1$, $p(e,h) = 1/10$, $p(e) = 1/10$. Then by Bayes's theorem, $p(h,e) = 1$. Using definition (2) we must conclude that e is evidence that h.

Can the problems with (1) and (2) be avoided by combining these definitions? Using a background-information formulation, it might be tempting to say that

(3) e is evidence that h if and only if *both* $p(h, e\&b) > p(h, b)$ *and* $p(h, e\&b) > k$.

Unfortunately, this does not provide a necessary condition for evidence. As demonstrated by the paradox of ideal evidence and the second lottery case, e can be evidence that h even though e does not raise h's probability (indeed, even if e lowers it). Does (3) provide a sufficient condition for evidence? Let us consider one more lottery, as follows.

The third lottery case. Let b be the background information that there is a lottery consisting of 1 million tickets, one of which will be drawn at random, and by Tuesday all but one of the tickets have been sold, of which Eugene owns 1. Let e be the information that on

Wednesday Jane, who owns no other tickets, bought the remaining ticket. Let h be the hypothesis that Eugene will not win. Since p(h, e&b) = 999,999/1,000,000 > p(h, b), (3) permits us to conclude that the fact that Jane, who owns no other tickets, bought the one remaining ticket is evidence that Eugene will not win. But that seems much too strong a claim to make. The fact that Jane bought the one remaining ticket is not a good reason at all for believing that Eugene will lose.

It is not my claim that probability is irrelevant for evidence, but only that the particular probability definitions (1), (2), and (3) – the standard definitions and their conjunction–are inadequate.

3. AN EXPLANATION DEFINITION

I turn then to a very different proposal which appeals to the concept of explanation:

(1) e is potential evidence that h if and only if e is true and h would correctly explain e if h were true.

This definition can be closely associated with at least two views. One is Hanson's account of retroductive reasoning, which takes the form

Some surprising phenomenon P is observed
P would be explicable as a matter of course if h were true
Hence, there is reason to think that h is true.[15]

The fact that phenomenon P has been observed is then potential evidence that h; it is so because h would correctly explain P if it were true. (1) is also closely associated with the hypothetico-deductive account of theories according to which if hypothesis h is a potential explanans of e (which, on this view, means roughly that h contains a lawlike sentence and entails e), then if e turns out to be true e is confirming evidence for h [see Selection II.]. Sympathy with (1) might then lead to the following simple definition of veridical evidence:

(2) e is veridical evidence that h iff h correctly explains e (i.e., e is potential evidence that h and h is true).[16]

---

[15] N. R. Hanson, *Patterns of Discovery* (Cambridge, 1958), p. 72 [cf. Selection III].

[16] (2) might be associated with a view, in addition to the above, that in any inductive inference one infers that a hypothesis correctly explains the evidence. This is Gilbert Harman's view in 'The Inference to the Best Explanation', *Philosophical Review*, lxiv (1965), 88–95. Later he revised it by requiring only that h correctly explains something, and also by stressing the global nature of inference, viz. that one infers to the best overall system.

Despite the emphasis in recent years on the role of explanation in inference from evidence, neither (1) nor (2) provides a necessary or a sufficient condition for potential or veridical evidence. Neither provides a necessary condition since, as noted earlier, e may be evidence that h even if h does not, and would not if true, correctly explain e. The fact that Jones has the chest wound he does may be potential or veridical evidence that he will die, even though the hypothesis that he will die does not, and would not if true, correctly explain why he has that chest wound. The explanation condition if necessary at all should be changed to require only some explanatory connection between h and e.

Nor do these definitions provide sufficient conditions. Suppose my car won't start this morning. The hypothesis

h: At precisely 2.07 last night 5 boys and 2 girls removed the 18.9 gallons of gas remaining in my tank and substituted water

would if true correctly explain why my car won't start this morning; indeed, suppose that h is true and that it does correctly explain this. In either case the fact that (e) my car won't start this morning is not evidence that h is true. There is too much of a gulf between this e and h for e to be evidence that h, even if h does or would if true correctly explain e. What this gulf amounts to I shall try to say later.

It is worth noting here that the earlier principle of reasonable belief is violated. According to this principle, if the fact that my car won't start this morning were evidence that h, then this fact would be at least some good reason for believing h. But (given the 'normal' background information one might imagine for such a case) the fact that my car won't start this morning is far too meagre a reason to believe the very specific hypothesis h. Indeed, innumerably many hypotheses in addition to h can be invented which if true would correctly explain why my car won't start. The hypothesis that

h': At precisely 3.05 last night 2 monkeys removed the remaining 3.7 gallons of gas in my tank and substituted crushed bananas

if true would explain why my car won't start. Is the fact that my car won't start evidence that h' is true? Does this fact provide any reason to believe such a hypothesis?

4. A NEW PROPOSAL

Although neither the probability nor explanation definitions are adequate, if these are combined in a certain way the outcome may be more successful. Here are my proposals:

(1) e is potential evidence that h if and only if (a) e is true, (b) e does not entail h, (c) p(h,e) > k, (d) p(there is an explanatory connection between h and e, h&e) > k.

(2) e is veridical evidence that h if and only if e is potential evidence that h, h is true, and there is an explanatory connection between the truth of h and e. (This is simply (1) of section 1.)

For e to be potential evidence that h we require, in addition to e's being true and not entailing h, the satisfaction of two probability conditions. One is that the probability of h given e be high. The other is that the probability that there is an explanatory connection between h and e, given that h and e are both true, be high; i.e., that it be probable, given h and e, that h is true because e is, or conversely, or that some hypothesis correctly explains both. Veridical evidence requires, in addition to this, that h be true and that there be an explanatory connection between the truth of h and e.

In section 1 the following features of potential evidence were cited: (i) e can be potential evidence that h even if h is false; (ii) potential evidence is objective, i.e., whether e is potential evidence that h does not depend on whether anyone believes e or h or anything about their relationship; (iii) e is potential evidence that h only if e is true; (iv) e is potential evidence that h only if e does not entail h. Features (i), (iii), and (iv) are obviously satisfied by (1) above, as is feature (ii) provided that the concept of probability used in conditions (1c) and (1d) is construed as an objective one.

To assess these definitions let us reconsider the counterexamples to the previous probability and explanation definitions.

The first lottery case. The fact that all the lottery tickets except those of John and Bill have been destroyed, that of the original 1000 tickets John has 100 and Bill has 1, and that one ticket will be drawn at random, does not make it probable that Bill will win. Hence by condition (1c) this fact is not potential (and therefore not veridical) evidence that Bill will win. On the contrary, as previously indicated, it ought to be potential evidence that John will win. And indeed it is on definition (1), since given the fact in question it is probable that John will win (1c); and given the same fact and the fact that John will win it is probable that a correct explanation of why John will win is that all the 1000 lottery tickets except those of John and Bill have been destroyed, that of the 101 remaining tickets John has 100 and Bill 1, and that one ticket will be chosen at random (1d). Definition (1) above gives us a reasonable analysis of this case in a way that the probability definition (1) of section 2 does not.

The paradox of ideal evidence. The fact that (e) the roulette ball has landed on numbers other than 3 approximately 35/36ths of the time during the second 5000 spins ought to be potential evidence that (h) it will land on a number other than 3 on the 10,001st spin, even if the probability of this hypothesis has not increased over its prior probability. Definition (1) gives us what we want, since the probability of h on e is high. And given that h and e are both true it is probable that both h and e are correctly explained by the hypothesis that on the roulette wheel there are 36 places of equal size for the ball to land, 35 of which show numbers other than 3.

The second lottery case. The fact that (e) by Wednesday 1001 lottery tickets have been sold, of which Alice owns 999, and no more tickets will be sold, ought to be potential evidence that (h) Alice will win—despite the fact that Alice's chances have diminished slightly from what they were on Tuesday. Again, definition (1) yields the desired result, since the probability of h on e is high. And given that h and e are both true, it is probable that the reason that h is that e: it is probable that the reason that Alice will win is that she owns 999 of the 1001 lottery tickets that have been sold and that no more will be sold.

The Wheaties case. The fact that (e) this man eats Wheaties should not be (potential or veridical) evidence that (h) this man will not become pregnant, even though the probability of h given e is high. And it is not evidence on definition (1) since condition (d) is violated. Given that h and e are both true, it is not probable that there is an explanatory connection between h and e: it is not probable that this man will not become pregnant because he eats Wheaties, or that he eats Wheaties because he will not become pregnant, or that there is some hypothesis that correctly explains both why he eats Wheaties and why he does not become pregnant. His eating Wheaties and his not becoming pregnant are not only probabilistically independent, they are (probably) explanatorily independent.

However, we might alter the example as follows. Let e' be the information that this man who wants to become pregnant believes that he never will and as a consequence becomes anxious and eats Wheaties to reduce his anxiety. In this case, it might be urged, given both h and e' it is probable that h does correctly explain e': it is probable that this man believes what he does, becomes anxious and eats Wheaties because in fact he will not become pregnant. Then by definition (1) e' is potential evidence that h. Assuming that h is true and that there is such an explanatory connection between e' and h, then e' is also veridical evidence that h, by definition (2). Is this reasonable?

A claim that it is not might be made on the ground that we do, after all, have extremely good evidence that h, viz. that this man is indeed a *man*, not a woman. And this is both potential and veridical evidence that there will be no pregnancy. However, the fact that there is other evidence whose support for h is stronger than that given by e′ does not by itself mean that e′ is not evidence that h. Here it is important to recall the distinction between something's being evidence that h and its being *someone's* evidence that h. In our earlier example at the end of section 1, the fact that Alan is receiving treatment T might be (potential or veridical) evidence that he has an i.c.b. without its being the *doctor's* evidence. (The fact that Alan is receiving this treatment may not be the doctor's reason for believing that he has an i.c.b.) Similarly, the fact that this man, who wants to become pregnant, is anxious because he believes he never will and eats Wheaties to reduce his anxiety can be evidence that he will not become pregnant without its being *anyone's* evidence for this. No one who believes that this man will not become pregnant may do so for the reason just given.

The third lottery case. The fact that (e) on Wednesday Jane bought the remaining ticket in the lottery should not be potential evidence that (h) Eugene will lose. This is so even if we assume as background information (b) that there is a lottery consisting of 1 million tickets and by Tuesday all but one of the tickets have been sold, of which Eugene owns 1. By definition (1), e is not evidence that h, since condition (1d) is violated. Given that Eugene will lose and that Jane bought the remaining ticket, it is not probable that the reason Eugene will lose is that Jane bought the remaining ticket, or that the reason that Jane bought the remaining ticket is that Eugene will lose, or that some hypothesis correctly explains both why Eugene will lose and why Jane bought the remaining ticket.

The case of the stalled car. The fact that (e) my car won't start this morning is not potential evidence that (h) at precisely 2:07 last night 5 boys and 2 girls removed the 18.9 gallons of gas remaining in my tank and substituted water. This is so because condition (1c) is not satisfied. The gulf mentioned earlier which prevents e from being evidence that h is a probabilistic one: it is not the case that h is probable given e.

The proposed definition of potential evidence thus avoids the counterexamples to previous definitions, and yields those evidence claims in the examples that we are willing to assert. Will it sanction other evidence statements that we are usually prepared to make? Is the fact that all the observed crows have been black potential evidence that all crows are black? Is the fact that the gases hydrogen and oxygen combine in a simple ratio by volume potential evidence that the gases nitrogen and oxygen do too (as Gay-Lussac thought)? Is the fact that electrons produce tracks in cloud chambers potential evidence that they carry a charge? Is the fact that Alan has yellow skin potential evidence that he has an i.c.b.? Whether these claims can be made depends on whether certain probability statements can be asserted. The fact that Alan has yellow skin is potential evidence that he has an i.c.b. only if it is probable that he has an i.c.b., given that he has yellow skin, and it is probable that there is an explanatory connection between his having yellow skin and his having an i.c.b., given that he has both. And whether these probability claims can be made depends on what background information is being assumed, and on the general relationship between probability statements and background information. What view we take of this relationship will determine what evidence statements we can assert, as will be shown next.

5. BACKGROUND INFORMATION

Two views about the role of background information are possible. One is that probability statements should be relativized to the background information to which any appeal is made. The other is that no such relativization is necessary. According to the former view the background information must be incorporated into the probability statement itself. If appeal is made to b in determining that the probability of h on e is r then we should write 'p(h&b) = r'. In the case of evidence, we could say that the conjunction of e and b is evidence that h, provided that the definitions of section 4 are satisfied. Or we can continue to say that e is evidence that h, provided that we relativize the evidence statement to the background information by writing 'e is evidence that h, given b', and reformulate the definitions of section 4 as follows:

(1) e is potential evidence that h, given b, if and only if (a) e and b are true, (b) e does not entail h, (c) $p(h, e\&b) > k$, (d) p(there is an explanatory connection between h and e, $h\&e\&b) > k$.

(2) e is veridical evidence that h, given b, if and only if e is potential evidence that h, given b; h is true; and there is an explanatory connection between the truth of h and e.

In what follows I will discuss that version of the relativization view given by (1) and (2). According to it the fact that Alan has yellow skin can be shown to be potential evidence that he has an i.c.b., given the doctor's background information on Monday (which includes the fact that people with that kind of skin usually have an i.c.b. and usually have that kind of skin because they have an i.c.b.). However, the fact that Alan has yellow skin is not potential evidence that he has an i.c.b., given the doctor's background information on Friday (which includes the results of tests).

By contrast to the relativization view, one might claim that background information need not be construed as a part of the probability statement itself, but only as information to which one appeals in *defending* or *justifying* that statement. Thus

(3) The probability that Alan has an i.c.b., given that he has yellow skin, is high

might be defended by appeal to the empirical fact that

(4) In most cases people with (that kind of) yellow skin have an i.c.b.

But on this view the fact that (3) is defensible by appeal to the empirical fact that (4) is true shows that (3) itself is an empirical statement. It does not show that (3) is an incomplete version of the (perhaps) *a priori* statement that

The probability that Alan has an i.c.b., given that he has yellow skin and that in most cases people with (that kind of) yellow skin have an i.c.b., is high.

On Monday the doctor defends (3) by appeal to (4). On Friday he has accumulated new information, which includes the results of tests, and he then defends the negation of (3) by appeal to this new information. By contrast, the relativist must say that on Monday the doctor is asserting a probability statement of the form '$p(h,e\&b_1) > k$', while Friday he is asserting one of the form '$p(h,e\&b_2) < k$'. And these are not incompatible statements.

Returning to evidence, a non-relativist with regard to background information can accept the definitions of evidence as these are given in section 4, and need not relativize them to the background information by writing either 'e&b is evidence that h' or 'e is evidence that h, given b'. He can consider statements of the form

(5) The fact that Alan has yellow skin is potential evidence that he has an i.c.b.

to be complete, even though appeals to background information will be made in defending (5) or its denial. On Monday, on the basis of the information available to him, the doctor affirms (5); on Friday, on the basis of the new information, he denies (5). The relativist, on the other hand, regards (5) as incomplete. If (5) is relativized to the background information on Monday it is true, and if relativized to the background information on Friday it is false.

I shall not here try to arbitrate between these views. Perhaps each reflects different tendencies in the way we speak about probability and evidence. Perhaps one is more dominant than the other in linguistic practice or is more advantageous for other reasons. But which of these views about background information we employ will affect what claims about potential and veridical evidence we are prepared to make.

Thus, in section 1 it was asked whether there is a concept of potential evidence according to which

(6) Alan's yellow skin was evidence of an i.c.b. (on Monday) and still is (on Friday)

is true, despite the fact that on Friday the doctor's tests prove negative. Using (1), a background-relative concept of potential evidence, (6) might be understood by reference to

(7) The fact that Alan has yellow skin is potential evidence that he has an i.c.b., given the background information of the doctor on Monday.

And (7) is as true on Friday as it is on Monday, since it is true timelessly. Of course if (6) is relativized to the information of the doctor on Friday then it is false timelessly. But the relativist who wants to explain the sense in which (6) is true can use definition (1) and relativize his evidence statement to the doctor's information on Monday.

The non-relativist will not be able to regard (6) as true, if construed as it has been so far. He will say that whereas on Monday he believed (5) to be true, on Friday he realizes that it is false; but he cannot assert that (5) was true on Monday and remains true on Friday, as (6) suggests.

Nevertheless, the non-relativist can resurrect (6) by claiming that it is true if it is construed as making a *general* claim rather than a particular one, viz.

(8) Having the kind of yellow skin which Alan has is (timelessly) evidence of (having) an i.c.b.

And he can provide the following set of necessary and sufficient conditions for statements of this type, using as a guide the previous definition of potential evidence:

(9) Having F is potential evidence of having G (for A's) if and only if (a) 'X is F' does not entail 'X is G'; (b) the probability of something's (an A's) having G, given that it has F, is high;

(c) the probability that there is an explanatory connection between something's (an A's) having F and its having G, given
that it has both, is high.

Using (9) the non-relativist can argue that (8) is true and therefore
that a sense of potential evidence can be provided which sanctions (6).
There is then a certain analogy between the relativist's and the non-
relativist's response to (6), since according to both (6) has different
interpretations. The relativist argues that (6) is true if construed as (7)
but false if construed as

The fact that Alan has yellow skin is potential evidence that he has
an i.c.b., given the background information of the doctor on Friday.

The non-relativist argues that (6) is false if construed as (5) but true
if constured as (8).

6. THE LOCH NESS MONSTER AND SEVERED HEAD CASES

Two objections to the definitions of section 4 will now be considered.
    There is a well-known photograph taken by a London surgeon in
1934 which purports to depict the Loch Ness monster.[17] Even if
the existence of the monster is very improbable despite the photograph, isn't the existence of the photograph evidence that the monster
exists? If so there is a violation of the condition for potential evidence
that p(h,e) be high. Those who favour the 'increase in probability'
condition for evidence may cite examples such as this in defence of
their position and in criticism of mine. Let us examine this criticism.
    We are being asked to consider the claim that

(1) The existence of this photograph which purports to depict the
    Loch Ness monster is evidence that the monster exists.

Someone who believes that (1) is true might defend it by providing
information about the surgeon who took the picture, from what
position, at what time of day, etc. He might also point out how the
camera used works and that photographs are generally reliable, i.e.,
usually when a photograph depicts what seems clearly to be X and the
photographer has not made efforts to be deceptive, then an X exists.[18]
But if this is how he defends (1) then, I think, he should not accept

[17] This photograph as well as three others taken between 1934 and 1960 are
reproduced in David James, *Loch Ness Investigation* (London).
[18] A non-relativistic notion of evidence is here being assumed in accordance
with which this background information is being used to defend (1). However,
the same argument could proceed with a relativized notion by relativizing (1)
to this background information.

the claim that the existence of the monster is very improbable despite the photograph. On the contrary, he should believe that it is probable. (Indeed, this is what Sir Peter Scott recently claimed about new photographs taken in 1972.) New information can cancel the negative effects of background information. Even if the existence of the Loch Ness Monster is improbable on the background information, a suitable photograph can make its existence very probable.

However, two other situations are possible. First, we may not know the reliability of the photographer, the conditions under which the photograph was taken, or indeed whether it is a genuine photograph (rather than a clever drawing). If so, and if there are independent reasons for doubting the existence of X, then we may be very unsure of the truth of claim (1). We should then assert not that the existence of this photograph *is* evidence that a monster exists, but that it *may* be evidence (we don't yet know), or that it is evidence that there *may be* a monster (a claim to which I will return in a moment). Secondly, we may know that the photographer was unreliable or that the conditions under which he took the photograph were. Given this and other background information, the existence of the Loch Ness monster is very improbable, let us suppose. But given the unreliability of the photographer and photographic conditions would we make claim (1)? I seriously doubt it.

The importance of the subjective concept of evidence should not be minimized here. A question such as 'Is there any evidence that there is a Loch Ness monster?' might be understood as 'Is there anything that people take to be evidence that the monster exists?' To which the answer is: emphatically yes! It is not that those who believe that the monster exists are unable to appeal to any facts as their reason for so believing. Quite the reverse. The existence of this photograph, among other things, is their evidence.

Finally, when the probability of h given e is low, although e is not evidence that h is true it can be evidence that h *may* be true (or that h is possible). One might claim that the existence of the surgeon's photograph is evidence that there may be a monster. The fact that Joe is one of 50 finalists in the state lottery is not evidence that he will win $1 million—that is too strong a claim to make. But it can be evidence that he may win $1 million or that his winning is a possibility. The fact that Bob is playing one round of Russian roulette is not evidence that he will die but that he may die, that his dying is a possibility. Such evidence claims, although different from the ones we have been considering, can be understood, I think, by altering the concept of potential evidence so as to require not high probabilities but non-negligible ones. That is

> e is evidence that h may be true (or that h is possible) if and only if (a) e is true; (b) e does not entail h; (c) the probability of h given e is not negligible; (d) the probability that there is an explanatory connection between h and e, given h and e, is not negligible.

The fact that (e) Bob is playing one round of Russian roulette is evidence that h may be true, where h is the hypothesis that Bob will die. This is so since the probability of h, given e, is not negligible; and given that h and e are both true, the probability is not negligible that there is an explanatory connection between Bob's dying and his playing one round of Russian roulette.

The second objection to definitions of section 4 will be dealt with more briefly. We saw that the requirement of an explanatory connection between e and h for e to be veridical evidence that h allows us to preclude certain unwanted cases. In view of the following gruesome example, however, it may be wondered whether this requirement is too strong.

Henry drops dead from a heart attack. Afterwards his head is severed by a fiendish decapitator.[19] Isn't the fact that his head has been severed from his body veridical evidence that Henry is not living, even though there is no explanatory connection between his decapitation and his not being alive? If so the explanatory requirement is not necessary for veridical (or potential) evidence.

The latter conclusion is too hasty. There are various reasons one may not be alive, not all of which need be reasons for which one died. Anyone whose head has been severed from his body is not alive because, among other things, his brain is unable to receive oxygen from the rest of his body. Consider an analogous case. Tom's TV set is not working because one of the tubes burned out. Later Tom accidentally drops the set breaking the remaining tubes. Now among the reasons the set is not working is that all the other tubes are broken (although this is not among the reasons that it stopped working in the first place). There is an explanatory connection between the fact that these other tubes are broken and the fact that the set is not working; indeed, the former is veridical evidence that the latter is true.

To this one might respond that we should change the case a bit. Let e be the information that someone severed Henry's head. Instead

---

[19] Brian Skyrms, 'The Explication of "X knows that p"', *Journal of Philosophy*, lxiv (1967), 373–389, uses this kind of case as a counterexample against certain causal analyses of 'X knows that p'.

of considering the hypothesis that Henry is not living, let h be that Henry died (i.e., that he went through some process that eventuated in death). Now e should be evidence that h despite the fact that there is no explanatory connection between e and h. I agree that we would speak of evidence in such a case, and yet there is something objectionable about it. The tension can be resolved, I suggest, by saying that the fact that someone severed Henry's head is potential, but not veridical, evidence that he died. The conditions for potential evidence are satisfied. For example, given background information which does not include the fact that Henry's death was due to a prior heart attack, and given that someone severed Henry's head and that Henry died, the probability is high that Henry died because someone severed his head. However, the fact that someone severed his head is not veridical evidence that he died, since there is no explanatory connection here. This is analogous to one of the examples in section 1 involving Alan and the i.c.b., viz. that in which Alan has yellow skin and an i.c.b. although his yellow skin did not result from the i.c.b. but from the chemical dye with which he was working. Although his having the yellow skin he does is potential evidence that he has an i.c.b. it is not veridical evidence.

7. THE DESIRABILITY OF EVIDENCE

In concluding, I shall briefly turn to the question of why evidence is desirable. When one has a hypothesis h why should one seek evidence that h?

The answer, which is straightforward, is that one wants one's hypothesis to be true or at least probable, and one wants a reason for believing it. To have evidence is to satisfy both desires, at least on the theory of evidence in section 4. If e is veridical evidence that h, then h is true, and if e is (only) potential evidence that h then h is probable given e. Moreover, given background information b, if e is potential or veridical evidence that h, then, following the principle of reasonable belief, given b, e is at least some good reason for believing h. According to the theory of section 4 evidence that h provides at least some good reason for believing h only if (a) h is probable given e, and (b) there is probably an explanatory connection between h and e, given h and e. The Wheaties example provides a case satisfying (a) but not (b), while the case of the stalled car satisfies (b) but not (a). And in neither case does e provide a good reason for believing h. The fact that this man eats Wheaties is not a good reason for believing that he will not become pregnant. And the fact that my car won't start this morning is not a good reason for believing the very specific hypothesis h of section 3.

On the other hand, the alternative definitions of evidence that I rejected do not jointly satisfy the twin desires of truth/probability and reasons for believing. The 'increase in probability' definition spawns the first lottery case in which the hypothesis that Bill will win is not probable (though its probability is increased over its prior probability); nor in this case does the information cited provide a reason for believing that Bill will win. The 'high probability' definition, although it satisfies the desire for probability, generates the wheaties case in which, as we have just seen, the 'evidence' provides no reason for believing the hypothesis. Finally, the explanation definition satisfies neither the truth/probability desire nor that for a reason for believing, as is shown by the case of the stalled car.

APPENDIX. GLYMOUR'S BOOTSTRAP THEORY*

Clark Glymour offers an account of evidence which is quite different from any of those so far discussed.[20] Indeed, it includes no probability or explanation conditions whatever.[21] Glymour's claim is that something is evidence for a hypothesis only in relation to a theory consisting of a set of hypotheses. His basic idea (the 'bootstrap condition') is that e is evidence that h with respect to theory T if and only if using T it is possible to derive from e an instance of h, and the derivation is such as not to guarantee an instance of h no matter what e is chosen. The specific conditions Glymour imposes are complex, and the account is most readily developed for hypotheses that are expressed quantitatively in the form of equations. . . .

Glymour's conditions for evidence for an equation can be stated as follows. Where e describes a set of observed values of quantities, and h is an equation containing quantities, and T is a theory consisting of equations, e is evidence that h with respect to T if and only if

1. e is consistent with T.
2. From the specific values in e a value for each quantity in h is computable.
3. The computation involves only equations in T and their consequences.
4. The equation representing h for the computations used is not a mathematical identity.

---

* From *The Nature of Explanation*, ch. 11, sec. 2.
[20] Clark Glymour, *Theory and Evidence* (Princeton, 1980), ch. 5 [see Selection VII].
[21] For a later attempt to introduce probabilities see his 'Bootstraps and Probabilities', *Journal of Philosophy*, 77 (1980), 691-9.

5. The values obtained from the computations used constitute a solution to the equation in h.[22]

These conditions invoke no probability requirements. In particular, for e to be evidence that h with respect to T there is no requirement that the probability of h be high, given e and T, or that this probability be greater than the probability of h given T. (Indeed, in the usual case of interest to us hypothesis h will be a part of T itself, so that p(h, e&T) = 1 and p(h, T) = 1. Thus h will have maximal probability, and its probability will not be increased by e.) Nor is there a requirement that the confirmed hypothesis h explain the observed values reported in e, or that given e&h&T the probability be high that there is an explanatory connection between h and e. (In a moment I shall consider an example violating such explanation requirements.) The basic idea is that observed values of quantities provide evidence for an equation in a theory if from these values together with equations in the theory computations can be made for all quantities in the equation which will yield (positive) instances of that equation.

Let me now suggest a simple example which will illustrate what I take to be a major shortcoming in the bootstrap approach. The theory that I will propose consists of a set of equations employing three quantitites. The first two quantities are familiar ones which I shall take to be directly measurable:

A = the total force acting on a particle
B = the product of a particle's mass and acceleration.

The third quantity, the 'theoretical' one, is not directly measurable:

C = the quantity of God's attention focused on a particle.

Theory T consists of two equations:

(i) A = C
(ii) B = C

Experimentally we determine specific values for A (total force) and B (product of mass and acceleration). From a specific value for B, using equation (ii) we compute a specific value for C (quantity of God's attention). The representative of (i) for this computation is A = B, which is not a mathematical identity. Therefore, if the value of C computed from B is the same as the experimentally determined value of A, we have confirmed the first equation A = C. In this case the statement describing the experimentally determined values of total force

[22] *Theory and Evidence*, p. 117.

and mass $\times$ acceleration is evidence that the total force on a particle = the quantity of God's attention focused on the particle, with respect to Theory T.

Similarly, a value for C can be computed from A using equation (i). If this computed value of C is the same as the experimentally determined value of B, then the second equation B = C has been confirmed. In this case the statement describing the experimentally determined values of total force and mass $\times$ acceleration is evidence that the product of a particle's mass $\times$ acceleration = the quantity of God's attention focused on the particle, with respect to theory T. Thus, the observed values of force and mass $\times$ acceleration provide evidence for each equation in this theory, with respect to that theory.

This result may strike one as absurd. How can information about experimentally determined values of the total force acting on a particle and its mass $\times$ acceleration provide evidence for how much of God's attention is focused on the particle? Given no other background information about God and his relationship to particles, and indeed given little if any idea of what it means to talk about 'the quantity of God's attention focused on a particle', such an evidence claim seems unwarranted. It would be precluded by the account of evidence I propose in [earlier sections]. In the absence of any other information, there is no reason to suppose that the probability that A = C is high, given that the specific values observed for force and mass $\times$ acceleration are the same. If not, the high probability condition is not satisfied. Neither is the explanation condition. There seems to be no reason to say that the probability is high of an explanatory connection between the fact that A = C and the fact that the observed values of A and B are equal, given these facts.

However, this objection may not be decisive. We must bear in mind that Glymour insists on relativizing evidence for a hypothesis to a theory. What he would (or could) say is that e (the sentence describing the observed values of A and B) is evidence for (i) *with respect to theory T* (consisting of equations (i) and (ii)); it need not be evidence for (i) with respect to some different theory T' (e.g., one that does not contain (ii)). Within T the observed values of force and mass $\times$ acceleration count as evidence for equations relating each of these quantities to the quantity of God's attention focused on a particle. Within some different theory T', say the theory consisting of Newton's first, second, and third laws of motion, the observed values of force and mass $\times$ acceleration will not count as evidence for equations relating each of these quantities to the quantity of God's attention focused on a particle. And—perhaps Glymour will say—it is because we are thinking of a theory of the latter sort, rather than of the former, that we find the present evidence claim so puzzling and objectionable.

This raises a fundamental question about the usefulness of the concept of evidence or confirmation that Glymour is defining. [Earlier] I took evidence to bear an important relationship to what it is reasonable to believe: if, in the light of the background information b, e is evidence that h, then, given b, e is at least some good reason for believing h. I also took a sentence of the form 'e is evidence that h, given b' to require the truth of b as well as e (see section 5). Accordingly, if e is evidence that h, given b, then we can say that in view of the truth of b, e is at least some good reason for believing h. Now a concept of evidence is a useful one only if it is possible for a person to come to know that e is true, that b is true, and that, given b, e is evidence that h—at least for a considerable range of cases in which, given b, e is evidence that h. Only then can persons have (legitimate) reasons for believing hypotheses. It would be useless for us to have a concept of evidence which is such that although e *is* evidence that h, given b, we would not be in a position to have e as our reason for believing h.

Returning to our 'God's attention' example above, on Glymour's definition, e (the sentence describing the observed values of A and B) is evidence that A = C, with respect to theory T. It is not part of Glymour's view that the latter claim entails or presupposes the truth of theory T. (Glymour's 'with respect to T' is not to be understood in the way I am construing 'given b' in 'e is evidence that h, given b'.) So from the truth of the claim 'e is evidence that A = C with respect to T' we cannot conclude that *in view of the truth of T* e is at least some good reason for believing that A = C. At most we can say this:

(7) If T is true, then e is at least some good reason for believing that A = C.

Now this conditional fact is a useful one in helping to form people's beliefs only if people can come to know the truth of T (or, at least, if they can come to have good reasons to believe that T is true). If they do come to know that T is true (or have good reasons to believe it is), and they do come to know that e is evidence that A = C with respect to T, then (I shall suppose) they have at least some good reason for believing that A = C. But how are people to come to know that T is true?

Presumably (since T is not *a priori*) by discovering that something is evidence that T; which means discovering that something is evidence for hypothesis (i) and that something is evidence for hypothesis (ii), or by discovering that something is evidence for the conjunction of (i) and (ii). Now we have shown that (on Glymour's definition) e, which reports the observed values of A and B, is evidence that (i) and also evidence that (ii). If this suffices to give us knowledge that T, then in view of (7) we get the absurd result that the observed values of force and mass × acceleration provide some good reason for believing that the total force acting on a particle = the quantity of God's attention focused on the particle. However, I doubt that Glymour will say that e's being evidence for (i) and (ii) suffices to give us knowledge that T, since e is evidence for (i) and for (ii) *with respect to T.* (It is not, e.g., evidence for (i) or (ii) with respect to T′, Newton's three laws of motion.) Although I know that (in Glymour's sense) e is evidence for (i) and for (ii) with respect to T, this fact does not enable me to know that T is true, Glymour will probably say. Nor, indeed, does this fact give me a reason to believe T. (It only gives me a reason to believe T with respect to T).

Glymour in his book does have a short section entitled 'Comparing Theories' (pp. 152-5). He claims that 'what makes one theory better than another is a diffuse matter that is not neatly or appropriately measured by any single scale' (p. 153). Glymour briefly mentions several criteria. For example, one theory may contain some hypotheses that are disconfirmed by the evidence whereas the other does not. (Presumably Glymour has in mind disconfirmation with respect to the theory in question.) One theory may contain more untested hypotheses than the other. The evidence may be more various for one theory than for another. And so forth. (My 'God's attention' theory T contains only confirmed hypotheses with respect to T, and no untested ones, although the evidence for it is less various than that for Newtonian theory.) However, if one theory is better than another according to Glymour's criteria for comparing theories, this does not mean that the former is known to be true whereas the latter is not; nor does it mean that there is a good reason to believe the former to be true and the latter false. Indeed, so far as I can make out from his brief description of the criteria, we can conclude nothing about the (probable) truth or falsity of a theory from the fact that it is 'better' or 'worse' in Glymour's sense than another theory.

On Glymour's conception of evidence it is difficult to see how one can come to know that T is true, or to have good reasons to believe it is, and hence to establish the antecedent of the conditional in (7). If one cannot do this, then one cannot come to know whether e is at least some good reason for believing that A = C. If Glymour's theories were entirely observational—if the equations contained quantities all of which are directly observable—then this problem would not arise. We could come to know the truth of each equation by making direct measurements of each quantity. There would be no computations at all. Each equation could come to be known without using any other equation, without, indeed, using any theory. But this is not the sort of case that interests Glymour. In general, his theories will contain 'theoretical' quantities whose values are determined not directly but only by computations from observable quantities using equations of that theory or some other. In such cases I fail to see how one comes to establish the truth of the theory, on Glymour's view of evidence. So even if the crazy theory T above is true, the fact that e is evidence that A = C, with respect to T, gives a person no reason whatever to believe that A = C (or to act on this assumption). In the absence of a method of coming to know the truth of a theory, or at least for coming to have good reasons for believing that it is true, Glymour's concept of evidence, I suggest, is not of sufficient use to us.

NOTES ON THE CONTRIBUTORS

CARL G. HEMPEL was Stuart Professor of Philosophy at Princeton until his retirement in 1973, and now teaches at the University of Pittsburgh. He is the author of *Aspects of Scientific Explanation, Fundamentals of Concept Formation in Empirical Science, Philosophy of Natural Science*, and of numerous influential articles in the philosophy of science.

R. B. BRAITHWAITE was Knightbridge Professor of Moral Philosophy at Cambridge University from 1953 to 1967. He wrote *Scientific Explanation* and *Theory of Games as a Tool for the Moral Philosopher.*

NORWOOD RUSSELL HANSON, the author of *Patterns of Discovery* and *The Concept of the Positron*, was a professor at Yale until his untimely death in 1967 at the age of forty-three. Before going to Yale he taught at Indiana University where he founded the first department of history and philosophy of science in the U.S.

NELSON GOODMAN, who retired from Harvard University in 1977, wrote the widely discussed works *Fact, Fiction, and Forecast, The Structure of Appearance,* and *Languages of Art.*

RUDOLF CARNAP, one of the central figures in the logical positivist movement in the 1920s and 1930s, later taught at the University of Chicago and UCLA. He is the author of the important work *Logical Foundations of Probability*, as well as of books and papers in logic, the philosophy of language, and the philosophy of science.

WESLEY SALMON, who teaches at the University of Pittsburgh, has written *The Foundations of Scientific Inference, Statistical Explanation and Statistical Relevance, Space, Time, and Motion,* and many papers on probability and induction.

CLARK GLYMOUR is the author of *Theory and Evidence* and of papers on the history and philosophy of modern physics. He teaches at the University of Pittsburgh in the Department of History and Philosophy of Science.

PETER ACHINSTEIN, a professor at Johns Hopkins University, wrote *Concepts of Science, Law and Explanation,* and *The Nature of Explanation.*

BIBLIOGRAPHY

An important general work in which the classificatory concept of evidence is discussed is

RUDOLF CARNAP, *Logical Foundations of Probability* (Chicago, 1950, 2nd edn., 1962).

Carnap's main focus is on developing a quantitative concept, but he has useful material on the classificatory concept in the preface to the second edition, and in chapters 1 and 7. A more introductory book on the quantitative concept which also discusses problems related to the classificatory concept is

RICHARD SWINBURNE, *An Introduction to Confirmation Theory* (London, 1973).

A recent book devoted primarily to the classificatory concept is

CLARK GLYMOUR, *Theory and Evidence* (Princeton, 1980).

Glymour develops his own bootstrap theory with applications to examples in the sciences; he also critically discusses Hempel's satisfaction definition, the hypothetico-deductive account, and the probability conception.

In addition to the selection by Carnap in this volume, and to material in Glymour's *Theory and Evidence*, Hempel's satisfaction definition of confirmation is critically discussed in

ISRAEL SCHEFFLER, *Anatomy of Inquiry* (New York, 1963), part 3
HELEN LONGINO, 'Evidence and Hypothesis: An Analysis of Evidential Relations', *Philosophy of Science*, 46 (1979), 55–86.

The paradox of the ravens, introduced in Hempel's article, has generated a large literature containing different solutions. The interested reader might consult W. V. Quine, 'Natural Kinds', in his *Ontological Relativity and Other Essays* (N.Y., 1969), and articles by R. E. Grandy, Nelson Goodman, and J. W. N. Watkins in Baruch A. Brody, ed., *Readings in the Philosophy of Science* (Englewood Cliffs, N. J., 1970), as well as bibliographic references in that volume. For some of Hempel's later thoughts about the paradox and his definition see his 'Postscript (1964)', *Aspects of Scientific Explanation* (New York, 1965), pp. 47–51.

The hypothetico-deductive account described by Braithwaite in selection II is also defended in

CARL G. HEMPEL, *Philosophy of Natural Science* (Englewood Cliffs, N. J., 1966).

BIBLIOGRAPHY 177

For a striking h-d viewpoint that completely eschews any concept of evidence that is based on inductive principles, see

KARL POPPER, *The Logic of Scientific Discovery* (London, 1959).

Recent defences of an h-d concept of evidence are given in

G. SCHLESINGER, *Confirmation and Confirmability* (Oxford, 1974)
G. MERRILL, 'Confirmation and Prediction', *Philosophy of Science,* 46 (1979), 98–117.

For a criticism of Merrill's theory and a claim that this criticism is applicable to all such h-d theories, see

CLARK GLYMOUR, 'Hypothetico-Deductivism is Hopeless', *Philosophy of Science,* 47 (1980), 322–5.

A good general discussion of hypothetico-deductivism is to be found in

WESLEY C. SALMON, *The Foundations of Scientific Inference* (Pittsburgh, 1966).

A number of the ideas about retroduction presented by Hanson in selection III were first expounded in

CHARLES PEIRCE, *Collected Papers,* ed. Charles Hartshorne and Paul Weiss (Cambridge, Mass., 1960). See particularly volumes 2 and 5.

See also

N. R. HANSON, *Patterns of Discovery* (Cambridge, 1958), ch. 4.

More recent accounts of retroduction can be found in

GILBERT HARMAN, *Thought* (Princeton, 1973)
PAUL THAGARD, 'The Best Explanation: Criteria for Theory Choice', *Journal of Philosophy*, 75 (1978), 76–92.

For a critical discussion of Hanson and Harman, see my

Law and Explanation (Oxford, 1971), ch. 6.

Goodman's theory of confirmation in selection IV was developed in response to his 'new riddle of induction' (the grue problem), which is formulated in

NELSON GOODMAN, *Fact Fiction, and Forecast* (Cambridge, Mass., 4th edn., 1983).

This riddle, like Hempel's ravens paradox, has spawned a good deal of controversy. For a few articles on the topic the interested reader might consult

STEPHEN BARKER and PETER ACHINSTEIN, 'On the New Riddle of Induction', *Philosophical Review*, 69 (1960), 511–22.
Articles by R. C. JEFFREY, JUDITH JARVIS THOMSON, and J. R. WALLACE, *Journal of Philosophy*, 63 (1966), 281–328.

For replies to these see

NELSON GOODMAN, *Problems and Projects* (Indianapolis, 1972), 402–10.

Goodman's positive theory of projection is discussed in

178   BIBLIOGRAPHY

DALE GOTTLIEB, 'Rationality and the Theory of Projection', *Nous*, 3 (1975), 319–28;

JOSEPH S. ULLIAN, 'On Projectibility', *Nous*, 3 (1975), 329–39 (this is a response to Gottlieb)

ANDRZEJ ZABLUDOWSKI, 'Concerning a Fiction about how Facts are Forecast', *Journal of Philosophy*, 71 (1974), 97–112. There are replies to this by JOSEPH ULLIAN and NELSON GOODMAN in *Journal of Philosophy*, vol. 72, 142–5, and vol. 73, 527–31, and responses by Zabludowski in vol. 72, 779–84, and vol. 74, 541–52.

In addition to the probability definitions of confirmation discussed in selections V and VI by Carnap and Salmon, the reader might consult the definitions given in

PAUL HORWICH, *Probability and Evidence* (Cambridge, 1982), Ch. 3.

MARY HESSE, *The Structure of Scientific Inference* (Berkeley, 1974), chs. 6 and 7

J. L. MACKIE, 'The Relevance Criterion of Confirmation', *British Journal for the Philosophy of Science*, 20 (1969), 27–40

KARL POPPER, *The Logic of Scientific Discovery*, 389.

A criticism of probability definitions of evidence is given in Glymour's *Theory and Evidence*, ch. 3. For a discussion of Glymour's criticism see papers by Roger Rosenkrantz, Daniel Garber, Richard Jeffrey, and Brian Skyrms in

JOHN EARMAN, ed., *Testing Scientific Theories* (*Minnesota Studies in the Philosophy of Science*, vol. 10), Minneapolis, 1983.

The bootstrap theory proposed by Glymour in selection VII is discussed in

ARON EDIDIN, 'Glymour on Confirmation', *Philosophy of Science*, 48 (1981), 292–307

PAUL HORWICH, 'An Appraisal of Glymour's Confirmation Theory', *Journal of Philosophy*, 75 (1978), 98–113

Papers by BAS VAN FRAASSEN, PAUL HORWICH, and ARON EDIDIN in the collection edited by Earman cited above.

The definition I propose in selection VIII is criticized in

MAYA BAR-HILLEL and AVISHAI MARGALIT, 'In Defence of the Classical Notion of Evidence', *Mind*, 88 (1979), 576–83.

I reply in

'On Evidence: A Reply to Bar-Hillel and Margalit', *Mind*, 90 (1981), 108–12.

I respond to other criticisms, and discuss Hempel's conditions of adequacy, the ravens paradox, and the concept of the variety of evidence, in

The Nature of Explanation (New York, 1983), chs. 10 and 11.

Finally, it might be noted that the selections in this volume presuppose that a definition of evidence or confirmation can be given that is applicable to the sciences generally. For a criticism of this basic idea and a defence of the claim that the standards of evidence and confirmation depend upon, and change with, the tenets of particular scientific theories, the interested reader should consult

THOMAS KUHN, *The Structure of Scientific Revolutions* (Chicago, 2nd edn., 1970)
PAUL FEYERABEND, *Against Method* (London, 1975)
IAN HACKING, ed., *Scientific Revolutions* (Oxford, 1981).

INDEX OF NAMES

(not including those appearing only in the Bibliography)